THE HERMITS AND
ANCHORITES
OF ENGLAND

BY

ROTHA MARY CLAY
AUTHOR OF "THE MEDIÆVAL HOSPITALS OF ENGLAND"

WITH FIFTY-FOUR ILLUSTRATIONS

METHUEN & CO. LTD.
36 ESSEX STREET W.C.
LONDON

Now Reissued by
Singing Tree Press
1249 Washington Blvd., Detroit, Michigan 1968

First Published in 1914

Library of Congress Catalog Card Number 68–21759

DEDICATED TO THE MEMORY OF

THE REVEREND CANON CHARLES HILL WALLACE

WHO, LIKE THE HONOURED HERMITS OF OLDEN TIME,

HAS BEEN TO MANY

FATHER, FRIEND, AND COUNSELLOR

PREFACE

I DESIRE to acknowledge my indebtedness to all those who have rendered assistance in the preparation of this volume, by the supply of materials, and the loan of manuscripts, books, engravings, and photographs. Particular mention must be made of Miss M. Leaf, who has kindly permitted her drawings of the " Prick of Conscience" window to be reproduced. The valued help of a large number of correspondents and helpers can of necessity only be acknowledged privately, but I should like to name Canon C. W. Foster, Mr. E. L. Guilford, Mr. H. B. McCall, Mr. W. Brown, Mr. J. W. Clay, Mr. A. G. Little, Rev. C. H. Evelyn-White, Canon Wilson, Rev. Dr. Wilson, Rev. B. Zimmerman, Canon Deedes, and Mr. W. Farrar. Mr. W. Rye, of Lammas, generously granted me access to his Norfolk MSS., especially to Mr. John L'Estrange's transcripts of wills from the Norwich Registers. Canon Wordsworth, Rev. R. M. Serjeantson, and Rev. H. Salter freely placed at my disposal notes relating to Wiltshire, Northamptonshire, and Oxfordshire; and to other good offices Mr. Salter has added that of proof-reading. To Rev. Dr. J. C. Cox I owe much, both in planning and carrying out this book. In conclusion, heartfelt thanks are offered to my friends, Miss Arnold-Forster, Rev. M. F. Peterson, Prof. G. H. Leonard, and Rev. C. S. Taylor, who have encouraged, advised, and greatly assisted me in this work.

I have sought documentary evidence for all the statements made in this book, taking as a motto the words of the faithful old historian, Thomas Habingdon, when describing a Worcestershire hermitage: "Other thinges which I receaved from uncertayne rumours I will rather conceale than hazard mysealfe to father an untruthe". I trust that my readers will point out errors, and will send me additional notes. The necessity of condensing my manuscript has led, I fear, to a sacrifice, in some cases of clearness, and in others of interest of detail.

ROTHA MARY CLAY

MILLER BRIDGE, AMBLESIDE
St. Cuthbert and St. Herbert's Day, 1913

CONTENTS

LIST OF PLATES

LIST OF ILLUSTRATIONS IN THE TEXT

ANCRES AND HERMYTES

For sum fleen from the world and closen hemsilf in wallis,
And steken hem in stones, and litil wole thei speken,
To fleen sich occasiouns as foly wole fynden ;
And thees we clepen ancres in the comoun speche.

Also in contemplacion there ben many other,
That drawen hem to disert and drye [endure] muche peyne,
By eerbis, rootes, and fruyte lyven for her goddis love,
And this maner of folk men callen hermytes.

—Friar Daw Topias (*Political Poems*, ed. Wright, ii. 64).

INTRODUCTION

IN every age and amongst all peoples a certain wonder
and reverence have been excited by the solitary life—a
life so abnormal that those who have watched it from
without have not only been interested in its eccentricity, but
also strongly attracted by its spiritual mystery. It has always
been felt that a life so independent of the common intercourse
of human relationships must possess a secret known only to a
few, and asceticism has therefore been venerated alike in the
Oriental fakir, the Stoic sage, and the Hebrew prophet.

This withdrawal from the world was not at first encouraged
by the Christian religion. Tertullian, writing about A.D. 197,
says: "We are not Indian Brahmans or Gymnosophists, who
dwell in woods and exile themselves from ordinary human
life . . . we sojourn with you in the world". During the
third century, however, the Church developed a monasticism
of her own which was in its beginning solitary (μοναχεῖν, to
dwell alone). Although Paul of Egypt—called "the first
hermit"—dwelt alone in his desert cave, his successor
Anthony attracted round him many followers, and in this
way the hermitage developed into the *laura* or group of cells.
The solitary monk frequently became the founder of a body
of cœnobites—monks dwelling in community. The great
Benedict himself was a son of the wilderness.

The history of many of the monastic houses of England
shows that they also were of eremitical origin. Guthlac and
his hermit companions dwelt in fenland solitude in a group of
single cells; but in course of time Crowland became a famous

abbey. The hermit Guy was joined by so many brethren at Malvern that he formed them into a large convent. Benedict, a Norman monk, lived in seclusion at Selby, and thus formed the nucleus of a monastery of which he was the first abbot.

It is, however, with the solitary rather than with the social aspect of monasticism that we are now concerned—with the solitary but not necessarily self-centred state of life to which the recluse felt himself called. From a modern standpoint this retirement from the world might perhaps be considered selfish; but it must be borne in mind that the problems of that time were different from those of to-day, and that those who thus withdrew themselves from their fellow-men did not become useless to the community. It is true that their primary object in retiring into solitude was the cultivation of the soul, but in so doing they became living witnesses to the reality of the spiritual world. Theirs was no easy religion. Indeed, hermits were regarded as heroes, because of the physical hardness they endured. Their life was one of strenuous effort. They strove after Christian quietude by bending all their activities to self-conquest. They upheld a lofty and austere moral ideal in the face of self-indulgence, and their manner of life was a silent rebuke to rudeness, and exercised a chastening influence in an age of violence.

Further, they could not but have some social intercourse. There were, indeed, two distinct classes of solitaries: the *anchorite*, enclosed within four walls, and the *hermit*, who went out of his cell and mingled with his fellow-men. The ideal of both was the contemplative life, but even in the case of the anchorite, this concentration upon religious exercises did not imply complete absorption in his own spiritual interests. Intercession was his appointed work. Aelred of Rievaulx mentions some of the needs which would call out the sympathies of the anchoress: the misery of the poor, the sigh of the orphan, the desolation of the widow, the need of pilgrims, the danger of voyagers, the hardships of soldiers, the vows and temptations of nuns and monks, the cares of bishops. It is evident that those who lived this life of contemplation were recognized as being qualified to exercise spiritual influence and give ghostly counsel. Awed by such austerity of life, the conscience-stricken and heavy-laden resorted to them in order to receive comfort and benediction after unburdening themselves of their sins and sorrows. In some cases anchorites devoted their quiet hours to study, and placed their literary or artistic powers at the service of others. The Lindisfarne Gospels were wrought and adorned with the aid of recluses. Scholars sent forth from their cells books of devotion, historical works, poetry, and at least one valuable dictionary. Anchoresses, too, found useful occupation in making clothes for the poor.

The hermit, with his larger measure of freedom and activity, had a still wider sphere of influence, and undertook many social duties. He taught and preached, celebrated divine offices in his chapel for the benefit of wayfarers, or acted as guardian of some shrine; he gathered alms for the relief of the poor at home, or for the freeing of those in captivity amongst the heathen; he helped to cultivate the waste places of the land and to clear the forest; he made roads and bridges and kept them in repair; he erected sea-marks and lighthouses for the guidance of mariners. In fact, the hermits were pioneers of philanthropic works which in these days are undertaken and carried out by public bodies.

All who embraced this separate life were under vows of some kind. They were subject to authority, and had a recognized place in the ecclesiastical system. The hermit, if a monk, needed only the approval of his abbot; if a layman, he applied to the bishop for his habit. No man or woman could become an anchorite without the permission of the bishop, who enclosed them in the cell with solemn rites. The Appendix contains a valuable translation of the *Office for the Enclosing of Anchorites*, contributed by the Rev. C. S. Taylor, to whose ready and generous help this book owes much throughout. It also includes, by the courtesy of Mr. F. C. Eeles, an *Office for the Benediction of Hermits*, transcribed by him from a sixteenth-century Pontifical in his possession. After pro-

b

fession in either of these orders, solitaries were under some definite Rule of Life. The best known is the *Ancren Riwle*— a book of wise and tender counsels for anchoresses, compiled by one who knew in an intimate manner not only the homely details of their outward circumstances, but also the special needs of their inner life.

The solitary life thus developed into an established institution. So widespread did it become that there was not a single county in England which had not at some time or another a recluse's cell. It will be seen from the Tables appended to this volume that there is evidence for the existence of at least 750 cells, whilst the actual names of over 650 hermits and anchorites occur in the following pages.

Dim traditions exist of solitaries in Celtic Britain. The Christian martyrs under Diocletian are said to have included two anchorites of Caerleon. We learn from Bede that a recluse was the oracle of the British Church at the time of the Conference with Augustine. Elgar the kidnapped slave, Kenyth the crippled prince, and the wonder-working women Keyne and Modwen, are shrouded in the mists of legend, it is true, but these and others, who like them lived apart from the world, helped to keep the faith alive in those early days.

Among the Saxon saints are numbered many hermits; Cuthbert, drawn from his northern retreat to become a bishop, and his faithful friend Herebert of Derwentwater; Guthlac, the soldier-monk of the eastern fens, whose presence transformed that grim wilderness into a "glorious plain," and Neot, the nobleman of the western wilds; Alnoth the serf, and Edwold the prince; Plegmund and Dunstan, archbishops of Canterbury; Werstan the martyr, and Wulsi the seer.

The religious revival of the twelfth century produced five great ascetics; Roger, the monk of Markyate; Christina "of the Wood"—remarkable alike for her fortitude and for her gifts of wisdom and counsel; Wulfric of Haselbury—prophet and confessor, stern and uncompromising alike with himself and his king; Godric—the sea-roving adventurer, the tender son, the pious pilgrim, the simple, stout-hearted solitary of

Finchale ; and that other undaunted northerner, Bartholomew of Farne—to whom, for the space of over two and forty years, people resorted for comfort and exhortation.

Amongst later hermits two famous Yorkshiremen must be named ; Robert of Knaresborough—the poor man's friend ; Richard of Hampole—an evangelist burning with the fire of love. Nor can we forget Dame Julian of Norwich "strong in sure trust in weal and woe," whose *Revelations of Divine Love* show the eager and joyous spirit of the writer. From the dawn of Christianity in England until the sixteenth century many men, perhaps even more women, continued to dedicate themselves to this separate life.

"The life of the recluse," says a recent writer upon mysticism, "is now seldom chosen and never respected." In the period which we are about to study, it was, however, regarded as the state nearest perfection. In the *Liber Vitæ* of the church of Durham, anchorites rank second to royal benefactors, and take the precedence of abbots and others. The life of action, indeed, was apt to be despised by religious teachers, save by such rare saints as Hugh of Lincoln, who would speak in this wise to persons unable to practise the more perfect life of contemplation : "By no means shall monks alone, nor yet hermits, nor even anchorites, attain to the kingdom of God"; adding, that when the Lord should judge any man at last, He would not require of him to have been a hermit or monk, but rather to have been truly a Christian—to have had love in his heart, truth in his mouth, purity in his life.

In the following account of the lives of English hermits and anchorites no attempt has been made to consider the scientific truth and value of the miraculous element in their history. To ignore it, however, would be not merely a loss of the picturesque, but also a denial of spiritual facts. Modern science forbids us to doubt the reality of the spiritual forces exercised by these self-disciplined men and women. To investigate and determine these imperfectly understood powers lies beyond the scope of these pages. Indeed, no attempt has been made to penetrate into the subject of Mysticism, which has recently been so ably dealt with by Miss Evelyn Underhill. The aim of this book is rather to give a picture of the daily life of the lonely dwellers in fen and forest, hillside and cliff, cloister and churchyard, and to show something of the way in which their influence made itself felt.

THE HERMITS AND
ANCHORITES OF ENGLAND

I. ISLAND AND FEN RECLUSES

When saynt Jone was in the yle of Pathmos, than God schewed hym his pryvytees.—RICHARD THE HERMIT

NO self-imposed barrier was so complete as that of the island-recluse. Surrounded as he was by an expanse of sea and sky, "the secrecy of solitude" was his. Only a devoted friend or an earnest penitent would venture forth to visit him who was sea-bound, or encircled by some wellnigh impassable morass. The hermit-inhabited islands of England and Wales include Farne and Coquet, in the north ; and in the west, Bardsey, off the coast of Carnarvon, the Holmes, St. Tiriac's Rock, and other islets of the Severn.

I. ISLES OF THE SEA

(a) *Farne and Coquet.*—About two miles from the Northumbrian coast lay a bare inhospitable rock which became famous as the abode of solitary saints. When St. Aidan, the island-monk of Iona, was Bishop of Lindisfarne, he used occasionally to retire to Farne for undisturbed prayer. Cuthbert afterwards sought in this spot the secret solitude for which he longed. It was a desert island, and ill-suited for human habitation. At the presence of the man of God, however, the evil spirits fled ; at his prayer water bubbled out of the rocky ground ; and by his manual labour he raised from the barren soil plentiful crops of barley. With the help of the brethren he built himself a small dwelling and an oratory, which are thus described by Bede :—

"The building is almost of a round form, from wall to wall about four or five poles in extent: the wall on the outside is higher

I

than a man, but within, by excavating the rock, he made it much deeper, to prevent the eyes and the thoughts from wandering, that the mind might be wholly bent on heavenly things, and the pious inhabitant might behold nothing from his residence but the heavens above him.   The wall was constructed, not of hewn stones or of brick and mortar, but of rough stones and turf. . . . There were two chambers in the house, one an oratory, the other for domestic purposes."

This simple beehive-hut was not the only building on the island, for it proved necessary to make a large guest-house to accommodate those who came continually to visit the saint. Many came, not only from Lindisfarne, but from the more remote parts of Britain :—

"At first, indeed, when the brethren came to visit him, he would leave his cell and minister to them. . . . At length, as his zeal after perfection grew, he shut himself up in his cell away from the sight of men, and spent his time alone in fasting, watching, and prayer, rarely having communication with anyone without, and that through the window, which at first was left open, that he might see and be seen ; but after a time he shut that also, and opened it only to give his blessing, or for any other purpose of absolute necessity."

When Cuthbert was elected bishop he would not consent to leave Farne, but the king and others went across and "drew him, weeping, from his retreat ".   At length he yielded to their entreaties.   Faithfully did the Bishop of Lindisfarne fulfil the duties which he had undertaken.   " He protected the people committed to his care with frequent prayers, and invited them to heavenly things . . . by first doing himself what he taught to others."   Amid the turmoil by which the hermit-bishop was surrounded, he ceased not to observe the severity of a monastic life.   His mission was manifold.   He visited parishes and religious houses, healed the sick, comforted lonely survivors of the plague, and protected the needy from the oppressor.   As the shepherd was visiting his folds, he came one day to a wild spot, where many people were gathered that he might lay his hands upon them.   Among the mountains no fit church or other building could be found, but at night the bishop and his flock were sheltered in tents and in booths roughly formed of boughs from the neighbouring wood.   " Two days did the man of God preach to the assembled crowds, and minister the grace of the Holy Spirit by imposition of hands."

After two years of strenuous labour, Cuthbert returned to Farne, knowing that the time of his departure was at hand. He used now to leave the cell frequently and converse with those who came to visit him. He died after a short illness on 20 March, 687—on the same day as his friend, St. Herebert (p. 12). He had earnestly desired to be buried on his island, but finally yielded to the wish of the brethren, who accordingly buried his body in Lindisfarne—a spot which became so sacred as to win thereafter the name of Holy Island.

Cuthbert's successor, Aethelwald, a priest of Ripon, was in seclusion at Farne for twelve years. When he arrived, he found the cell in a dilapidated condition. Crevices made by the violence of the winds had been roughly filled up with timber, hay, or mud ; and the walls were crumbling. Aethelwald therefore begged the brethren who came thither to bring him a calf-skin, which he fastened in the spot where he, like Cuthbert, was wont to pray.

Bede relates how Aethelwald stilled a tempest when Guthfrid and certain other brethren were in peril. The story was told to Bede by Guthfrid himself. When the monks were returning to Lindisfarne a tempest arose, so great that neither sails nor oars availed aught :—

" Looking out as far as we could see, we observed, on the island of Farne, Father Oidiluald, beloved of God, who had come out of his cell to watch our course ; for, hearing the noise of the storm and the raging of the sea, he had come out to see what would happen to us. When he beheld us in distress and despair, he bowed his knees to the Father of our Lord Jesus Christ, in prayer for our life and safety ; whereupon the swelling sea was calmed, so that the violence of the storm ceased on all sides, and a fair wind attended us even to the very shore." [1]

When they were safely landed the storm immediately returned and raged throughout the day, so that it was clear that the brief cessation had been granted at the hermit's request. It was this Aethelwald who with Billfrith assisted in illuminating the Lindisfarne Gospels (see chapter XIII).

[1] Bede, *Ecc. Hist.*, ed. Stevenson, 492-3.

During the time of Felgeld, the third inhabitant of the place, the hermitage was rebuilt from the foundations by Bishop Eadfrid. "By means of the ruins of the holy oratory," Felgeld himself was said to have been cured of a dreadful disease and deformity. In earlier life he had been subject to the swelling; "but now that he was living alone, and bestowed less care on his person, whilst he practised still greater rigidities, and, like a prisoner, rarely enjoyed the sun or air, the malady increased". When the cell was being restored, devout persons begged of Felgeld relics of his predecessors. Having cut into pieces the calf-skin which Aethelwald had nailed in the corner where the hermits used to pray, Felgeld determined to apply the relics to his own need. Steeping a piece of the covering in water, he washed his face therein, and the blemish was removed. When Bede wrote his account of St. Cuthbert (before 721), Felgeld, then seventy years of age, was still dwelling on the island.

For a considerable period history is silent about Cuthbert's cell, but Gaufridus, the twelfth-century chronicler, states that the island lapsed into a wild state, until at length the desecrated, time-worn oratory was cleansed and repaired by the monk Edulf.

Bartholomew of Farne, the most famous of Cuthbert's followers, was born at Whitby about the year 1120. His life was written by Gaufridus,[1] the contemporary biographer of the famous hermits of Finchale and of Farne. He seems to have been of Saxon origin; but as his name Tosti met with disfavour he adopted that of William. He was a careless youth, and does not appear to have been awakened to spiritual things even by two visions which were vouchsafed to him. Desiring to travel, William sailed to Norway, where he came under religious influences and was ordained priest. When the wanderer came home to Northumbria, his zeal led him to seek the stricter life of a monk. On entering the monastery of Durham, William assumed the name Bartholomew. Before long St. Cuthbert appeared to him, bidding him become a hermit at Farne. In obedience to the vision, Bartholomew went thither, and there he spent the remainder of his days.

[1] Printed in Rolls Series (75), as Appendix to *Symeon of Durham*, I. 295-325. See also *English Saints*, III.

PLATE I

ST. CUTHBERT'S CHAPEL, FARNE

Like St. Cuthbert he lived frugally by his own labour, and devoted himself to meditation. Farne became once more a spiritual centre, and the guest-house was in constant use. Fishermen from the mainland and seamen from all parts visited the solitary, and relied on his advice, whether it concerned their ships or their souls.

In this convenient harbour sailors and traders were frequently detained by stress of weather. Sometimes the hermit-host suffered from a scarcity of provisions, but so hospitable was he that upon one occasion he killed his only cow to supply the needs of his guests. Pirates frequently carried off his slender stores. During the reign of Stephen, Aeistan, King of Norway, ravaged the English coast, and landing on Farne he killed and roasted the sheep of the hermits Bartholomew and Aelwin, and even repaired his ships with the timbers of their cell.

Bartholomew lived at Farne for over forty-two years, and he persevered in ascetic habits to old age. He would have no couch, no pillow, no prop to support his body. As long as he was able, he would sit upright, or walk round the island, and all the while he never ceased from prayer. During the last nine days he was very ill; but, despite the diseases of his body, he kept all the faculties of his mind, nor did the brave old man shrink from dying in solitude. When, therefore, the brethren had administered the last holy rites, they left him ; and on their return from Lindisfarne they found his body lying not far from the stone coffin which he had prepared for himself. It was remembered that when the coffin had first arrived, Bartholomew, finding it too short, had with his own hands hewn it out to fit his body. He was buried in the oratory on the south side, in the spot where his great predecessor had desired to lie. The monks would gladly have carried the remains to Lindisfarne, but Bartholomew's love for his island-home was strong, and he had expressed a wish that he should be buried there in order that the place might not again become deserted. Echoing the words of St. Cuthbert, he declared: " I would have my body lie here, where I hope that my spirit will be received by its Creator, and where I have fought during a very little time for the Lord ".

The mediaeval chapel shown in Plate I is still standing.

It has been restored, and services are occasionally held there for the lighthouse men.

South of Farne, near the mouth of the river Coquet, was another sanctuary of the sea.   In the days of St. Cuthbert, who visited Coquet Island, it was remarkable for the number of its monks.   Little is known of the place, however, before the time of St. Henry, early in the twelfth century.   This young Dane of noble family was about to be forced into marriage, when, in obedience to a vision, he determined to serve God all the days of his life upon a certain rock on the Northumbrian coast.   Sailing, therefore, from Denmark, he obtained permission of the prior of Tynemouth to build a small cell on Coquet Island.   Messengers followed him, urging him to return to the land of his birth, where there were deserts to which he might withdraw.   Strong was the longing of the exile, but before making his decision he cast himself down before the crucifix set up in his oratory, and implored a revelation of the Divine will.   It seemed to him that the lips of the figure moved, and that Christ, reminding him of his call, promised eternal life if he should persevere.   " Play the man, and strengthen thine heart, and in nowise abandon this place of solitude unto thy life's end."   Fearing lest he should again be tempted to forsake the island, the hermit prayed to be stricken with some infirmity which should render this impossible.   He was afterwards afflicted with a loathsome disease in his knee, which he bore with fortitude.   Leaning on a crutch, he continued to cultivate his plot of land.   The ulcerated leg caused him agony, but he refused assistance.   Alone in his cell, without fire or light, Henry passed the winter, until one night (January, 1127), there was heard a choir of angels singing.   The music ceased, and suddenly a bell tolled.   When a monk reached the hermitage, he found Henry in the sleep of death, seated on a stone, holding the bell-rope, and beside him burned a candle lit by no human hand.[1]

In the thirteenth century the office of " keeper of the island " was held by an energetic recluse named Martin, who raised thereupon at great expense a windmill.   But Robert Fitz Roger, considering Martin's act as detrimental to the

---

[1] Roscarrock's *Life; Nov. Leg.* II. 22-6.

PLATE II

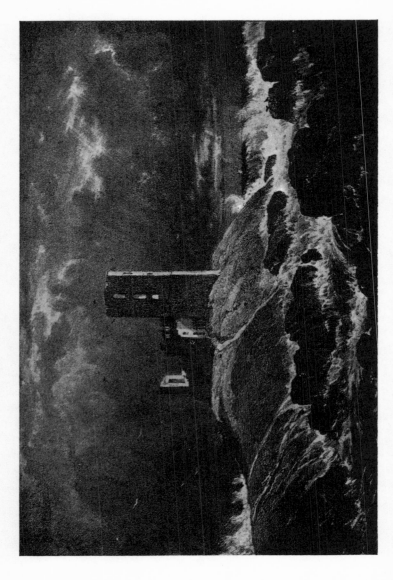

COQUET ISLAND

overlord, sent thirty men with axes and mattocks to destroy the mill. The terror-stricken hermit made no protest, and when his servant ventured to remonstrate, they treated him so ill that he barely escaped with his life. This curious story of enterprise and persecution breaks off abruptly with these words : "Moreover, the said Martin was blamed by no one in that he was wont to prefer to lead the solitary life. He desired to attract neither the approach nor the noise of people of either sex, because often in mills and play-houses irregular and unlawful things are done." [1]

The island was under Tynemouth Priory, which in its turn was subject to St. Albans. When the latter convent was replying to a Benedictine inquiry in 1253, it was noted that no monk dwelt apart, save one hermit in a certain little island called Coquet, and another in a wood. A tower, possibly used as a lantern, adjoined the chapel. It is mentioned in 1415 as belonging to the prior of Tynemouth. At the Dissolution of Monasteries the buildings included a chapel served by a chaplain. Mediæval remains may still be traced in and about the modern lighthouse. The tower shown in Plate II was standing a century ago.

(b) *Isles of the West.*—The West, like the North, had her isles of saints ; nor can the recluses of the Welsh coast be excluded, although not strictly within the scope of this volume. The ascetic life was eagerly embraced by the fervent-natured Celt, and from shadowy traditions it would seem that many a rocky islet had its cell.

The "Book of Llandaff" opens with an account of Elgar, hermit of Ynys Enlli (Bardsey), a native of Britain, who had been carried off as an infant from his home in Devon, and became a slave in Ireland. After serving King Roderic in the office of executioner, Elgar obtained freedom and became a sailor. Being wrecked on Bardsey, a holy island where many martyrs were buried, he resolved to stay there and to lead the contemplative life.

"Having spent the space of seven years with a religious community of brethren, and sometimes in solitude, led a holy, glorious, and chaste life, with scant food, slight clothing, and an emaciated

[1] Chr. S. Alb., *Annales, Edw. I* (Rolls, 28, ii.), 477-8.

countenance, he, in the following seven years . . . dwelt in his hermitage, and had nothing for his maintenance except the support which he received, through the providence of God, from the fish of the sea, and what the eagles, or as we may say, angels, brought to him."

By the ministry of the eagles, Elgar's table was prepared in the wilderness with fishes, herbs, and water; and once when he was hungry he found a large white stag which supplied him with food for some time. The hermit " led his life, present to the Lord, and unknown to man ". At length, having prepared a grave for himself in the oratory, he lay down beside it and expired; and the sailor-saint was afterwards buried by sailors. The details of his life were told by him at the entreaty of the teacher Caradoc who came to visit him.[1]

Upon a rocky promontory on the coast of Glamorgan dwelt Kenyth, a Welsh prince cast adrift on the waves in an osier coracle. Friendly sea-birds bore the hapless babe to Ynys Weryn—Worms Head, which is an island at high tide— where they made him a nest of feathers, and drove the serpents from the place. According to the legend, an angel brought a brazen bell, which was regularly replenished with milk by a doe. The child was found and taken home by a shepherd, but when the sea-gulls gathered in flocks and attacked his home, the affrighted rustic carried him back to his rocky nursery. There, on a ledge of rock, the little cripple grew up with no companions save the gulls. An early Celtic representation of this legend is found on the Cumberland cross-shaft of Dearham, near Maryport. It is strange that the story of a solitary of the Severn Sea should thus reach the shores of the Solway. The rude but graphic sculpture (Fig. 1) shows a sea-bird with a bundle in its claws, and a deformed human figure holding out a bell-shaped vessel.[2]

Kenyth, who after eighteen years of solitude found a companion to share his ascetic life, spent the rest of his days at Burry Holmes, an island-promontory on the north shore of Rhosilly Bay. He built a cell of osiers and thatched it with

---

[1] *Liber Landav.*, ed. W. T. Rees, 281-7.
[2] W. S. Calverley and W. G. Collingwood, *Early Sculp. Crosses*, 127-30.

reeds. The hermit was revered by all. Once some starving robbers, coming to those parts, said among themselves :—

"There is a certain saint not far from here, who loves and instructs all, and he refreshes the strong as well as the weak ; he invites the destitute and wayfarers, and even to evil-doers he is gentle. Let us go, therefore, to him that he may succour our need. And when they arrived there they were quickly received into the hospice."

After the hermit's death, his remains were removed to a neighbouring church. William Worcester records his "translation" to St. Keneth's in Gowerland. Many centuries later a custom prevailed of taking solemn oaths upon his relics. In a quarrel which arose in 1472, the arbitrator adjudged that the claimant should swear to the rightfulness of his title "in the chirche of Langenytt upon Seint Kenythis hedde".[1]

FIG. 1.—The Hermit and the Seagull.

The cell at Burry Holmes was inhabited from time to time. Possibly the oratory there was the "deserted church of St. Kined," to which Caradoc retired early in the twelfth century.[2] The hermitage of St. Kenyth "atte Holmes in Gowers-

---

[1] *Nov. Leg.* II. 105-9 ; J. D. Davies, *W. Gower*, Pt. III.; Birch, *Penrice and Margam MSS.* v. 114.

[2] Caradoc left the Court of Rhys, became a monk at Llandaff, then a hermit on the Isle of Ary. His final retreat was near Haverfordwest. He died in 1124. *Nov. Leg.* ii. 105-9.

land" was still occupied during the fifteenth century, when Philip Lichepoll, William Bernard, etc., were hermits.[1]

Steep Holme, Flat Holme, and Barry, were often inhabited by solitaries—not always as permanent abodes, but for periods of seclusion between missionary journeys or during Lent. These islands of Severn were a wilderness to which it was easy to retire, and a centre from which work could be resumed. Two famous friends abode upon Ronech and Echni (The Holmes), namely, Cadoc, who chose the flat island nearest to Wales, and Gildas, who inhabited the craggy rock lying off the English shore.   Gildas built a cell and an oratory in honour of the Blessed Trinity, but his rocky bed was under the precipitous cliff, where he was wont to watch and pray until midnight. These holy men used to visit one another during their seven years' sojourn in the Severn.   Being troubled by pirates, however, St. Gildas left Steep Holme, and went to Glastonbury, where he became abbot and wrote his history (chapter XIII.). Not far from Glastonbury, on the river, he built a church, and there he lived once more as a hermit, clad in a hair-shirt. People came from remote parts of Britain to hear his wisdom and his teaching.   St. Cadoc, returning to Wales, became Abbot of Llancarvan.   One of his disciples, Barroc, gave his name to Barry, near Cardiff.   "His remains," says Giraldus de Barri, "are deposited in a chapel overgrown with ivy."   This "fair little chapel of St. Barrok" was a place of pilgrimage in Leland's day.[2]

Prince Fremund was the son of the Saxon King Offa. Whilst his father was yet alive the pious youth was crowned as his successor; but, fired with love to God, he determined to leave home and country and seek the desert.   Fremund and his two companions set out for Caerleon.   When they reached the sea they took a little barge, and without oar and without food committed their passage to God's ordinance (Plate III).   Driven to and fro by the wind for five days, they came to land "up an yle froward to kome to"—deserted of inhabitants, but with fair mountains, running rivers, crystal

---

[1] See Pat. Rolls, 1398, 1428, 1482, etc.

[2] Possibly the same saint to which the fine old Derbyshire church of Norbury was dedicated, "St. Barlok," mentioned in Fitzherbert wills, and commemorated in the glass of the S. chapel.

PLATE III

THE VOYAGE TO ILEFAYE

BUILDING THE CHAPEL

ST. FREMUND

wells, green meadows, and trees laden with wholesome fruits—
a place divinely ordained for them.

> And Ilefaye men that yle calle
> Off old tyme desolat and sauage
> More agreable than was his stalle
> To hooly Fremund thouh he were yong off age
> And ther he bilte a litel hermytage
> Be side a ryuer with al his besy peyne
> He & his fellawis that were in noumbre tweyne.
>
> A lytil chapel he dide ther edefie
> Day be day to make in his praiere
> In the reuerence only of marie
> And in the worshepe off hir sone deere
> And the space fully off seuene yeere
> Hooly Fremund lik as it is found
> Leued be frut and rootis off the grounde.

Despite privation, trial, and temptation, Fremund kept to
his purpose : " stable as a wal he stood in his degre ".   At
length Offa, hearing of the arrival of the Danish chieftains
Hinguar and Hubba, and of the death of St. Edmund (his
queen's brother), sent to seek his son through that region and
all strange isles.   The messengers told the prince of the desolation brought by the paynims and besought his aid.   Then
stood Fremund in a sore plight.   By his profession he was
pledged to live apart and to eschew bloodshed ; yet in that
world which he had forsaken, the helpless were oppressed,
the Church despoiled, and Christ's faith brought to destruction.
Perplexed, the hermit fell to prayer, and he was bidden in a
vision to hasten home to his country, and be strong in spirit
like Christ's champion.   Fremund straightway left Ilefaye, and
was victorious when he led his people against " the miscreants
of Denmark ".   Whilst he knelt in thanksgiving, however, he
was murdered by a Saxon renegade to the faith who was in
league with the Danes.   The hermit-martyr's story is depicted
in the beautiful MS. of Lydgate's " Life of St. Edmund." [1]
    Near the old passage of Severn, at the mouth of the Wye,
is Chapel Island with its " chapel of St. Tiriac the anchorite".
The earliest known record concerning this place is a licence of
the Bishop of Hereford, given in 1290 to Brother John Sterre,
a Benedictine monk, to officiate in the chapel of St. Tryak of

[1] B.M. Harl. MS., 2278.

Beachley.[1]   In the year 1405 "a multitude, both of English and Welsh," were wont to resort thither on pilgrimage.   In the time of Henry VIII, the *capella S. Triaci*, standing in the sea, is described as being worth nothing.   The ruined oratory, which measured 31½ feet by 14½ feet, was drawn by Miss Eleanor Ormerod many years ago (Plate IV).

There is no clue as to the identity of the dedication-saint. *St. Triaculus* occurs on one Patent Roll.   William Worcester refers to *Sanctus Tiriacus anachorita*, and to *Rok Seynt Tryacle*. Leland speaks of *S. Tereudacus Chapel*.   Modern maps complete the confusion by printing St. Tecla.

II. Inland Isles

(*a*) *In Lakes.*—Many a saint sought solitude upon some inland-islet, shut off from the world by the waters of the mere, the marsh, or the river.   The holy Herebert dwelt upon an island in Derwentwater :—

"There was a certain priest, venerable for the probity of his life and manners, called Herebert, who had long been united with the man of God, Cuthbert, in the bonds of spiritual friendship.   This man, leading a solitary life in an island of that great marsh from which the Derwent flows, was wont to visit him every year, and to receive from him advice concerning his eternal salvation."

In the year 696 Cuthbert and Herebert met in Carlisle for the last time.   The bishop told his friend of his approaching death, and the hermit won from him the assurance that his own soul should depart at the same time.

More than eight centuries later, Leland writes of "St. Herebert's Isle wher is a Chapel".   It had long been visited as a hallowed place.   In 1374 Bishop Appleby of Carlisle offered an indulgence to such parishioners of Crosthwaite as should accompany the vicar thither when the mass of St. Cuthbert was celebrated on St. Herbert's Day (the 13th of [the kalends of] April, i.e. 20 March).   "What a happy holy-day must that have been for all these vales ; and how joyous on a fine spring day must the lake have appeared, with the boats and banners from every chapelry, and how must the

[1] Reg. Swinfield (Cant. and Yk. S.), 238-9.   Beachley is in Tidenham, near Chepstow.

PLATE IV

CHAPEL OF ST. TIRIAC THE ANCHORITE

chapel have adorned that little isle, giving a human and
religious character to the solitude!"   "Its ruins are still
there," adds Southey, "in such a state of total dilapidation
that they only make the island, mere wilderness as it has
now become, more melancholy."[1]   One of Wordsworth's
Inscriptions was written for the spot where the hermitage
stood :—

> . . . Stranger! not unmoved
> Wilt thou behold this shapeless heap of stones,
> The desolate ruins of St. Herbert's Cell.
> Here stood his threshold; here was spread the roof
> That sheltered him, a self-secluded Man,
> After long exercise in social cares
> And offices humane, intent to adore
> The Deity, with undistracted mind,
> And meditate on everlasting things,
> In utter solitude.—But he had left
> A Fellow-labourer, whom the good Man loved
> As his own soul.   And, when with eye upraised
> To heaven he knelt before the crucifix,
> While o'er the lake the cataract of Lodore
> Pealed to his orisons, and when he paced
> Along the beach of this small isle and thought
> Of his Companion, he would pray that both
> (Now that their earthly duties were fulfilled)
> Might die in the same moment.   Nor in vain
> So prayed he :—as our chronicles report,
> Though here the Hermit numbered his last day
> Far from St. Cuthbert, his beloved Friend,
> Those holy Men both died in the same hour.

There was an island cell "within the water of Winder-
mere," on Lady Holm near Bowness.   The earliest known
reference is to "the hermit brethren of St. Mary's" (1272).
The Chapel, also described as hospital or chantry, was
served by two priests, some of whom came from Segden
hermitage, near Berwick-upon-Tweed.   After the Dissolution
of Religious Houses, the Survey mentions "a Fre Chapel
within the parishinge of Wynondermere called our ladie
Chapelle of tholme".   According to local legend it was a
monk of Lady Holm who silenced for ever the ghostly
"Crier of Claife".   Travellers from Kendal to Hawkshead
crossed the narrow lake by ferry.   The fell between Winder-
mere and Esthwaite is called Claife Heights.   Thence one
stormy night a fateful voice cried "Boat!"   The ferryman

---

[1] Southey, *Colloquies* (More), I. 337.

rowed across expecting some passenger, but he saw some dreadful apparition, and returned speechless to die. The story of the boatman's last voyage struck terror into all hearts, and after nightfall none would venture upon the lake. At length a priest of St. Mary's went forth to lay the ghost, and henceforth the awful "Crier" was heard no more.

(*b*) *In the Fens.*—Encircled by fenny swamp or flooded river, Saxon solitaries took up their abode at Crowland, Peakirk, Thorney, Huneia, Bethney, and other islands.

Felix, himself a monk of Crowland, describes the terrible marsh which Guthlac made his home—with its stagnant pools, its spongy moss, its wreaths of dark vapours, its watercourses winding between woods and islands. Now when the young monk of Repton heard of this huge desert he went straight thither. Inquiring of the inhabitants their knowledge of this vast solitude, Guthlac heard of a more uncultivated part of that wide wilderness. One of those who stood by, Tatwine by name, declared that he knew another island in the hidden parts of a yet more remote desert, which many who had tried to live there disliked on account of unknown monsters and terrors of different kinds. Guthlac, who in youth had ever been ready for a wild raid, was still eager for holy adventure. He was guided by Tatwine to the place of dreadful desolation. The voyage to Crowland is shown upon the fine Harley Roll (Plate V), which also depicts the construction of the chapel under the hermit's direction.

Traces of Guthlac's church and cell remained until last century on a mound not far from the abbey.[1] The cistern or well mentioned by the eighth-century chronicler has also been uncovered. A cottage here was known in the eighteenth century as "Anchor Church House".

Pega, Guthlac's famous sister, settled as a recluse at Peakirk, "being the first dry land she reached after coming by water from Croyland". On the traditional site of her dwelling stands a chapel, which was formerly known as the hermitage of St. Bartholomew—the saint who appears constantly in the life of Guthlac as his patron. According to the continuator

---

[1] *Brit. Archæol. Journal*, XXXV, facing p. 133.

PLATE V

ST. GUTHLAC'S VOYAGE TO CROWLAND

of *Ingulph's Chronicle*, the chapel of St. Pega was rebuilt by Abbot John Wysbech about 1469, "after the same had been for many years levelled with the ground". If this be true, the nave (now used as a reading-room) may represent the abbot's work. The chancel is older, dating probably from the latter part of the thirteenth century.

At Thorney (once Ancarig, island of anchorites) dwelt, according to uncertain tradition, Thorncred, Thortred, and Bosa. To this spot in the tenth century Athelwold, Abbot of Abingdon, and Bishop of Winchester, was wont to retire at certain seasons, and a monastery was afterwards founded there. In Thorney Abbey were preserved the relics of Huna, the chaplain of St. Etheldreda. The priest had long practised great austerity of life, and after he had performed the last offices for the holy abbess, he spent the rest of his days in seclusion upon a small island near Ely, called Huneia after the saint. Near Hunney farm, on the borders of Chatteris, traces have been found of an ancient building, supposed by some to have been the chapel where Huna was buried, before the translation of his body to Thorney.

(*c*) *In Rivers.*—Bertellin or Berthelm (by some identified with Beccel or Beccellin, Guthlac's disciple), a wild young prince who had become a penitent recluse, went in disguise to his father, the King of Mercia, and begged from him a little island in the river Sow, where now is Stafford. After his father's death, the hermit was dispossessed, and, leaving Bethney, he retired to the desert places of the mountains. This last retreat is supposed to have been Dovedale, possibly near Ilam, where the shrine and well of *St. Bertram* are still to be seen, and also certain ancient cross-shafts which may once have marked the saint's grave. [1]

Modwen is said to have dwelt upon a plot of ground between two branches of the river, near Burton-on-Trent. "Returning to England from Rome, she came to the place which is called Scaleclif, by the hill where the river Trent makes, as it were, an island. Having built an oratory in honour of St. Andrew, she lived the anachoritical life for seven years." A sixteenth-century rental mentions "Andrew's Isle, alias Mud-

---

[1] Bishop of Bristol, *St. Bertram's Shrine at Ilam.*

win's chappell ".   The story of St. Modwen's hermit-friend, Hardulch, is told in chapter III.

Plegmund, the learned friend of King Alfred, once lived the solitary life upon "an island of Chester, called by the inhabitants Plegmundesham"—probably Plemondstall, about four miles from Chester.   The good priest was summoned from his place of retirement by Alfred, whose instructor and counsellor he became (chapter XIII.).   The Saxon Chronicle for the year 890 records that: " This year was Plegmund chosen of God, and of all the people, to the Archbishopric of Canterbury ".   " At this time," says another historian, " Archbishop Plegmund, so faithful and so famous, ruled the Church of Christ ; a reverend man, bright with the fruits of wisdom." He is said to have crowned Edward the Elder, and to have died at an advanced age in 914.   The memory of the hermit-archbishop was treasured in his former retreat, where his name was adopted.   The " Christening Well," near the church of Plemstall, was called " St. Plegmund's Well " in the time of Edward VI.[1]

An island called Andersey, by the river Parrett in Somerset, was inhabited during the twelfth century by Herduin, a venerable solitary ; the place was granted to him by charter, and he afterwards presented it to Athelney Abbey.   The Wye had a hermit's isle near Winforton, in Herefordshire ; it was about a quarter of a mile south of the church, and had a chapel dedicated to St. Kenedr.   The first occupant of the cell was Walter the priest.   His successor, Brother Stephen, planted a quickset hedge about the hermitage, finding, perhaps, that even the river did not protect him sufficiently.

[1] Hook, *Archbishops*, 1. 312 *sq.* ; E. Conybeare, *Alfred in the Chroniclers*, 106, 127, 156, 203 ; *Chester and N. Wales Hist. S.*, N.S., XVI, 56, 67.

II. FOREST AND HILLSIDE HERMITS

A little lowly hermitage it was,
Down in a dale hard by a forest's side.
—SPENSER, *Faerie Queene*

THE densely wooded wilderness or hidden cave of the mainland afforded seclusion almost as complete as that of the sea-girt sanctuary. Celtic recluses in particular seem to have loved the depths of the forest. Several of these have left their memory in Somerset. The village of Keynsham, for example, is supposed to derive its name from the Welsh princess Ceneu or Keyne, who is believed to have lived the contemplative life in those parts ; whilst Congresbury and St. Decumans are associated with Cungar and Degeman. The watery, woody spot where Cungar—otherwise called Docwin—settled in the days of Ina, King of Wessex, became under his care flowery meadows; so cultivated, indeed, did the Congresbury valley become that the holy man crossed the Severn to seek a more fit hiding-place in the wilds of Glamorganshire. Crossing the Severn Sea—the hermit's highway—the Welsh prince Degeman disembarked from his rude raft in the neighbourhood of Dunster. The tract between Exmoor forest and the Quantocks, with its high hills and deep ravines, was densely wooded. There he dwelt for many years, subsisting upon herbs and roots, and he was martyred at a spot afterwards known as St. Decuman's Well.

Another hermit-martyr was Alnoth, a herdsman of St. Werburg, who, winning favour by his faithfulness, was released from serfdom, and became a solitary :—

This foresayd Alnotus by synguler grace
Refused this worlde pleasures and vanyte
Went unto wyldernesse and machoryte was
Whome theues martyred to heuen blysse went he
At Stow besyde Bukbrydge buryed was trule.

The place of his murder was Stow Wood in Bugbrooke, near Weedon.[1]

FIG. 2.—St. Werstan.

The Saxon saints included prince as well as serf.   After the martyrdom of St. Edmund the people desired to make his

[1] H. Bradshaw, *Lyfe of St. Werburge* (Chetham S. 1848), 101, 103.

brother Edwold king in his stead. From his youth up Edwold

FIG. 3.—The Hermit-Martyr of Malvern.

had given himself to the exercises of religion, and had earnestly
longed to retire into the wilderness. It was revealed to him

that he should depart from East Anglia and travel far until he should reach a fountain called " the silver well ".   After traversing many shires Edwold reached Dorset, where on a hillside, some four miles west of Cerne, he found the spring and built his hut.   The spot which he sought was indicated to him by a shepherd, who afterwards supplied him with milk and bread, and received from the solitary in return silver pennies.   When St. Edwold died, he was buried in his cell, but his body was eventually translated to Cerne.

Of the martyr-monk of the Malvern Hills little is known. Leland notes that near the priory stood the chapel of St. John Baptist, where St. Werstan suffered martyrdom.   Within the priory church is a series of painted glass windows (c. 1460), which depict a part of his story.   On a flower-covered hill kneels the hermit.   Above is seen a vision of angels, apparently indicating the spot where he should build his hermitage.   In the next window (Fig. 2) angels are represented as assisting in the consecration of the oratory.   In the third compartment a figure of St. Edward the Confessor is introduced, which suggests that he was in some way Werstan's benefactor or protector.   The last subject (Fig. 3) is the death of the saint, whose head is being struck off at the window of his cell.[1]

William of Malmesbury tells of another solitary who dwelt "in that vast wilderness which is called Malvern".   Aldwin lived with a fellow-hermit named Guy, and he was minded to accompany Guy on a pilgrimage to the Holy Land.   He sought counsel, however, of Wulstan, Bishop of Worcester (1062-1095), who urged him to stay at Malvern, foreseeing that a great work lay before him.   Aldwin therefore remained, and he lived to see the establishment through his influence of the priory at Great Malvern.   An inquisition entered in Bishop Giffard's Register (1268) states that in the time of Edward the Confessor or earlier, Aldwin lived in a wood granted to him by Hudde, Earl of Gloucester, where now stood the priory.   The foundation is elsewhere attributed to Urso d'Abytot.[2]

Early in the twelfth century a group of fen and forest re-

---

[1] Albert Way, in *Archæological Journal*, II, 48-65.
[2] Reg. Giffard (Worc. Hist. S.), II, 178; *Abbrev. Placit.* (Rec. Com.), 331.

cluses were dwelling miles apart in the counties of Hunting-
don, Bedford, and Hertford, whose lives were interwoven in a
singular manner. Edwin lived on the island of Higney, near
Ramsey. He surrounded his hermitage by a dyke, over which
there was a drawbridge. When he endeavoured to make an
outer dyke—because, for some unknown reason, certain shep-
herds of the neighbourhood endeavoured to burn down his
hut, but failed in the attempt—the men of Saltrey succeeded
in hindering him, and indeed drove him away; but after a
while he returned and made himself secure.

The assistance of Edwin, probably the hermit of Higney,
was sought in time of distress by Theodora (afterwards called
Christina), the young daughter of a certain Autie of Hunting-
don, and Beatrix his wife. Although vowed to maidenhood,
she had been forced into marriage by her parents, and cruelly
persecuted :—

"She had noe means to free herself but by flight; being ascisted
by one Edwine an Erimite, who procured her a horss, and a boye to
Convaye her, to one Alfwina an Anchorisse of Flamsteed . . . ;
from thence she went to one Roger a holie Ermitt, whoe lived in a
desert not farr from Dunstable."

Roger's hermitage was situated "by the wayside on the
right hand as you go from St. Albans to Dunstaple, hard by
the village which in these days is called Markyate"—a spot to
which he was said to have been led by the ministry of angels
on his return from pilgrimage to Jerusalem. Christina was
destined to become the devoted disciple of Roger, but family
claims and church order had first to be satisfied :—

"But before she came thither, Edwine, by Roger's means, whoe
refused to admitt her, imparted her case to Radulfe, Archb. of
Canterburie. . . . After this Burfred her husband together with the
Preist whoe had maried them, came with others to the Ermitage of
the forenamed Roger, and there in the presence of five Ermittes gave
her leave, notwithstanding that which had passed, to dispose of her
self as she pleased; and Thurstane Archb. of Yorke disolving the
Match with their consent, permitted him to Marrie, and shee to enter
into Religion." [1]

When the Archbishop of Canterbury died, Roger turned to
the Archbishop of York. As a monk of the proudly inde-

[1] N. Roscarrock, *Life of St. Christina*, in *Nov. Leg.* ii. 532-6.

pendent Abbey of St. Albans, he would acknowledge no
allegiance to the Bishop of Lincoln ; indeed, he had himself
been ordained sub-deacon by an Irish bishop, who had been
called in by the abbot to perform certain rites.   Archbishop
Thurstan, moreover, was a personal friend of Roger, whom he
revered for his goodness.   The archbishop, wishing to speak
privately with the maiden concerning her purpose, bade Roger
send her to him at Redbourn.   Travelling thither with
Godescal of Caddington and his wife, Christina was received
by Thurstan, who, having bestowed salutary counsel upon her,
sent her back to Roger :—

> " Now there was a building adjoining the oratory of the said
> Roger, with which it made an angle.   This [angle], having a board
> before it, might so be concealed as to lead the outside beholder to
> suppose that no man was in this space. . . . In this prison Roger
> placed the joyful Christina, and set for a door a proper oaken plank,
> which was so heavy that the anchoress could by no means move it
> either to or fro. . . . If she would have had Roger come to her she
> must call to him or smite upon the door, and how could the hidden
> virgin do this, who dared not utter even half a sigh ?   For she feared
> lest some other than Roger might be near, who at the mere sound of
> her breath might discover her hiding-place ; and she would rather
> have died in her prison than make herself known at that time to
> any person outside." [1]

There the recluse dwelt for over four years, enduring misery
with great fortitude (chapter X.).   So did she grow in grace that
the old monk cherished the hope that she should become heir
to his hermitage, and it was revealed to her that it should be
even so.   " At last Roger, leaving this world at the call of the
God whom he served, went the way of all flesh."

Hearing of Roger's death, Thurstan sent for Christina,
treated her with great kindness, and offered to provide for her.
" After this, she havyng Choyce of sundrie places, preferred
Sainct Albons, where she had vowed virginitie, and where her
deare frind Roger laye buried : and Alexander Bishop of Lin-
colne vailing her, she lived under the obedience of the Abbott
of St. Albons as Roger before had done."

It is noteworthy that no less than two archbishops, three

---

[1] *Gest. Abb.* (Rolls, 28, IV.) I. 98-9, trans. G. G. Coulton, *Mediaeval
Garner*, 510.

bishops, two mitred abbots, and a pope are concerned in the life story of this young recluse. Her case is committed by one friend to Ralph d'Escures, Archbishop of Canterbury (*d.* 1122), and by another to Thurstan, Archbishop of York (*d.* 1140); she is persecuted by Ralph Flambard, the wicked Bishop of Durham (*d.* 1128); Robert Bloet of Lincoln (*d.* 1123) is amongst her detractors, but she receives the veil from his successor, Alexander.   She becomes the counsellor of the powerful Abbot Geoffrey, who appoints her first prioress of Markyate; whilst Abbot Robert uses her as an instrument in his dealings with the English Pope, Adrian IV, whose favour he won by the gift of three mitres and a pair of sandals exquisitely embroidered by Christina.   Lastly, Henry II makes a grant for her support, fifty shillings a year being paid out of the exchequer (1155) "in corn which the king gives to Lady Christina of the Wood ".[1]

Nor was Christina the only woman in that neighbourhood who lived thus in seclusion.   In a wood close to St. Albans two holy women made a wattled hut of boughs and twigs and logs covered with bark.   They lived "in wonderful abstinence" for some years, until Abbot Geoffrey, who approved the lives of these recluses, added to their number, and the settlement at Eywood became Sopwell Nunnery.   In one charter it is stated that this *cellula* was rebuilt by Roger.

Sigar, another monk of St. Albans, dwelt at Northaw. In that richly-wooded part of Hertfordshire nightingales abounded, and their chorus disturbed the hermit's devotions. He, therefore, made supplication that they might be removed "lest he might seem to rejoice rather in the warbling of birds than in the worship whereunto he was bound before God ". John Amundesham declares that in his own day nightingales not only never presumed to sing, but never appeared within a mile of the hermitage.   Sigar was wont to walk every night to St. Albans in time for matins.   He was buried in the abbey in the same tomb as "St. Roger" (see p. 113).

A northern hermit now arose to fame.   Godric of Finchale dwelt in various waste places before he finally settled down beside the river Wear.   In his youth he followed successively

---

[1] *Pipe R.*, ed. Hunter, 1844, 22.   The priory, called Holy Trinity *de Bosco*, was in Caddington, at Markyate, now Market Street.

the callings of sailor, trader, and household steward.   The first longing to embrace the solitary life came to him as the result of a visit to Farne, although he did not at once become a follower of St. Cuthbert, but went on pilgrimage to St. James of Compostella in Spain, to the hermitage of St. Giles in France, and to Rome.   When he resolved to make the journey to Rome a second time, he was accompanied by his mother.   The pilgrims set out on foot, and when they came to ford or ditch Godric carried Aedwen on his back.   Beyond London there met them in the way a lovely maiden, who asked permission to join in their pilgrimage.   They readily assented, and henceforth she served them with grace and diligence.   They knew not who she was or whence she came, and none of the company save themselves saw the mysterious maiden.   When they were returning, and had reached the place where they had first met, she bade farewell with words of benediction.

After Godric had restored his mother in safety to his father's protection and had received their blessing, he sold all that he had and made his way to Carlisle, where, in the neighbouring forest of Inglewood, he searched for the empty den of some wild beast.   Desiring to follow the example of John Baptist in the wilderness, he lived on herbs and wild honey, with acorns, nuts, and crab-apples.   He slept upon the bare ground, and, rising at daybreak, went forth to gather food, falling on his knees in prayer every few paces.   Godric then became the disciple of an aged hermit at Wolsingham in Weardale (p. 128).   After Aelric's death, the wanderer went off a second time to the Holy Land.   There he worshipped at the sacred Sepulchre, and bathed in the Jordan ; and whilst staying in Jerusalem he ministered to his fellow-pilgrims in St. John's hospital.   The attraction of the solitary life was irresistible, and he went to see the hermits dwelling in the subterranean caves of the Judean deserts.

On Godric's return to England, he found a secret place in the forest near Whitby, and for over a year dwelt in a turf-covered log hut in Eskdale.   He at length discovered, in the forest north of Durham, the unknown valley of Finchale, where St. Cuthbert in a vision had bidden him ultimately settle ; whereupon he made a cave in the earth near the bank of the river Wear.   Possibly this was at the place still called

PLATE VI

ST. GODRIC OF FINCHALE

"St. Godric's Garth," in the lower whin-covered open ground nearly a mile above Finchale. The hermit afterwards betook himself to a more favourable spot, "well fitted both by situation and view for habitation". It was a level plot at the bend of the Wear, sheltered by the rushing river, with its steep, rocky, densely wooded banks. During a part of his sojourn it became an island, encircled by the flood which rose so high on one occasion that he was nearly swept away. He encountered many perils. He was once bound and all but killed by marauding Scots, who broke into his cell in the hope of securing treasure. He would have been in danger from the beasts of the forest, had he not possessed that mysterious power over the lower creation which has been attributed to many saints, and especially to those of the desert. Upon his arrival at Finchale (which was the bishop's hunting-ground), a wolf rushed at him as though it would tear him to pieces. He made the sign of the cross and adjured the creature to depart, whereupon it crouched at his feet as if begging pardon. "The number of serpents was fearful, but they were all tame towards the man of God". Sometimes, as he sat by the fire, they would coil themselves round his legs, or settle in his dish. They so multiplied, however, that they hindered his devotions, and he bade them enter no more. The picturesque legends describe Godric as a gentle companion, but firm master, of the wild creatures, forbidding the stag to touch his trees, or the leveret his herbs. He was the protector of beasts pursued in the chase; he delivered birds from the snare of the fowler; he nursed back to life little animals which were half-dead through the severity of the northern winter.

The legend round the figure of *Goderyke heremit*, depicted in Plate VI, runs thus :—

In wasterne and in wildernes . whare nane wont bot wilde
I went and in halines . a heremitage i plylde
The fendes with faindinges of my flesche . fayne walde me haue filede
Bot gode his grace to me gune dres . elles hade i bene gilde.[1]

There are two graphic descriptions of Brother Godric, one

[1] B.M. Cott. Faust. B. vi, pars. ii. f. 16 *b*.

    wont, dwelt; *plylde*, ? build ; *faindinges*, temptations; *filed*, defiled; the last line may be translated "unless God had begun to address (or direct) his grace to me, I should have been beguiled ".

recalling his strength in the prime of life, the other portraying him in the grace and dignity of advanced years :—

" He was a man earnest in spirit and fond of work, in body vigorous, of undiminished strength, moderate in stature, having broad shoulders, a wide chest, a long face, eyes grey and brilliantly flashing, thick eyebrows, a broad forehead, wide nostrils, a well-shaped hooked nose, a narrow chin, with a beard thick and rather long, a comely mouth, lips moderately full, the hair of his head and of his beard black in his younger days, but in old age of a hoary whiteness.   His neck was short and thick with full lines of sinews and veins; shins moderately thick, feet with good insteps, knees thickened and hard through his often kneelings; the skin of his body was very rough, but in old age all that roughness was turned to softness." [1]

This stalwart, steadfast solitary remained at Finchale for sixty years.   His extraordinary asceticism seemed only to harden him ; but at length he was conquered by infirmity, and was stricken with disease.   The last stage of life is thus described by an eye-witness, William of Newborough :—

" When then he had lived to a feeble old age, he lay for a few years before his death in great weakness of body, and for a long time preserved some measure of life in his perishing body by small draughts of milk.   In those days I was privileged to see him and to speak with him as he lay in his own oratory near the high altar. When then he appeared to be in his body under the shadow of death, he nevertheless spoke readily enough those words which were often on his lips : ' In the Name of the Father and of the Son and of the Holy Ghost,' repeating them over and over again.   In his countenance, moreover, there appeared a certain dignity and beauty unknown before.   Thus he passed away, old and full of days, and his body now occupies the very spot of ground in which he was wont to lie prostrate in prayer or in sickness." [2]

St. Godric died on 21 May, 1170.   The grave which he had himself prepared became the resort of thousands of pilgrims.   The priory of Finchale (Plate VII) grew up round the shrine, where many miracles of healing were wrought.

Not infrequently, as in the case of Finchale, the cell developed into a monastery.   It happened that Ralph Aldlave, chaplain of Henry I, fell ill at Pontefract.   Going one day

---

[1] Anon. chronicler (probably Reginald).   See *Vita*, 30, 31 n.
[2] *Hist. Rerum Angl.* (Rolls, 82), i. 150.

PLATE VII

FINCHALE

into the woods on his recovery, he found there certain men living in seclusion—probably Gilbert, hermit of St. James, Nostell and his brethren, mentioned in an early charter. Adlave (or Adelwold) became the first prior of the community of St. Oswald's.[1] Radmore, in the royal chase of Cannock, was granted to Clement and Hervey ; but finding the foresters troublesome, the hermits removed to Stoneleigh where they built a priory. Beaulieu Priory grew out of the hermitage of Moddry Wood, once tenanted by Ralph de Nuers, a monk of Lichfield.

Many monasteries sent forth monks to inhabit desolate parts of their territory. Whitby Abbey appointed monks to lonely outposts at Goathland, Eskdaleside, Saltburn, and Mulgrave. About the year 1220 there was a hermit at Shap in Westmorland, probably a brother from the abbey, who received by the will of Agnes de Clifford one mark.

In the Cumberland forest of Inglewood there were hermitages at Sebergham and Ilekirk. That of St. Hilda at Ilekirk was held by Roger Goky, and was afterwards granted by royal charter to Holme Cultram Abbey. In 1223 the abbot himself, Adam de Kendal, retired thither. He had become insane after the failure of ambitious schemes, and dwelt there until his death under the care of the monk Ralph.[2]

There were cells also in Charnwood Forest. Charley Hall, with the field called Priests' Close, occupies the site of St. Mary's hermitage. It was at one time under Luffield Priory, but the Earl of Winchester became patron both of Charley and Ulverscroft. The hermitage of Ulverscroft developed into an abbey. That of Haliwell Haw was under Garendon Abbey.

Several solitaries dwelt in the forests of Wychwood and Brill. The king, as lord of the forest, was usually the original patron of the cells, but in course of time they were placed under religious houses : Loughborough ("Lovebyri" or Low Barrow, near Leafield) was granted to Lechlade, Lockeslegh to Deerhurst, Muswell to Missenden, and Brill to Chetwode. The foregoing were actual hermitages, but the word was occasionally given to semi-parochial chapels served by secular

[1] Nostell MS. in *Scott. Hist. Rev.* No. 26, pp. 153-4; cf. *V.C.H. Yorks*, III. 234.

[2] Fordun, *Scotichron.*, ed. Goodall, II. 12.

priests.   Thus Chetwode had a so-called " hermitage " (distinct from that of Brill), founded by Robert, lord of Chetwode. Lord Ralph nominated to it a chaplain, who was " canonically instituted therein as perpetual guardian with the duty of a vicarage".   Bishop Grosseteste enters in his register the following illuminating memorandum : " This place is commonly called by lay people a hermitage, on account of its loneliness, not because any hermit at any time was accustomed to dwell there, but a chaplain serves there, after the manner of a secular, and is bound to live there with a suitable household ".

In the Forest of Dean there were cells at Ardland, St. Briavels, and Taynton.   Ardland, or Ertlond, seems to have been between Cinderford and Newnham-on-Severn.   Henry II gave this place to a certain William the hermit, who afterwards, in the days of Richard I, entered stricter seclusion at that chapel.   He was taken under the protection of the Abbot of Flaxley, who promised him food and clothing.   In 1225 Panye de Lench became a recluse at Ardland, and was granted by Henry III four acres of land and also two oaks for the construction of her dwelling.

The hermitage of St. Briavels is mentioned early in the twelfth century.   It was afterwards granted by Henry III to Grace Dieu Abbey (Monmouthshire), on condition that three priests should celebrate there for the souls of his ancestors. The wildness of the spot is shown by the fact that, as late as 1361, the chantry was removed to the abbey on account of the depredations of the beasts of the forest.   There are said to be traces of the chapel at Stowe Grange.

Whilst the twelfth and thirteenth centuries were pre-eminently the period of the solitary, there were throughout the fourteenth century some retreats in wood and wilderness.   In 1323, for example, there was a hermit at Dalby in Pickering Forest.   Again, the chapel of Losfield in Clewer (now called St. Leonard's Hill), which had been occupied by a certain William the hermit in Henry III's time, was afterwards inhabited by a succession of solitary priests.   In 1355 it was held by another William, and seems, from the following petition, to have been a place of pilgrimage :—

" Whereas William the hermit, chaplain of St. Leonard, Loffield, in Windsor forest, lives a solitary life, and serves God alone, and

PLATE VIII

A FOREST HERMIT

whereas a multitude of people flock to the chapel, the pope is prayed to grant an indulgence to those who visit the said chapel . . . and give alms to the fabric." [1]

In the same year there was, as formerly, a hermit living on the slopes of the Wrekin. The first tenant of this cell on *Mons Gilberti* was Nicholas de Denton, a clerk, who received a piece of land from Shrewsbury Abbey. The king granted him another plot for an oratory, and also contributed six quarters of corn every year in order to give him greater leisure for holy exercises, and to support him so long as he should be a hermit on the mountain.

The woods and hills of Somerset and Dorset had their solitaries. In 1317 a chaplain was instituted to the hermitage in Rechych or Neroche Forest. At Winscombe on the Mendips there was a hermit at the place commonly called *locus S. Romani* (1331). Polden Hill had a cell made for herself by the chapel of St. Thomas by a woman named Elneva. In 1505 John the hermit of St. Thomas super Powldon received 4*d.* as the bequest of a neighbour at Cossington. The chapel in the forest near Wimborne was inhabited in 1395, when Lady Alice West bequeathed 40*s.* "to the Reclus frere Thomas atte seynt Iames in the Holte".

A succession of chaplains dwelt at Clipston in the royal forest of Sherwood. To one of these King John paid 40*s.* a year, and Henry III continued the grant to one Benedict, hermit of St. Edwin at Birkland. Priests were instituted to this chantry throughout the fourteenth and fifteenth centuries. The sixteenth-century commissioners reported that "itt hathe no mancyon butt a parlor under the chappell of no valewe".

Turning from history to romance, Sherwood is the scene of the exploits of the hermit-poacher who unwittingly entertained his king. It befell in good King Edward's days—so runs the popular minstrel's tale of the fourteenth century [2]— that the king went a-hunting. Towards eventide he missed his way, and espying a hermitage, asked harbour. The inmate replied that it was but a poor place, yet since it was far from the town he consented to receive the stranger. " I dwell here

---

[1] Papal Reg., *Petitions*, I. 270; *Lett.* III. 572.
[2] W. Carew Hazlitt, *Early Pop. Poetry*, 11-35.

among wild beasts in the wilderness, living upon roots and rinds," says the solitary. "Did I dwell in this forest," exclaims the other, "when the foresters were asleep, then would I cast off my habit and stalk deer, to glad me and my guest —for the king needs not the venison!" The man replies piously that his work is not archery, but prayer and penance; as for himself, he eats no meat. He sets before the king bread and cheese and thin ale. After a while the hungry huntsman discovers that the cell can produce not only white bread, but collops of deer's flesh. "Wyllym Alyn," the serving-lad, goes out to feed the horse, and when host and guest are left alone, they make merry over a pot of wine. The huntsman admires the skill and strength that can bend such a bow as hangs over the bed, and invites the hermit to visit him in the town, adding: "Jhake Flecher, that is my name; all men knowys me at home". Next morning the solitary shows the stranger his way; after leaving him the king blows his bugle, and at the blast come anxious knights and foresters who had sought him in vain. They ride away, and the MS. breaks off before the hermit has fulfilled his promise of visiting his whilom guest. This old tale was retold by Sir Walter Scott in "Ivanhoe," where the Clerk of Copmanhurst entertains the Black Knight.[1]

Mention must also be made of the murdered monk of Eskdaleside. In the time of Henry II, certain barons were hunting in a wood belonging to the Abbot of Whitby. Having found a great wild boar, the hounds ran him near about the hermitage of Eskdaleside, where dwelt a solitary monk of Whitby. The boar, hotly pursued, went in at the chapel door, and there died: whereupon the hermit shut the hounds out and remained within at his meditations. Following the cry of the hounds, the huntsmen came to the cell, where they found the boar lying dead. In fury they rushed violently at the hermit with their boar-staves, and he died soon afterwards. Before his death, however, the monk desired the abbot to send for those who had wounded him, and freely forgave them, but he enjoined a certain penance upon them for the salvation of their souls.

[1] The cave cell of Friar Tuck is shown at Copmanhurst near Fountain Dale.

The names and dates incorporated in the legend are not confirmed by records. The date given is the fifth year of Henry II ; the murderers are William de Bruce and Ralph de Perci, whilst the abbot is Sedman, a name unknown in the annals of Whitby. The cartulary of Meaux shows that about this time a hermit called Sedeman was dwelling at St. Leonard's, near Egton, in Whitbystrand. This cell, however, did not belong to Whitby; it was at first in the hands of William le Gros, Earl of Albemarle, and was granted by him to Meaux.[1]

The popular story of the monk of Whitby passed into " Marmion " :—

> In wrath for loss of sylvan game
> Saint Hilda's priest ye slew.

[1] B.M. Cott. Vesp. E., xix. f. 80 *b* ; Burton, *Monast. Ebor.* 78-9.

III. CAVE DWELLERS

Far from men in the wilderness . . . enclosed in a cave . . . deep down in the grey rock.—*Life of Edward the Confessor*

THE solitary dwelt not only in desert or mountain, but in dens and caves. It seems natural to associate him with hidden haunts in deep valleys or riverside crags.

Hollowed out at the base of the Cratcliff rocks, near Stanton-in-Peak, is a cave, small and bare indeed, but perhaps the most impressive of our hermitages. There dwelt a solitary whose name has not been recorded, but graven in the rocky wall is a lasting memorial of his faith. In a recess at the eastern end is a simple, striking rood (Plate XXXI). The crockets on the cross suggest the budding foliage of the tree of life. The features are defaced, but the sacred figure is boldly executed. A manuscript Rule of hermits, dating from the fourteenth century (probably contemporary with this sculpture), says: " Let it suffice thee to have on thine altar an image of the Saviour hanging upon the cross, which represents to thee His passion which thou shalt imitate, inviting thee with outspread arms to Himself ".[1]

In the same county, near Repton, is the cave-pierced rock called Anchor Church (Plate IX), which from its name is believed to have sheltered an " anker ".[2] It has been suggested that this was the abode of the hermit mentioned by John of Tynemouth, who used to visit Modwen, the legendary lady of Burton (chapter I.). The tradition of his name and dwelling-place has been preserved in a fragment of an early printed book :—

" [One] tyme dwelled an holy heremyte, whose name was [Ha]rdulche in a place named Bredon. He herde tell

[1] Camb. Univ. MS., VI, 17, f. 74 *b*, 75.
[2] Compare Anchor Church House, Crowland, Nichols, *Leicestershire*, IV, Pt. I, p. 2.

PLATE IX

ANCHOR CHURCH

[of Mod]wen's holy lyuynge and wente oft to her and bare
[boke]s of holy sayntes lyues.　On a daye this holy man
[left h]is boke at home, and therfore she made great
[*wailing*] and sayd, Father why bringest thou not thy
　　booke
[like a]s thou were wonte to do.　Madame he sayde I
[haue] forgoten.　That tyme saynt Hardulche had a
　　celle in
[a c]lyffe a lytell frome trent." [1]

Then St. Modwen sent two of her maidens in a boat to his
hermitage to fetch the book.　A tempest arose and overturned
the boat, but (needless to relate) they were rescued by the
miraculous intervention of their mistress.　Anchor Church is,
it is true, some miles from Breedon-on-the-Hill (where the
church is dedicated to St. Mary and St. Hardulph), but in
those remote times the parish of Breedon, or the lands of its
monastery, may have extended to the Trent.　Probably the
original hermitage—if such it was—consisted of "church" and
cell.　There are now four chambers in a semicircle, one of
which commands a view of the Trent valley.　The river no
longer runs beneath the rock, but a pool indicates its former
course.

There was perhaps no hermitage which possessed a more
beautiful situation than that of Guy's Cliffe, near Warwick.
This rugged precipice, washed by the Avon, is clad in living
green.　Leland saw in this spot—with its mossy caverns,
clear springs, and flowery fields—a place of more than ordinary
beauty.　Its silence was only broken by "the river rollynge
with a praty noyse over the stones ".

In the time of King Athelstan—so the story goes—this
cliff became the retreat of Guy of Warwick.　Returning from
pilgrimage, the famous warrior arrived at Warwick, and received an alms from Felicia his wife, who failed to recognize
him in his pilgrim's weeds.　He then carried out his resolve
to retire into a cave not far distant from his lady's castle :—

"He repaired to an heremite that resided amongst the shady woods
hard by, desiring . . . to receive some spiritual comfort, where he

---

[1] Sir Matthew Joyce's pamphlet on "St. Hardulph" contains a facsimile of
the page of black letter bound as a flyleaf into a volume in Lord Kenyon's
library.

abode with that holy man till his death, and . . . succeeded him in that Cell . . . and continued for the space of two years after; but then discerning death to approach, he sent to his Lady their wedding Ring by a trusty servant, wishing her to take care of his burial: adding also, that when she came, she should find him lying dead in the Chapel, before the Altar; and moreover, that within xv dayes after she her self should depart this life. She came accordingly, and brought with her the Bishop and others, and did honourably interre [his body] in that Heremitage."

This romantic tale, derived from Gerard of Cornwall, is recorded in the chronicle of Hyde Abbey, under the date 927.[1]

The hermit's cave (Plate X) is small, narrow, and almond-shaped. It is about 14½ feet long, and barely 5 feet at its widest point. The rudely-hewn entrance, being 5 feet above the floor, is more like a window than a door. Opposite this opening is a panel in the rocky wall, bearing an obliterated inscription. According to an ingenious, but doubtful, reading, it is rendered: *Remove, O Christ, from thy servant this weight —Guthi.*[2] If this were a genuine record of some recluse's prayer, it would add a living interest to the cell, but the semi-runic characters are regarded with suspicion by scholars.

Guy's cave and Guy's well are mentioned by Leland. "Men shew a cave there in a rok hard on Avon ripe, where they say that he used to slepe. Men also yet showe fayr springs in a faire medow thereby, where they say that Erle Guido was wont to drinke." The well, reached by a path along the riverside, is in an arched recess. Richard Beauchamp "enclosyd the silver welles in the medow with pure whit slike stone like marble". The carved slab in which the twin-basins are scooped, is time-worn and overgrown with creeping liver-wort, but a never-failing spring bubbles out of the rock into the well.

Early in the thirteenth century Brother Wiger, canon of Oseney, took up his abode in the hermitage, having determined, with the consent of his abbot, to lead the solitary life at the place called Gibbecliff.[3] Gilbert, described in an ordination list (1283) as the hermit "of Warwick," may have dwelt

---

[1] *Liber de Hyda* (Rolls, 45) 122-3; Dugd., *Warwickshire*, I. 273, 275; see also *Romance of Guy of Warwick* (E. E. Text S., 1875), 302-7.

[2] R. Carr, 1870, "Anglo-Saxon Epigraph " (Warwick Museum).

[3] B.M. Cotton. Vitell. E., xv., 186, per Rev. H. Salter.

PLATE X

HERMIT'S CAVE, GUY'S CLIFFE

PLATE XI

GUY'S STATUE

THE CLOISTERS

GUY'S CLIFFE

here. The names of Thomas de Lewes, Robert Maudith, and John Burry also occur as hermits of Gibbecliff.

At one time the cell was under the care of the priory at Warwick, but the earl, recovering the patronage, converted it into a chantry. In the Rows Roll, Richard Beauchamp is represented bearing the chapel in his right hand and the young king in his left. He was the kinsman and guardian of Henry VI (see p. 155) in the first year of whose reign he obtained licence to found a perpetual chantry in the chapel called Gibbecliff, wherein two priests should perform divine service for the souls of the king and of the founders. He did so " that God would send him heir male," prompted thereto by the prophetic visions of an anchoress at York :—

" He did hyt by the styrryng of a holy anchoras namyd dam Em Rawghtone dwellyng at all halows in the northe strete of york and for hyt to her apperyd our lady vii tymes in on yer and seyd that in tyme to cum . . . hyt shuld be a gracious place to seke to for eny dises or gref and on of Seynt Gyes Eyris shuld bryng hys Reliks a geyn to the same place." [1]

William Worcester notes in his *Itinerary* that Richard Beauchamp caused a fair house to be made for the priests called hermits, and Leland mentions " a praty howse of stone for the cantuary prists by the chapel ". It is uncertain to which of the rock-hewn dwellings the travellers refer. The lofty hall with pillars and arches, surrounded by an ambulatory, is known as the cloisters [2] (Plate XI). There is a range of cells in both upper and lower cliffs. Some of them have small square-headed windows and other signs of habitation.

The " right goodly chapell of St. Mary Magdalene " is still in use, after careful restoration in 1875. The ancient door is massive, carved and iron bound. A huge oak chest has been preserved. Within the chapel, cut in the rock, is a gigantic statue of Sir Guy ; it is about 9 feet high and represents him as warrior, the victor over Colbrand the Dane. Shakespeare doubtless had this figure in his mind when he writes : " I am not Samson, nor Sir Guy, nor Colbrand, to mow them

---

[1] *Rows Roll*, ed. 1845, sect. 50 (John Rows was chantry priest at Guy's Cliffe ; he was aged in 1491. His *Vetustates Clivi Guidonici* perished by fire.) Dame Emma was instrumental in the appointment of Richard Beauchamp as Regent, see chapter XII.

[2] Dimensions 32 × 28 ft., or excluding ambulatory 23 × 12½ ft.

down before me". It appears to date from the early part of the thirteenth century, although according to Leland it was Earl Richard who set up there "an ymage great lyke a giant". Richard Beauchamp held his famous ancestor in especial honour. Like Guy he went on pilgrimage, and like Guy did deeds of prowess. Richard Neville, "the king-maker," purposed "to have woltyd and butracyd sir Guys caue for fallyng downe of the hangyng rok . . . and to let peynt Sir Gyes Image". His further scheme to enlarge the chantry as an almshouse was never carried out, owing, probably, to the Wars of the Roses.

Fuller, after describing the charms of Guy's Cliffe, adds :—

"Many hermites . . . being sequestred from the world, retreated hither. Some will say it is too gaudy a place for that purpose, as having more of a paradice then wilderness therein. . . . But seeing hermits deny themselves the company of men, let them be allowed to converse with the rarities of nature."

The hermitage near Bridgnorth (Plate XII) is said to date from the tenth century, and the rock of Athelardston, in the royal forest of Morf, was, by the tradition preserved by Leland, the habitation of a brother of Åthelstan. Nothing authentic is known before the fourteenth century, when the Crown nominated several persons. A Patent Roll entry sets forth that :—

"Whereas Roger de Burghton, chaplain, inflamed with the fervour of devotion, has arranged to take the habit of a hermit, and has made instant supplication to the king to grant him for life the hermitage at Atherlaston on the high road by Bruggenorth now void, wherein to dwell, that he may pray for the king, queen Philippa and their children : the king has granted his petition."

Athelardston, now Hermitage hill, is near the top of the sandstone ridge above the Severn valley. The rock consisted of four chambers. A small door opens into the largest cave, about 33 feet long, including the chapel (Plate XII), which is the most complete part remaining. A passage and flight of steps lead to the upper cave, which, like the lower side cave, is now roofless, the soft stone having crumbled away.[1]

The county of Worcester had several habitable caves, as,

[1] Hubert Smith, *Shropshire Arch. Trans.* I.

PLATE XII

THE HERMITAGE, BRIDGNORTH

PLATE XIII

THE CHAPEL, BRIDGNORTH HERMITAGE

for example, those at Redstone, Blackstone, and Southstone. That of Redstone (Plate XXII), near Stourport, contained a chapel with an altar and several chambers, all hewn in the rock. Over the altar there was formerly a wall-painting which depicted an archbishop saying Mass, and above it an inscription declaring some indulgence to those who frequented this place with devotion. Those who trafficked on Severn used to make offerings of their commodities to the hermit as they passed. Some suppose that Layamon dwelt here when compiling his translation of Wace's *Brut*. "It appearethe the Hermittes weare buryed heere, althoughe the stone hardly yeeldethe a grave."

In some unknown cave in the neighbourhood of Evesham dwelt one of the most influential recluses of the west. "On the slope of a wood, enclosed in a cave, deep down in the grey rock," Wulsi lived in seclusion through the troublous reigns of Cnut, Edward the Confessor, Harold, William the Conqueror, and William Rufus. He was brought up in Worcestershire, but became a Benedictine monk at Crowland. He was unskilled in literary pursuits, and could neither sing in the choir, nor cater in the market ; but he felt that he had a vocation for the contemplative life. He therefore sought to become an anchorite, that he might pray unceasingly for the whole community and for himself. A few years passed peacefully, but upon Cnut's death there was an upheaval in the kingdom. A multitude of men, women, and children took refuge at Crowland, and they "everlastingly" disturbed the whole monastery. But more than all, they distracted Wulsi ; for day and night they consulted him, crowding to the doors of his humble cell as though it were some royal palace. The din made Wulsi weary of his life, and he had not time for devotion. Worn out, and fearing lest, while people called him holy, he should fall into utter desperation and rush headlong into depths of wickedness, he at length, by the advice of the prior, sought tranquillity at Evesham, and there in a cavern and in the chapel of St. Kenelm hard by, he served God in all holiness of life.[1]

Some years later, a vision was vouchsafed to the hermit.[2]

---

[1] Peter of Blois, Continuation of Ingulph's *Chron.*, ed. Riley, 252-5.
[2] Flete, *Hist. of Westminster* (ed. J. A. Robinson), 45, 46, from Aelred's *Life of St. Edward* (R. Twysden, *Hist. Angl. Script.* x., col. 382).

One night, after much prayer and meditation, the Apostle Peter, bright and beautiful, appeared saying :—

"Fear not, brother; I am Peter, who keep the keys of Heaven. Tell Edward the king that his prayer is accomplished; of all his sins he has pardon, and absolution from his vow . . . on the condition that to me he make a house, where he may have a convent of monks. . . . At London is the spot marked out, two leagues from the city, at Thorney, where is a church, ancient and low . . . towards the west on the Thames. I myself will consecrate the spot with my hands. . . . Whatever I have here said to you, clearly put it in writing."

Wulsi delayed not. In the morning he wrote it on parchment, and caused it to be carried as from St. Peter to the king (Plate XIV). The writing and receiving of the roll are well depicted in the thirteenth-century manuscript.[1] Meanwhile the messengers (who had gone to obtain a release from the king's vow to go on pilgrimage) returned from Rome, and since the two messages agreed, the Divine will seemed clear : "For the one comes from the east, and the other from the west . . . hence every one is assured of it, because no tidings could have reached the recluse, who was very far away in the country of Worcester, far from men in the wilderness."

After living in seclusion for seventy-five years Wulsi died, and was buried at Evesham. The shrine of "St. Wlsin" was one of the treasures of that abbey.

The solitary life was embraced by persons of every estate, not only by the noble lord of Warwick and the high-born monk of Worcester, but by a baker of Derby and a citizen of York. The narrative concerning the pious townsman of Derby —"not a tale, but a circumstance which most certainly happened"—is recorded by Thomas de Musca.[2] The baker was a Godfearing man, intent on good works, "being in a measure another Cornelius". Whatever food and clothing he could procure during the week beyond what was needful for his family he would bring on Saturday to St. Mary's church, for distribution amongst the poor. At length, yielding to a call

---

[1] *La Estoire de S. Aedward*, Camb. Univ. MS. Ee. 59. See *Lives of Edward* (Rolls, 3), p. 8; Kemble, *Cod. Dip.* IV. 175.

[2] Trans. by Mr. W. H. St. J. Hope.

PLATE XIV

ST. WULSI, THE HERMIT-SEER

which seemed unmistakable, he exchanged social life for solitude, commerce for contemplation, prosperity for privation.

"It happened that on a certain day in autumn when he had given himself up to repose at noon, there appeared to him in his dreams the Blessed Virgin Mary, saying: "Thy alms are acceptable before my Son and me. But now if thou wilt be perfect, leave all that thou hast and go to Depedale and there thou shalt serve my Son and me in solitude."

Awaking, he straightway left all that he possessed. Ignorant of the place for which he was bound, he turned eastwards, and in passing through a village, heard a woman bidding a maiden drive the cattle into Depedale; he followed forthwith.

"He found that the place was a marsh, exceeding dreadful, and far distant from every habitation of man. And turning himself to the south-east of the place, under the side of the mountain, he cut out for himself in the rock a very small dwelling, and an altar turned to the south which has been preserved to this day, and there, by day and night, he served God in hunger and thirst, and cold and nakedness."

Now Ralph Fitz Geremund was hunting one day in his woods of Ockbrook. He caught sight of smoke ascending from the cave, and was indignant that anyone had dared to make himself a habitation. But seeing the miserable case of the man of God who was clad in rags and skins, the baron was smitten to the heart, and granted him the place, giving him also for his support the tithe of the mill of Burgh. Lacking water, the hermit wandered about near his abode until he found a spring, beside which he made a hut and built an oratory in honour of God and the Blessed Virgin. In almost unendurable solitude the hermit of Dale steadfastly carried out his resolve, until at length "having finished the struggle of his life laudably in the service of God, he passed happily from the prison of his body to the Lord".

Dale hermitage (Plate XV) is situated in a steep wooded hillside above the dale and its ruined abbey. The rock is overhung with beeches which seem to be embedded in the sandstone. The cave is about 20 feet long, 9 feet wide, and 9 feet high. Possibly it was originally of two compartments. It has a doorway and two other openings. The walls are much defaced, but there is a niche to the west. In an orchard at the foot of the hill a spring which never runs dry is still called "the hermit's well"

Robert of Knaresborough was a citizen of York. According to a fourteenth-century chronicle, his surname was Koke. Leland calls him "one Robert Flowr, sunne to one Robert Flowr, that had beene 2 tymes Mair of York". Other authorities give his father's name as Touke or Tok Flour, and his mother's as Onnuryte, Simunina, or Sunniva.[1] The pious youth became a lay brother of Newminster in Northumberland, but after a few months he sought stricter seclusion. Being doubtless well acquainted with Knaresborough (only eighteen miles from his home), he determined to join a certain knight, rich and famous, who, having fled from the lion-like wrath of Richard I, was living apart from men on the banks of the Nidd. The two men dwelt together in a cave; but, after the king's death, the fugitive warrior returned to the world :—

> Langir lyked hym noght that lyffe
> Bott als a wreche wentt to hys wyffe,

leaving the "soldier of Christ" alone.

The young solitary was befriended by a virtuous matron named Helena, who gave him the chapel of St. Hilda at Rudfarlington in Knaresborough forest.[2] There he abode for a while, but when thieves broke into his hermitage, he moved on to Spofforth. Then, fearing lest the crowds which followed him should move him to vainglory, he accepted the invitation of the monks of Holy Trinity, York, to join some of their number at Hedley. The young zealot, clad in an old white garment, who would eat nought but barley bread and vegetable broth, was not a comfortable companion, and Robert, regarding his fellows as "fals and fekyll," returned to St. Hilda's. The noble dame was passing glad to see him, and provided a barn and other buildings for his use. William de Stuteville, Constable of Knaresborough, passing by, saw

---

[1] *Lanercost Chr.* (Bannatyne Club, 1839), 25-7 ; *Metrical Life* (Roxburghe Club); N. Roscarrock's *Life*, Camb. Univ. MS. C.Add. 3041, 377-9b.

[2] R. Stodley, *Vita*, B.M. Harl., 3775 f. 76; "ubi quondam uilla grandis que Rothferlington vocabatur". Rudfarlington, once a large township, is now a farm. A field towards Crimple Beck is called Chapel Garth.

PLATE XV

DALE HERMITAGE

the dwelling, and when he heard that one Robert, a devoted servant of God, lived there, he cried: "This is a hypocrite and a companion of thieves!" and bade his men "dyng doune hys byggynges". The homeless hermit took his book and fared through the forest to Knaresborough :—

> To a chapell of sayntt Gyle
> Byfor whare he had wouned a whyll
> That bygged was in tha buskes wyth in
> A lytell holett: he hyed hym in.

But again the lord of Knaresborough went a-hunting, and when he saw smoke rising from the hut, he swore that he would turn out the tenant. That night there " appered thre men blakker than Ynd," who roused him from his restless sleep. Two of them harrowed his sides with burning pikes, whilst the third, of huge stature, brandished two iron maces at his bedside: " Take one of these weapons and defend thy neck, for the wrongs with which thou spitest the man of God ". William cried for mercy and promised to amend his deeds, whereupon the vision vanished. Early in the morning the terrified tyrant hastened to the cell, and humbly sought pardon :—

> Roberd forgaff and William kyssed
> And blythely wyth hys hand hym blyssed.

The penitent baron then bestowed upon Robert all the land between the rock and Grimbald Kyrkstane, besides horses and cattle.

William de Stuteville was succeeded by Brian de Lisle, who regarded the hermit as his faithful friend. It was he who besought King John to visit Robert (see p. 153). This visit resulted in the further endowment of the cell. John bade Robert ask what he willed, but he replied that he had enough, and needed no earthly thing. When Ive found that alms for the poor had not been asked, he persuaded his master to follow the king, from whom he received the grant of a carucate of land. This land was appropriated to the use of the poor, and Robert refused to pay tithe for it to the rector, to whom he indignantly granted "crysts cursynge" for his covetousness. Robert was "to pore men profytable". He gathered alms for the needy, fed them at his door, and sheltered them in his cave. The complaint made by the angry baron that the hermit was a receiver of thieves had some truth in it.   In the rhyming life, Robert speaks of the corn required for "my cayteyffes in my cave".   His favourite form of charity was to redeem men from prison :—

> To begge an brynge pore men of baile,
> This was hys purpose principale.

St. Robert died on the 24 September, 1218.[1]   He had been a benefactor to many, and great was the grief of the mourners.   As he had foretold on his death-bed, the monks of Fountains sought to bear away his body, but Ive carried out his master's wish to be buried in the chapel of the Holy Cross, where he had himself prepared a rock-hewn grave.

> I wyll be doluen whar so I deghe
> Beried my body thare sall ytt be
> Wyth outen end here wyll I rest
> Here my wounyng chese I fyrste
> Here wyll I leyud here wyll I ly
> In this place perpetuely.

The chroniclers call St. Robert's first hermitage " the chapel of St. Giles," describing it as a dwelling under the rock formed by winding branches over stakes in front of a cave.   They relate how his brother Walter, who was mayor of York, thought this cavern and wattled hut no fitting habitation for him, and suggested that he should join some community. Robert replied : " This is my resting-place for ever : here will I dwell, for I have chosen it "—an answer which recalls the antiphon sung when a recluse was about to enter his life-long retreat.   Walter therefore sent workmen from the city who laid the foundations of a chapel in honour of the Holy Cross, built of hewn stone.   Evidently this chapel adjoined the cave, and replaced the humble oratory of St. Giles.

St. Robert's Cave is about a mile below the castle.   On the north bank of the river is a low cliff about 20 feet in height.   The descent is made by a narrow flight of steps, which ends in an uneven platform of rock about 40 feet in length of two levels, the upper one being the floor of the chapel, with traces of an altar at the eastern end (Plate XVI). Before the altar-steps is the tomb, deeply cut in the rock,

---

[1] 8 kal. Octobris, 1218, *Chr. Lanercost*, 25.   The *Dict. Nat. Biog.* gives c. 1235, but Chart. R. 1227 grants land of Brother Robert " formerly hermit there " to Ive.

PLATE XVI

CAVE AND TOMB OF ST. ROBERT, KNARESBOROUGH

which has a groove for a slab to cover it.[1] A mossy lichen-covered wall on the south shows the extent of the original building. On the north of the chapel (which now has a natural roof of beech and trailing greenery) is the picturesque ivy-clad cliff of a warm yellow and red tint. A low doorway gives access to the cave.[2]

After Robert's death, the cell was claimed as Crown property. A writ was issued (1219) to the Constable of Knaresborough to cause "our hermitage" to be given into the custody of Master Alexander de Dorset. The original grant was afterwards confirmed to Brother Ive, hermit of Holy Cross (1227).[3] The chapel became a place of pilgrimage, and many miracles of healing were wrought there, especially about twenty years after the saint's death. "The same year (1238) shone forth the fame of St. Robert the hermit at Knaresborough, from whose tomb medicinal oil was brought forth abundantly." Matthew Paris, naming in 1250 the chief personages of the last half-century, mentions in particular St. Edmund of Pontigny, St. Robert of Knaresborough, and St. Elizabeth of Hungary.[4] Although there seems to be no record of actual canonization, the hermit was universally regarded as a saint. The Papal records for the year 1252 contain an offer of indulgence to those who should help in completing "the monastery of St. Robert of Gnarebur, where that saint's body is buried". This new priory (or "House of St. Robert") was granted to the Trinitarian Friars, and it was fitting that the "Order of the Holy Trinity for the Redemption of Captives" should become successors of the saint who had delighted in releasing men from prison. The name Holy Cross or Holy Rood was superseded by that of the hermit. In 1257 Richard, Earl of Cornwall, confirmed to the Order the chapel of St. Robert. In the following century, letters of

[1] The grave measures 6 ft. 5 in. and is from 14-21 in. broad ; at the bottom is a hole 15 × 6 in.

[2] The cave is 16 ft. 8 in. from east to west, and is about 8 ft. at its widest; it is 5 ft. 10 in. high. At the N.E. corner is a recess 3 ft. 9 in. long. It is also known as " Eugene Aram's Cave," from the tragedy rendered famous by Lord Lytton and by Hood.

[3] The metrical life affirms that Ive gave the place to Coverham Abbey by charter.

[4] *Chr. Maj.* (Rolls, 57) III. 521 ; IV. 378 ; V. 195.

protection whilst collecting alms were granted by Edward
III to a follower of the saint who was also his namesake
and fellow-citizen, "Brother Robert of York, hermit of the
chapel of St. Robert".

Henceforth St. Robert was "the peirles patrone of this
place". Other chapels were built and dedicated to his
memory. Nothing is known of the history of the chapel
now called "St. Robert's," in the crag below the castle.
The tiny building contains an altar (Plate XVII), piscina, niche,
and seat, all carved out of the rock.[1] Near the entrance is a
figure with a drawn sword, the origin and meaning of which
are alike unknown (Plate XVII). Leland alludes but briefly
to this place : "A litle beneth March-Bridge . . . I saw an
old Chapelle yn a Rok hewen owte of the mayne stone".
There is no ground for believing that it was ever the habitation of St. Robert.

The rock-hewn cells of Pontefract and of Bristol will be
described in chapter VI. The history of St. Vincent's hermitage, Clifton (Plate XIX), is obscure. William Worcester
describes it as situated in the dangerous rock called Ghyston
Cliff. He speaks of "the hermitage with the church," and
again of "the hermitage and chapel". The "hall" and "kitchen" must refer to the caverns, but it is possible that the
chapel stood on a projecting ledge of limestone, now fallen.
An episcopal brief relating to it is preserved as a memorandum
in the episcopal register of Ely (1492). An indulgence is
offered to such as should assist and relieve Thomas Dene,
warden of the chapel of St. Mary and St. Vincent, and should
visit the chapel by way of pilgrimage or contribute to its preservation or the maintenance of lights and ornaments.[2] The
word "preservation" seems to suggest that the oratory had
been constructed, not merely hewn out of the rock. Some
support is given to this theory by the fact that an encaustic
tile and the fragment of a small Gothic window have been
found. It is evident that the chapel was the chief feature
of the place. It was a landmark, for Worcester records the

---

[1] The chapel is not more than 12 ft. long, including a miniature apse about
3 ft. in which the altar stands ; it is 8 ft. wide. In the centre of the floor is a
shallow cavity, 17 × 11 in.
[2] Reg. Alcock, f. 79-83.

PLATE XVI

ST. ROBERT'S CHAPEL, KNARESBOROUGH

PLATE XVIII

WARKWORTH HERMITAGE

height from the chapel to the summit of the lofty cliff, and down to the water below. Measurements would hardly have been given to him in this form had the chapel been out of sight. Worcester was struck with its perilous position ; but even this steep wall was by no means inaccessible, and the indulgence, dated within twelve years of the famous traveller's visit in 1480, shows that Thomas Dene expected his chapel to be the resort of the faithful.

Warkworth hermitage (Plate XXXVII), overhung by trees, with its well-defined architectural features, is a striking contrast to the rude caverns in the bare and precipitous rocks of the Avon gorge. It is pictured thus in the ballad *The Hermit of Warkworth :*—

> Then scoop'd within the solid rock,
>   Three sacred vaults he shows ;
> The chief a chapel, neatly arch'd,
>   On branching columns rose.
>
> Up to the altar's ample breadth
>   Two easy steps ascend ;
> And near, a glimmering solemn light
>   Two well-wrought windows lend.[1]

The hermitage is approached from the riverside by a flight of steps (Plate XVIII). The chapel of the Holy Trinity is reached through a tiny vestibule, in which is a rood. The chapel (about 20 feet long and $7\frac{1}{2}$ feet high) is of three bays (see ground plan, Fig. 4). It contains an altar, piscina (A), quatrefoil window (H), and hagioscope (J). These, with the shafts and capitals and the ribs of the roof are graven in the rock. In a recess to the south-east is a recumbent effigy, apparently that of a female, and above it a figure of a knight— monuments which suggested Bishop Percy's romantic ballad. The west wall is pierced with four lancet windows, beyond which is a small chamber, now open at the west end, having a window looking south upon the river. A long narrow chamber adjoins the principal chapel on the north and communicates with it by a doorway and by a fine Decorated window (Fig. 5). At the eastern end there is a small roughly-hewn oratory (C) containing traces of an altar, stoup (B), aumbry (D), and a hagioscope commanding the altar in the adjoining chapel.

[1] Percy, *Reliques*, III. 310.

Probably this narrow chamber was the original cell, entered from the west (I) by stone steps, some of which remain.   It

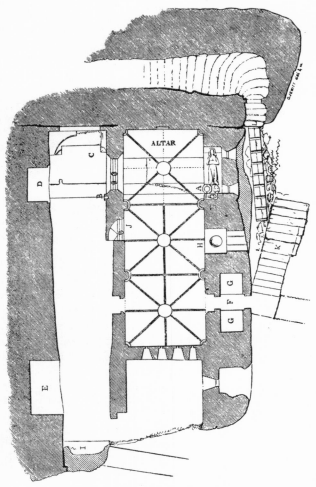

FIG. 4.—Warkworth Hermitage.

was perhaps the inmate's living room, and the recess (E) may have held a bed.

There are considerable remains of a later building erected at the south-west corner.   These were probably the hall and kitchen mentioned in Stockdale's *Survey of the Lands of the Percies* (1586) :—

"There hath been in the said parke one house hewen and wrought in a cragg or rock of stone, called the Harmitage, having in the same a hall, kytchen, chamber, and chapell, with a little orchard and garden adjoyning the same; in which house hath been kept in times past an heremity or priest to doe and celebrate divine service."

Fig. 5.—Window in Warkworth Hermitage.

The garden above is reached by winding steps. The holes in a rock near by may be traces of a lean-to byre. The hermit was allowed pasturage for horses and cattle, and received twenty marks a year and twenty loads of firewood. Once a week he might net salmon, for he had the right to "one draught of fishe every Sondaie in the yere, to be drawn fornenst the said army-tage, called the Trynete draught". The hermit's well is still shown.

Nothing is known of the foundation of Warkworth hermi-tage. The occupants were sometimes called "chaplains of the chantry "; but in 1515 Edward Slegg is described as "hermit in the chapel of Holy Trinity". In 1531 Henry, Earl of Northumberland, in consideration of the services of his chaplain Sir George Lancastre, appointed him to "myn armytage bilded in a rock of stone within my parke of Warkworth," whilst he on his part should pray for the good estate of certain persons (see p. 190).

There was a dwelling not far from the church at Sneinton near Nottingham, excavated, probably, in the low sandstone cliff by the Trent. A rental of 1544 notes : "There is a house under the ground in a rock of stone that some time was called Hermitage "; and again (1591) : "the Ermitage of Sneynton being a house cut out of rock and payeth yearly 2s.". A later deed mentions "Hermitage Close on the top of the rock of the hermitage near Sneinton church ". It is not unlikely that some of the Rock Holes in Nottingham Park were occupied by hermits. Two monks used to minister in the chapel of St. Mary of the Rock under the castle.

There is a subterranean oratory cut in the chalk at Royston, the walls of which are carved with rude figures— a Crucifixion, St. Katharine, and St. Christopher. At Oxton, near Exeter, there is a "hermit's cell" cut in the red rock. The chamber has a Gothic doorway, a lancet window, a niche, a ledge round the walls, and a kneeling-place with a cross carved above it. Other caverns remain which may have been the abode of recluses, although documentary evidence is wanting. On the banks of the Eamont, near Brougham, are the chambers hewn in the rock, mentioned by Leland ; and above the Eden at Wetheral are "St. Constantine's Safeguards ". Another cave-dwelling is the " Holy Austin Rock " at Kinver Edge in Staffordshire. The "Hermit's Hole" is shown in the midst of Culver Cliff in the Isle of Wight. Tradition says that the caves on the seashore at Buxsted and Hastings were once used as hermitages. A separate chapter must, however, now be devoted to some of the sea-coast solitaries.

PLATE XIX

HERMITAGE IN GHYSTON CLIFF, CLIFTON

IV. LIGHT-KEEPERS ON THE SEA COAST

It is a pious work to help Christians exposed to the dangers of the sea, so that they may be brought into the haven out of the waves of the deep.

(Patent Roll, 1247)

WHILST the hermits of the island, the forest, or the cave, chose their haunts chiefly with a view to solitude, there were others who took up their abode with more regard to the direct service of their fellow-men.

The Church was the pioneer in many works of mercy and utility, including the provision and maintenance of beacons, bridges, roads, harbours, and even forts. Tynemouth Priory kept up a lamp on St. Mary's Island near South Shields, and in foggy weather a bell used to ring from the chapel for the benefit of mariners. Probably the towers upon Inner Farne and on Coquet Island (Plate II) were designed for a similar purpose. When a sea-mark was required on the coast of Ireland, a tower was built at Hook (Co. Wexford) by the monastery of St. Saviour, with the assistance of the Earl of Pembroke. [1]

The chapel of St. Nicholas on Lantern Hill, about 100 feet above the haven of Ilfracombe, was, and still is, used as a lighthouse. Year by year throughout the winter a beacon burned on the top of this chapel "as if it were a star flashing in the night": so wrote Bishop Veysey in 1522, when he testified to its usefulness in stormy weather, and invited people to stretch forth a helping hand for the upkeep of the guiding light. [2] On the promontory near St. Ives, there was another conspicuous sea-mark. "There is now," says Leland, "at the very point of Pendinas a chapel of S. Nicolas,

---

[1] G. B. Hodgson, S. Shields, 287; Pat. 31 Hen. III, m. 6.
[2] Oliver, Monast. Exon. 29 n.

and a pharos for lighte for shippes sailing by night in those quarters."

Hermits used frequently to act as coastguards and light-keepers at these lonely stations. In the days of Edward III, John Puttock settled on the seashore near Lynn, where he erected, at his own great cost and charge, " a certain remarkable cross of the height of 110 feet," which proved a boon to seamen sailing up the Wash. Recognizing the services of the solitary of " Lenne Crouche " (who dwelt in a cave in the bishop's marsh), the mayor and commonalty petitioned the Bishop of Norwich to admit him to the order of hermits (1349). Possibly some such ministry was performed by the hermits of Cley by Blakeney Haven and of Cromer.

It seems probable that a leading light was shown from the chapel at St. Edmund's Point. Near the old village of Hunstanton, the low-lying shore of the Wash is broken by a ridge, rising at places to 60 feet in height. On the highest part of the cliff, near the lighthouse, are the ruins of St. Edmund's chapel (Plate XX), founded, as tradition says, by the saint after he had escaped from shipwreck. The building seems to date from Norman times, with doors and windows of later date. The site has been recently excavated, and the walls (3 feet thick), show that the chapel was 79 x 24 feet. Possibly this was the cell occupied by Thomas Cooke the hermit, who in 1530 was maintained by the L'Estranges of Hunstanton.

There were other hermitages on the shores of the North Sea, at Saltfleet Haven, at Skegness (near Ingoldmells Point), and at the mouth of the Humber. The last-named, the chapel of Ravenserespourne, was re-built at great expense by Matthew Danthorpe, shortly before 1399. Because it was situated "where the king landed at the last coming into England," Henry IV granted the place and the chapel of St. Mary and St. Anne to this hermit and his successors " with wreck of sea and waif and all other profits on the sand for two leagues round ". The possession of these privileges seems to have called out the sympathies of the succeeding chaplain, for in 1427 Richard Reedbarowe had much on his heart the dangers of the Humber and the frequent disasters, for lack of sea-mark and lighthouse :—

PLATE XX

ST. EDMUNDS-ON-THE-CLIFF, HUNSTANTON

So that the seid Richard, havyng compassion and pitee of the Cristen poeple that ofte tymes are there perisshed, and also of the Godes and Marchaundise there lost, hath begunne in weye of Charite, in Salvaĉon of Cristen poeple, Godes and Marchaundises comyng into Humbre, to make a Toure to be uppon day light a redy Bekyn, wheryn shall be light gevyng by nyght, to alle the Vasselx that comyn into the seid Ryver of Humbre.[1]

This enterprising man had begun his tower, but needed assistance in finishing it. He accordingly made a petition to Parliament, setting forth that the tower "may not be made nor brought to an ende withouten grete cost," and proposed that a tax should be levied on every ship entering the Humber ; to this suggestion the merchants and seamen of Hull had already agreed. The Commons, in response to these business-like proposals, made special request to the king's Council, and the matter was settled. It was arranged that for ten years the mayor should take tolls from each ship at a fixed tariff according to her tonnage, and that the money thus raised should be applied under the survey of certain merchants and mariners in completing the tower to serve as a beacon, and in finding a light to burn therein. Whether Richard Reedbarowe ever saw the fulfilment of his enterprise does not appear.

The terrible frequency of wrecks is shown by the duty incumbent upon the coastguard-chaplain of Reculver. On that cliff was a chapel " ordeyned for the sepulture of suche persons as by casualty of storms or other incident fate or mysaventures were perished ". When the hermitage was founded is not known ; but it was becoming ruinous in 1486, when Thomas Hamond, " hermyte of the chapell of St. Peter, St. James, and St. Anthony being at our lady of Rekcolver," was granted a commission to collect alms for the rebuilding of the roof which had fallen down.[2] Perhaps he was not successful in his quest for alms, or it may be that another fifty years of exposure to the winds had reduced it again to a state of disrepair, for Leland notes : " Ther is a neglect chapel, owt of the church-yard ". The sea was rapidly encroaching, and eventually the cliff was swept away at that point.

A hermit kept watch at St. Margaret's-at-Cliffe on the South

---

[1] P.R.O. Anc. Petitions, No. 1232 : *Rot. Parl.*, iv., 364-5.
[2] B.M. Harl., 433 f. 216.

Foreland.   In 1367 Brother Nicholas de Legh dwelt in this hermitage of " St. Margaret atte Staire " : the " Stair " was probably (like " St. Margaret's Gate ") a passage from the Bay to the cliff.   Local tradition declares that the cell was cut in the chalk cliff, near the modern lighthouses, and that a lantern was hung up there to guide ships at sea.   Possibly the hermitage on the Sussex cliff at Seaford was used for a similar purpose.

Upon Chale Down, in the Isle of Wight, there was in 1312 a hermitage and chapel in honour of St. Catherine.   Two years later a shipwreck occurred, which led to the foundation of a lantern tower at St. Catherine's.   A French ship belonging to a religious house was wrecked, and the mariners, who sold the cargo to certain men of the island, were afterwards charged with sacrilege for having appropriated Church property.   It is said that a papal bull was issued threatening the chief offender, Walter de Godeton, with excommunication.   In expiation he was charged to build a lighthouse on the Down near Nyton, above the scene of the disaster.   A letter of Bishop Stratford proves that the tower had already been erected in 1328.   A chantry priest was to keep up a bright light to warn mariners sailing by night on that dangerous coast.   A survey of 1566 shows the buildings as they then existed, with little stacks of wood ready piled for the beacon.   The octagonal tower with its conical roof is about 35 feet high (Plate XXI).   It is in good preservation, having been strengthened during the eighteenth century as an important sea-mark.   It stands 750 feet above sea level.   Into the walls of the old lighthouse a piscina is built, which probably came from the oratory, now demolished.

There stands on the Dorset coast another mediaeval lighthouse from which an idea may be gained of the kind of provision formerly made upon our shores.   The chapel on St. Aldhelm's Head (in the Isle of Purbeck) is 440 feet above the sea.   Within this oratory, which was in existence in 1291,[1] prayers were offered on behalf of mariners, whilst without, a beacon blazed for their benefit.   There is no actual record that St. Aldhelm's was served by a hermit, but the fact

---

[1] Hutchins, *Dorset*, ed. 1774, I. 228.

PLATE XXI

A LIGHTHOUSE HERMITAGE

that no institutions occur in the Sarum registers suggests that this lonely chantry was held by some semi-independent person.

Plymouth Hoe had a hermitage beside which stood a cross for a sea-mark. The chapel is described as an old one in 1413. Indulgences were frequently offered by the bishop to those who should give alms for its preservation. In 1511 there was a "hermyt of Seynt Kateryn". Leland writes : " Ther is a righte goodly walke on a hille without the toun by south caullid *the How*, and a fair chapel of S. Catarine on it ". Several other seacoast cells were standing in his day. Describing Branksea (or Brownsea) Island in Poole Haven, he observes : " Ther is yet a chapelle for an heremite ". An earlier traveller, William Worcester, mentions one dedicated to St. Anthony, in the midst of " the island of Camber," near Winchelsea. This chapel was destroyed by Flemish pirates in 1536. "The men of Rye say that these men burnt the hermitage of the Camber in despite and hewed an image of St. Anthony with their swords, bidding it call upon St. George for help."

There was also a hermit's cell in the cliff [1] at Dover, sometimes called the Chapel of Our Lady in the Rock. A reference to this place is found in the disbursements of John, King of France, before embarking for Calais in July, 1360 : " Un homme de Douvre, appellé *le rampeur*, qui rampa devant le Roy contremont la roche, devant l'ermitage de Douvre, pour don fait à li par le Roy, 5 nobles, valent 33*s*. 4*d*. ".[2]   One David Welkes was hermit of Dover in 1399 when Henry IV continued to him a life-annuity of 40*s*. granted by Richard II. When Henry VIII returned from France in 1532, he visited the oratory and gave alms : "Item . . . paied to the kings owne hands for his offering to our lady in the Rocke at Dover iiij*s*. viij*d*. ".

The hermitage had recently been rebuilt (1530) by Joachim de Vaux, the French ambassador, who afterwards declared that the little chapel in the cliff had been restored by himself " in honour of Our Lady and of that holy peace of which their majesties made him the instrument ".   Discord, however,

---

[1] Arclif, cf. hermit of Occlive near Dover (Pat. 1308).
[2] *Comptes de l'Argenterie* (Soc. de l'Hist. de France), p. 274.

arose in connexion with the chapel, because it was served by a French chaplain, Jean de Ponte, who was always in trouble with the comptroller of the king's works at Dover, or with the mayor and townsmen.   The arms of England and France were impaled over the door.   A letter written to Thomas Cromwell in 1535 set forth that "certain naughty persons have razed out the French king's arms from a table that stands upon the altar".   Henceforth there was constant trouble about the chaplain.[1]   On one occasion he was arrested by the mayor and put in prison.   He was released, but not long afterwards he was attacked one evening by some labourers working at the new fortifications.   By the friar's own account he was much ill-used.   "One," says he, "knelt on my breast, and with a stone knocked me on the mould of the head till I was as dead."   Froude, indeed, paints the man as a martyr :—

"While the harbours, piers, and the fortresses were rising at Dover, an ancient hermit tottered night after night from his cell to a chapel on the cliff, and the tapers on the altar, before which he knelt in his lonely orisons, made a familiar beacon far over the rolling waters.   The men of the rising world cared little for the sentiment of the past.   The anchorite was told sternly by the workmen that his light was a signal to the king's enemies, and must burn no more.   And when it was next seen, three of them waylaid the old man on his way home, threw him down, and beat him cruelly." [2]

By the men of his own day, however, the friar was regarded as a "false French knave".   The comptroller of the works himself begged Cromwell to command the mayor to expel him, because he advertised strangers of all that was done in those parts.   It is of interest to notice that it was partly the light shown in the hermitage which provoked ill-feeling. "These persons," complained Jean de Ponte, "because I have a light in my chapel at night when I go to bed or to my book, say I have a light for the king's enemies, which is not true." But the light was soon to be extinguished.   At this opportune moment (1537), the authorities determined to extend the harbour works to Arcliff, nor is it surprising that the Sieur de Vaux sought in vain to turn from their purpose those who

[1] *L. and P. Hen. VIII*, Vols. IX-XII.
[2] *Hist.* ed. 1858, III. 256-7 *n.*

intended to destroy the chapel by the contruction of a bulwark. For some years, indeed, a fisherman peacefully occupied the cell; but the place having been undermined by Arcliff fort, it was eventually swept away by a tempestuous sea.

The great sea-mark on the cliffs of Dover was the ancient Roman watch-tower which still stands by the church of Dover Castle. It is always known as the Pharos,[1] although there is no record of its use as a lighthouse. There was formerly a second tower, but this was already ruinous when Leland visited Dover. He describes it as " a ruine of a towr, the which has bene as a pharos or a mark to shyppes on the se ".

During the sixteenth century many of the old beacons were destroyed or fell into disrepair owing, doubtless, in many cases, to the suppression of religious houses. It was, however, a happy circumstance that the Fraternity of the Blessed Trinity had recently been founded at Deptford. This religious guild was instituted in 1514 for the benefit of mariners. In 1536 a similar guild of the Holy Trinity was founded at Newcastle-upon-Tyne, and was empowered to erect stone towers at the mouth of the Tyne for " signals, metes, and bounds," and the two towers were to be " perpetually lighted at night ".[2] By an Act of Parliament the erection of sea-marks for the guidance of navigators was afterwards committed to the sole charge of the Trinity House, Deptford. This Act (1566) contains a tribute to the work done by way of charity in bygone days :—

" Forasmuche as by the dystroyeng and taking awaye of certaine Steeples Woods and other Markes standing upon the mayne Shores . . . being as Beakons and Markes of auncyent tyme accustomed for seafaring Men to save and kepe them and the Shippes in their Charge from sundry Daungers thereto incident, divers Shyppes . . . have by the lacke of suche Markes of late yeres ben myscaried peryshed and lost in the Sea, to the great Detryment and Hurte of the Comon Weale, and the perysheng of no smale number of People," [3] etc.

---

[1] So called from the Island of Pharos, whereon Ptolemy Philadelphus built his famous lighthouse tower, one of the seven wonders of the world. It was of white marble, and could be seen at a distance of 100 miles. On the top fires were kept burning to direct sailors into the Bay of Alexandria (Lemprière, *Classical Dict.*).

[2] *L. and P. Hen. VIII*, xi. 376.   [3] Statute, 8 Eliz., c. 13.

Henceforth the story of the watchers of our coasts must be sought in the annals of the Trinity House. The scientifically-equipped lighthouses on Coquet Island, Spurn Head, St. Edmund's Point, and St. Catherine's, form, it is true, a striking contrast to the ancient cells upon those headlands, but it is well to remember that, in the day of small things, even the simple signal was to the seafarer a " bright beacon of God," and that the hermit helped to lay the foundations of the present elaborate system for the distribution of maritime lights.

PLATE XXII

REDSTONE HERMITAGE

V. HIGHWAY AND BRIDGE HERMITS

"To ordain a hermit to stay in the hermitage and labour with his hands for the maintenance of the highway, which has long been a nuisance for lack thereof."—*Patent Roll*, 1447

SIR Thomas Malory, looking back in imagination to the golden age of King Arthur, says that "in these dayes it was not the guyse of heremytes as is now a dayes". Formerly, they had been men of worship and prowess: "and the heremytes helde grete housholde, and refresshed peple that were in distresse". During the Middle Ages, however, ministering hermits, often of the peasant class, were found throughout the country, dwelling beside the highways, bridges, and fords. Their duties were those of host, guide, light-bearer, labourer, alms-gatherer, turnpike man, or bridge-warden.

Before the year 1114, Goathland hermitage, on the moors near Whitby, was a house of hospitality for the poor. It was under the care of Osmund the priest and other brethren. Another philanthropic solitary was Hugh Garth, "an heremyt of great perfection," who, after gathering alms for that purpose, founded a hospital—probably to shelter travellers—at Cockersand, in the sandy wastes between the estuaries of the Lune and Coker, a place described by Leland as "standing veri blekely and object to all wynddes". This refuge, founded shortly before 1184, afterwards developed into an abbey.

Other hermits acted as guides at the passages of rivers. There were cells above Rownham Ferry near Bristol; by the Severn at Redstone; by the Itchen at Southampton; at several Norfolk fords; and by the ferry and haven at Gorleston.

The work of light-bearer at the riverside is illustrated by the story of St. Christopher. In that beautiful legend it is a hermit who bids Offerus serve travellers, and lights the giant in his pious labours.   In many drawings of St. Christopher depicted on the walls of our ancient churches, the solitary stands on the bank with a huge lantern, to light him as he fords the river, carrying the Christ-Child ; as, for example, in the wall-paintings at St. John's, Winchester (now destroyed), and at Poughill (restored).   The painting in Shorwell church shows on one shore a cell, and on the other, a tripod-beacon and cross.[1]   That in St. Laurence, Winchester, depicted a flaming beacon outside the chapel, and on the opposite bank, a cottage.

Road-hermits begin to appear early in the fourteenth century.   Throughout the Middle Ages the upkeep of highways was left to the charity of the few.   Some of the religious houses did their share, and the bishops encouraged almsdeeds in this form.   Langland, the fourteenth-century social reformer, exhorted the charitable to repair "wikked ways" and "brygges to-broke".   The complaint of the ancient rhyme that "London Bridge is broken down" was echoed in other towns, and how to build it up again was often a problem.   A considerable amount of work was undertaken during the fourteenth century. The state of the common ways at this period has been so fully described by M. Jusserand in his *Wayfaring Life* that it is not necessary to say more about the subject than actually concerns the office of the hermit.

The bridge-maker's chief duty was to raise funds for materials and wages.   Brother John le Mareschal went about the country collecting alms for the sustenance of himself and of the men working at the causeway between Blyth and Mattersey, and at Mattersey Bridge.   This fourteenth-century stone bridge over the Idle is still standing.   It was begun in the previous century, for Archbishop Wichwane issued a brief for it in 1284.   The privilege of raising pavage or pontage —to use the technical terms—was occasionally given for a term of years.   Tolls were levied at Doncaster in order to fill up certain pits near the king's highway, and to repair the pavement near the bridge.   Geoffrey de Bolton, "who out of charity undertook that work," was permitted to take a penny on every cart, and a farthing on every pack-horse laden with goods for sale.

[1] *Journ. Brit. Arch. Ass.* x. pl. 10, 11 ; P. G. Stone, *Antiq. I. of W.*, pl. cxi.

PLATE XXIII

ST. CHRISTOPHER AND HERMIT

The office of these bridge-keepers was at once secular and religious. One of the hermits of Lancaster bought twenty-six oaks from John of Gaunt; he paid for them in advance and selected them with the chief forester of Wyresdale.[1] Another, thirty years later, received from Henry of Lancaster, after his accession, a gift of vestments of his chapel : *Item, a lermite de Lancastre un chesible, aube, amite, stole, et fanon, deux draps dor ragmas rouges, un corporas et un towaille.*[2] The keepers of this "Bridge of Loyne" received a yearly grant from the Duchy.

The overlord sometimes granted material assistance. The king, as Earl of Chester or Duke of Lancaster, supported work which was designed to benefit his tenants. By writ of Richard II, the forester of Mara was ordered to deliver to the hermit of Tarvin one oak for the repair of "Holmestrete" and of Stanford bridge. Henry IV granted five timber oaks for Warrington bridge.

The power that lay in the hands of such men is illustrated by the story of one keeper of Bow Bridge. An abbot of Stratford Langthorne once appointed a certain Godfrey Pratt (not necessarily a hermit) as his agent. He was given a house on the causeway and an allowance of food. Perceiving that, by the alms of passers-by, Godfrey was a gainer, the abbot withdrew his daily dole. But the man was a match for his master; he barred the bridge and refused to let cart or horse-man pass without fee. "At length, wearied with toyle"—so Stow charitably has it—"hee neglecteth his charge, whereof came the decay and ruine of the stone bridge and way."[3] This bridge of Stratford-le-Bow afterwards had a chapel dedicated to St. Katherine, which in 1344 was in the custody of Brother John de Ware, hermit.

In the forest, the labours of the roadmender were most necessary. The rough tracks were often impassable on account of fallen trees, and deep ruts in the mire, whilst the low wooden bridges of remote country districts were frequently swept away in flood-time. Several instances from the neighbourhood of

[1] John, "called the hermit of Syngelton," was at Ribble bridge before he went to the Lune (Loyne; the Lancaster toast is "luck to Loyne").
[2] P.R.O., Pat. 4 Hen. IV. pt. 2, m. 27.
[3] *Archæologia*, xxvii. 80.

York occur on the *Patent Rolls*. Adam de Whenby, who dwelt by St. Helen's chapel at Shipton in the parish of Overton, undertook to make a convenient road in certain dangerous parts. He was granted protection and safe conduct " while seeking means of carriage and alms to enable him to make a safe way in the forest of Galtres, at a place called *les Polles*, where many accidents have occurred by reason of the depth of the ways ". Adam continued his labours there between 1327 and 1332, but was succeeded by Robert de Skitheby, hermit of St. Augustine's chapel at Huntington by York. This Brother Robert, formerly of St. Augustine's chapel at Skeeby, near Richmond, had collected for the building of a bridge over the Gilling beck. There are other records of work going forward in the vicinity. The hermits of Skip Bridge and Stainforth Bridge spent large sums in repairing the ways over the moors. Similar improvements were effected in other wild districts. At Wragmire, about six miles from Carlisle, in the parish of Hesket in the Forest, dwelt John of Corbridge, who in 1354 was occupied in mending the highway between Carlisle and Penrith. It was small wonder if this lonely road, through the heart of Inglewood Forest, was a " foul way," for at this very time the paved streets of London were a disgrace, that between Temple Bar and Westminster being full of bogs and holes.

Travellers in the fens were constantly in peril. It can have been no light task to keep open several miles of highway, which, in that land of watercourses, suffered from serious inundations. The absolute necessity of the work is set forth in an indulgence issued by the Bishop of Ely (1458) in order to facilitate communication with the cathedral city :—

" Since our church of Ely is surrounded by waters and marshes, and the relics of the Holy Virgins lying in it can only be visited over bridges and causeys, requiring daily repair, we commend to your charity William Grene, hermit, who, at our command and with consent of our church of Ely, has undertaken the repair of the causeys and bridges of Stuntneye and Some ".

About the year 1400 there are frequent grants of a similar character in the episcopal registers.[1] At Cambridge one man

---

[1] See notes by Rev. J. H. Crosby in *Ely Diocesan Remembrancer*.

had charge of the great bridge at the Castle end of the town, and of two lesser ones over branches of the river at Newnham, and also of the road to Barton ; another kept the road towards Trumpington. A certain John Lucas kept the bridge and causeway between Great and Little Shelford ; later, he made Whittlesford Bridge his centre, and constructed a chapel there. " Foulmire," a place-name in that neighbourhood, suggests the discomforts which travellers had to endure. Hermits worked between Royston and Arrington, between Waterbeach, Denny, and Stretham, between Haddenham and Earith. The bishop issued a brief to hold good for life on behalf of John Thompson of Earith causeway, offering indulgence to all who should supply him with food, or contribute to the work committed to him.

When funds were being raised, the collector required either an episcopal or royal certificate, which might run as follows :—

" Edward the king [*no date*] hearing that Newbrygge and the two causeys leading from it, the one to Standlake and the other to Kingston, all of which were made of charity by John Golofre, knight, deceased, are out of repair and dangerous, gives his protection to Thomas Brigges, hermit dwelling by that bridge, who, moved by piety, proposes to collect money in Oxon, Berks, and Gloucester for the repair of the bridge and causeys ".

About the year 1434 there was a hermit of Newbridge who was highly respected. He made his office an opportunity for talking openly on the subject of temptation and sin. The learned Thomas Gascoigne, who doubtless heard him when on his way to Oxford, gives in his theological dictionary a brief account of " good William of Cornwall ".[1]

The office of bridge-warden was one which was liable to abuse. Some of the persons placed in these independent positions proved untrustworthy. In *Piers Plowman*, Langland inveighs against false hermits that " edify " the highway—men who were once labourers and ill off, but took the habit for the sake of an idle life, preferring alms to wages. He pictures a time of dearth, when even hermits seized spades and dug, in dread of death by hunger. Langland would have rich men give to the lunatic rather than to the " loller," who gathers alms at eventide to roast his back by the hot coals, drink deep, and

---

[1] Gascoigne, *Liber Veritatum*, ed. J. E. T. Rogers, 105-6.

go to bed; rising when he will, he roams out to espy where he may get a repast—a round of bacon, some meat, a loaf or at least half a loaf, a lump of cheese—and carries it home to his cot. Thus does he live "in ydelnesse and in ese and by others trauayle". The roadmender, indeed, was much in the world and might readily fall into bad company. Langland's *Glutton* finds a hermit in the tavern with a pedlar, a ratcatcher, and the hangman of Tyburn.[1]

The hermitage of St. James near Chester (at Handbridge, beyond the Dee) fell into bad repute. John Bennet was indicted for receiving robbers there, and keeping a house of ill-fame. His successor, Ieuan ap Blethyn ap Caswet, was nominated by the king, who directed the mayor and sheriffs to inquire into his conduct and rule of life (1455). The following entries on the *Patent Rolls* show that there were others who disgraced their habit: "Pardon to Thomas de Anderstowe, hermit of Corbridge, of the king's suit for the stealing of a pig worth 3*s.* whereof he is indicted or appealed, and of any consequent outlawry". Thomas Shelve, hermit of St. Katharine, dwelling on Teme bridge, Ludlow, late hermit of Leintwardine, was pardoned "for all felonies, trespasses, and misprisions committed by him".

The vow of Richard Ludlow of Maidenhead shows the abuses to which this office, at once religious and secular, was liable. He undertook to have the minister's profession in worship and reverence, to live to his life's end in temperance, soberness, and chastity, to eschew all open spectacles, common scot-ales, taverns, and other suspect places of sin; to hear Mass, pray, and fast; and lastly, he undertook that whatever he should receive by way of charity, he would expend truly, without deceit, upon the mending of the bridge and common ways of the town, reserving only sufficient to support himself. The bishop's charge in the office for the benediction of a hermit (see Appendix B), included a clause declaring that he must labour with his hands in order to obtain food, and also in making roads and bridges: "for idleness is the enemy of the soul".

In too many cases, however, these men were expected

---

[1] Ed. Skeat (*E.E. Text S.*) *Text C*, ix. 183; x. 140-52; vii. 368.

to fulfil important duties without being responsible to any competent local authority. This seems to have been remedied to some extent during the fifteenth century. Henry IV when granting pontage to the hermit of Stony Stratford appointed overseers of the repairs. The public-spirited wardens of St. Christopher's gild, Thame, took the matter in hand, themselves proposing to found a hermitage at Tetsworth "and to ordain a hermit to stay in the hermitage and labour with his hands for the maintenance of the highway between Stokenchurch and Hareford Bridge, which has long been a nuisance for lack thereof". The hermits of Stratford-on-Avon were members of the town gild, which was a guarantee of good conduct. The appointment to such posts was often made by the commonalty of the town. Letters-patent sealed by the mayor of Oxford were granted to Nicholas Wadekyns, keeper of Pettypont, who found pledges that he would mend the bridge according to his ability. The mayor, bailiffs, and aldermen appointed William Cardon to be warden of the South Bridge. Evidently he was to go about the town collecting, for the deed asks people in general that when he comes to them and asks alms, they will trust him and contribute to the repair of the bridge and of dangerous places in the ways about the town. At Henley, the hermit was under an official "Bridgeman," who even supplied his clothes.

The making and mending of roads continued to be regarded as a work of individual piety and private enterprise. Simon Cotes of Westbourne had the needs of travellers much on his heart; he therefore founded on his own property the hermitage of St. Anthony, and himself set to work to improve the means of communication in that neighbourhood. At his death in 1527, he bequeathed the house, chapel, and garden to the Earl of Arundel, to the intent that a professed hermit might dwell there, to pray for the souls of his own ancestors and those of his lord, and to maintain the bridges and highways which he had made.

Such labours, faithfully carried out, were appreciated by the people, as appears from bequests. A butcher of Northampton defines in his will (1528) the work which he desires to be done: "Also I wyll that Stonton the Hermyt of Saynt Thomas chapell have delyvered to him . . . vj^s viij^d· to the men[ding]

the cawsey " ; after describing the situation of the stony bit of
street, the testator offers a like sum for the repair of a little
causeway between the Tabard Inn and the stone bridge ; whilst
a third instalment is to be expended " at the dyscretion of the
sayd Armytt " in filling up with ramell (rubbish) the holes in
the street towards Coton.

As late as 1532 Nicholas Wodhull directs his executors to
repair the hermitage " at the Brigg foot " at Banbury (i.e. in
Grimsbury on the Northamptonshire side of the river), to place
therein an honest man to pray for him and his friends.

The repair of bridges and of the adjoining highways became
a matter for legislation in 1530-1.   Justices of the Peace were
charged to inquire " of anoysances of bridges broken in the
highe wayes to the damage of the Kynges liege People ".   In
cases where no person was liable to repair them, taxes might
be levied for this purpose by appointed collectors.[1]

There followed close upon this statute, however, the Suppression of Religious Houses, which resulted in the crippling of
communications for many years.   After the Dissolution bridge-
cells disappear, like other religious institutions directly or indi-
rectly associated with the monastic life.   Leland notes : " At the
very end of Thrapeston Bridge stand ruines of a very large
Heremitage and principally welle buildid but a late discoverid
and suppressid ".   The hermit of Chippenham causeway lin-
gered on until the days of Edward VI, when it was recorded
that : " Tharmyte holdyth without copye iij acres of pasture
. . . by th' armytage ".   In 1554 the causeway became charge-
able upon the borough.

Wayfaring men suffered sadly through the suppression of
religious houses.   The new owners of church property did not
consider themselves to be under any obligation to carry on
charities of this kind.   The people preferred to be almsgivers
rather than ratepayers.   In 1588 they were complaining that
since the Suppression they were burdened, taxed, and charged
for the repair of divers great bridges.   Even in the time of
Queen Elizabeth, when the hermits of the highway were already
dim figures of a bygone age, their work, however imperfect,
won recognition as useful to their own days and to the days

[1] Statute 22 Hen. VIII, c. v.

that followed. In 1596 the story was being handed down in Highgate that : " Where now the Schole standeth was a hermytage, and the hermyte caused to be made the causway betweene Highgate and Islington, and the gravell was had from the top of Highgate hill, where is now a standinge ponde of water ".

In due course, when the social upheaval of the sixteenth century had righted itself, things were placed on a sounder basis. It was, of course, far better that the maintenance of roads should become a public charge, organized by a local body which had continuity. The work of the pioneer need not, however, be forgotten, and it merits at least the slight record which has been attempted in this chapter.

VI. TOWN HERMITS

If a hermit dwell in a borough, town, or city, or nigh thereto where each day he can well beg his daily bread, let him before sunset distribute to Christ's poor that which remains of his food.—Rule of Hermits, Bodleian MS.

THE city of London seems a strange place in which to seek solitude, yet there were hermits by Cripplegate, Aldgate, Bishopsgate, and also near the Tower. In the present Monkwell Street stood the cell of St. James, "in the corner towards the west near Cripplegate," that is, in the comparatively retired spot formed by the north-west angle of the city wall, between the gate and the bastion which may still be seen in the churchyard of St. Giles. It was an ancient foundation, for the architectural features of the crypt below the chapel were Norman. Brother Warin, chaplain of Richard I dwelt here. It was afterwards granted to Robert Bat, rector of St. Bride's, with the provision that he entered the hermitage [1] immediately and religiously stayed therein. Probably he did not comply with the condition, for Jordan de Eston was subsequently appointed to serve it. One of Henry III's last nominees was Robert de S. Laurencio. After remaining there for over twenty years, he became incapacitated, and William de Wyntreburn, chaplain, was admitted to the cell—"provided that he behave himself well and honourably, that he devote himself to his sacred office, minister to Brother Robert, the hermit of the place, who is feeble, and maintain him in a fitting manner for as long as he lives". Three months later the old man died, and was succeeded by his companion, who stayed four years and then resigned.

In 1311, the Bishop prohibited Thomas de Byreford, who, living as hermit there, took upon himself to hear confessions, administer sacraments, offer indulgences, and do other un-

---

[1] Usually hermitage, but *inclusorium* occurs 1253 (Nicholas, *Leic.*, III. Pt. II. 840). In 1265 Richard de Ginges became a *recluse* there.

authorized things.   Some time previous to 1290, St. James's hermitage was enlarged, and, in 1332, the king granted the custody thereof to William Lyons and two other priests, and to Alan Chauns, hermit.   When in old age William Lyons was "broken with bodily weakness," a chaplain was sent to his aid.

All these men were nominated by the Crown, but the cell changed hands frequently, and, during voidance, damage was done to the muniments, ornaments, and goods.   Edward I committed the custody of the place to the mayor, and afterwards to the Constable of the Tower.   Edward III, however, granted the advowson to the abbot and convent of Garendon. One of their nominees, John de Flytewyk, stayed only one year. He was a priest on the staff of the lazar-house of St. Mary de Pré near St. Albans.   He failed to obtain permission to depart, but went nevertheless to the Cistercian Abbey of Garendon, by whom he was admitted to the hermitage.   He afterwards resumed the Benedictine habit.[1]

About this time the Cripplegate cell became a chantry chapel.   In 1347, new endowments were provided by the Countess of Pembroke, who founded a chantry for the soul of Aymer de Valence.   John *Ayobanensis* (formerly bishop-suffragan in the sees of Canterbury and Exeter) dated his will from this place in 1380.[2]   During the fifteenth century it appears to have been a corporate body with a common seal.[3] After the Dissolution, the property came into the hands of the Clothworkers' Company, and became known as " Lambe's chapel ".

There was also a hermitage on the south side of Aldgate. This cell was built in a turret of the city wall by John the hermit—possibly that John le Megre, who in 1259 was allowed to "transfer himself from the hermitage of Alegate, where he has lived for some years," to that of Cripplegate.   The *Hundred Rolls* record that the building encroached on the highway to the extent of 4 feet in one direction and 33 feet in another.   Brother Berengar afterwards dwelt at the chapel of St. Mary and St. Nicholas in the *torella* of the city wall, by

---

[1] Pap. Lett. II. 554.
[2] *Ex. Reg. Brantyngham*, I. 3.
[3] B.M. Seals, LXVIII. I.

the Tower.   During the fourteenth century, this place was in the hands of the mayor and aldermen, who granted it to Sir John de Elyngham, chaplain, on condition that he should keep it in repair and protect it against wind and rain.   In this document it is described as being near Bishopsgate.

Of the Bishopsgate cell little is known.   In 1342 the custody of the king's hermitage within Bishopsgate was given to John de Warrewyk.   Four years later, protection was granted to Robert, hermit of Bishopsgate, who was dependent upon alms.[1]

Another hermitage was situated by St. Katharine's hospital, near the Tower.   It was visited in 1360 by John, the captive King of France, who gave two crowns as alms on Ascension Day, and a fortnight later, attended Mass and offered 12d.[2]   This was evidently the place called " le Swannesnest," where in 1371 John Ingram was hermit.   In the same year one Sir Robert was " a recluse monk near the Tower ".

A more rural spot was the hermitage of St. Katharine, on the site now occupied by Charing Cross Post Office.   Henry III granted to the Bishop of Llandaff permission to lodge " in the close of the king's hermitage of La Charryng ".   In 1268 he appointed Simon de Bragham to succeed Richard de la March as chaplain of " the free chapel of the hermitage of la Cherring ".   The *Exchequer Roll* of 1272 mentions two chaplains who performed divine service there for the soul of the king's father..   In 1361, a bequest was made to the hermit near Charrynge-crouche.

In other parts of the kingdom, too, the " solitary " made his habitation in many frequented places.   Lawrence Burgeys (or Abingdon), bailiff of Reading, obtained permission from Abbot Helyas to build a chapel in honour of St. Edmund, beside which he might dwell as a hermit.[3]   This chapel was situated on rising ground nearly opposite the west end of the friary.   In a memorial issued against the abbot of Reading in the fifteenth century this allegation was made: " a chapelle at

---

[1] *Comptes de l'Argenterie* (Soc. de l'Hist. de Fr.), 248, 252.

[2] Possibly this cell became the abode of stricter recluses ; cf. " the anchorite within the gate of Bishopsgate on the wall towards Cripplegate," etc.

[3] B.M. Cott. Vesp. E. v. f. 81 *b*.

the west end of the towne, of Seynt Edmunds, and feyre londs therto, for to have God worshyppyd in that chapelle, wherein lyeth the bonys of many chrysten people, and now they have made a barne therof, and put therin corne and hey, and tye therin horse and bests ". When the remains of St. Edmund's were discovered a few years ago, some stones were removed to the museum at the abbey gateway.

There was a hermitage in the suburbs of Salisbury. The bishop licensed the hermit of Fisherton to celebrate divine service in the chapel there, but his office was usurped by a certain layman who assumed clerical dress and pretended to be a hermit. This schismatic person was in the habit of ringing a bell to collect the people in the slums of Fisherton, thus " tempting the people, as Jeroboam did Israel ". Offering years of pardon to those who attended the Mass which he presumed to say, he in this manner deceived the simple and extorted money from them. Bishop Wyvil therefore laid the chapel under an interdict (1352). Bishop Mitford afterwards licensed Thomas, hermit of St. Anne's chapel, to conduct service, subject to the vicar's consent. In 1418, the hermit John petitioned that he might be shut up in a confined place at the end of the chapel to lead the stricter life of an anchorite. Bishop Chandler commissioned two of the canons of Salisbury to inquire whether there were any impediment to his complying with this request, and empowered them to perform the ceremony of inclusion if the inquiry proved satisfactory.[1]

Some hermits lived in the heart of the town, and others on the outskirts. At Shrewsbury, for example, there was one at Cadogan's Cross, and another at Spelcrosse, a waste place on the Meole road. We hear of hermitages at Durham, Leicester, Ely, Colchester, Coventry, Crewkerne, Canterbury, Lydd, Chichester, etc.

There were two cells in the town of Pontefract, and another on the hill of St. Thomas. The series of underground chambers in or under Back Lane is evidently the place " in a certain lane leading from Malfaygate to the house of the Friars Preachers," which was granted in 1368 to Brother Adam. The rent paid by the inmates was a white rose at midsummer.

---

[1] Reg. Wyvil, I. f. 210 ; Reg. Mitford, f. 115 ; Reg. Chandler, III. f. 5.

The grants made to the various hermits of Pontefract are difficult to ascertain. West of the cell founded by the Layrthorps
and occupied by Adam and afterwards by the priest Laurence,
lay a garden (90 × 30 feet) in which Thomas Elys permitted
John de Crayk to build a hermitage ; and eastwards the land
belonged to the prior of Nostell, to whom eventually this
second hermitage passed. The present garden is surrounded
by walls, three of which are ancient. The ground below is a
network of cellars, one of which is an oratory and contains a
stone altar : another, the dwelling-place, has a hole in the floor
for fuel, and a flue cut out of the rock. The inmates obtained
water from a clear well, which was reached by a winding
staircase. A ground-plan and description of these excavations
were prepared for a visit of the Society of Antiquaries, and
may be found in the *Proceedings* for 1869.

A solitary used to dwell on the hill near the castle at
Pontefract. John of Gaunt permitted William de Byngham
to inhabit certain houses by the mount where Thomas, Earl of
Lancaster (the popular hero and "saint") had been put to
death. These buildings, which were then in a ruinous condi-
tion, the tenant agreed to keep up at his own charges. Lord
Scrope made a bequest to John the hermit of the hill at
Pontefract.

Brandon Hill by Bristol (Plate XXIV), from a fancied resemblance to Mount Calvary, was regarded as a holy place.
The summit was in the possession of Tewkesbury Abbey.
Probably there was already a cell in 1192, when the place
is referred to as "waste land at St. Brendan's". In 1313,
Walter, a monk of Garendon, sought permission to lead a solitary life in St. Brendun's chapel.[1] Walter de S. Cruce seems,
nevertheless, to have remained at Garendon, where he eventually became abbot ; and in 1350 he was translated to be the
first abbot of St. Mary Graces, London, at the invitation of
Edward III. At this very time, Lucy de Newchurch, was
beseeching the Bishop of Worcester to allow her to be enclosed
at that hermitage (p. 91). In 1403, the famous Bishop of
Winchester, William of Wykeham, issued letters of indulgence
to benefactors of St. Brandan's chapel, Bristol, or of Reginald

---

[1] *Reg. Sede Vac.* (Worc. Hist. S.), 147.

PLATE XXIV

BRANDON HILL, BRISTOL.

Taillour, a poor hermit there.[1] A later inmate was visited by William Worcester (1480). This hermit told the chronicler that sailors and discreet men declared that the hill-chapel was higher by 18 fathoms than the spire of Redcliffe or any other church. The length of the chapel was about 25 × 15 feet (8½ × 5 *virgas*). The wall enclosing the cell measured 180 steps. The chapel is said to have been frequented by mariners arriving at Bristol port.

In Bristol itself, or rather, in Redcliffe, is the picturesque hermitage shown in Plate XXV. William Worcester describes it as situated on the west side of the church (i.e. the hospital chapel) of St. John, above the river Avon in the red cliff. It stands in the Friends' Cemetery, Jones Lane. The chamber cut in the sandstone is only 9 feet by 8 feet, with an arched doorway and a rough recess which forms a seat. This cell was founded in 1347 by Thomas, Lord Berkeley, who placed there one John Sparkes to pray for him and his family.

Town-hermits often undertook definite employment. There were those, as we have seen, who kept the bridges and roads of Lancaster, Chester, Derby, Doncaster, Northampton, Oxford, Cambridge, Marlborough, etc. Some dwelt by the gates, as at Lynn and Bury St. Edmunds. At Norwich, a hermit used to inhabit a chamber over St. Stephen's Gate, and there were others near most of the gates. According to Blomefield, the hermit of Magdalen Gate presided over the lepers. Such men were sometimes employed by hospitals to gather alms on their behalf. Letters of protection were granted by Edward III to Richard de Breton, hermit of the leper-house at Southbroom outside Devizes, and also to John Trewe, of St. Thomas's hospital by Marlborough. At the end of the town of Bicester (in St. John's, now Sheep Street) there was a hermitage-chapel, of which the hermit, Nicholas Jurdan, obtained permission " to found a hospital for poor and infirm persons ".[2]

In two disused Norfolk churches solitaries acted as resident-caretakers. About the time of the Black Death, the Norwich parish of St. Margaret, Newbridge (or Colegate) being depopulated, the monastic patrons converted the church into a hermitage. When St. Giles's, Thetford, was annexed to

---

[1] *Reg. Wykeham*, Pt. III. f. cccLVII.
[2] *Pat. R.* 1337, 1338, 1340, 1355.

St. Cuthbert's, the church was let to a hermit at a yearly rent of 16*d.* The tenant, doubtless, gathered alms for its repair.

In the fifteenth century we still find churchyard-cells. At Sudbury, a hermitage was built in the churchyard of St. Gregory's at the cost of the parish, and one John Levynton was dwelling there in 1433. At this time, another townsman, Richard Appelby by name, applied to the bishop to be admitted to the order of hermits, but the bishop declined until he could be assured that the man would dwell " in a solitary place, wher virtues myght increase and vice be exiled "; whereupon the mayor of Sudbury and certain parishioners of St. Gregory's undertook that Richard should share John's abode, and they made supplication to the bishop to admit Richard.

In the busy seaport of Sandwich, the hermit seems to have acted as a special chaplain. It was his duty to minister to strangers and the poor, and to pray for the people. His chapel of St. James, near St. Mary's church, had a burial-ground, which was afterwards used as the cemetery of the parish. The churchwardens' accounts for the year 1447 show an expenditure of 12*d.* upon reparation of the chapel. The sum of 4*s.* 11*d.* was paid " for a stone to lay ovyr sir Williem ye herimyte withyn seynt Jamys chirchezerd ". The last chaplain, John Steward, who as late as 1538 received a bequest as " Sir John the Heremit," became vicar of St. Mary's. The churchwardens probably secured his appointment in recognition of his services to the parish. The chapel was destroyed in the time of Edward VI.

Solitaries in towns, and especially in churchyards, usually belonged to the stricter order of anchorites, and to them we must now turn our attention.

REDCLIFFE HERMITAGE, BRISTOL

VII. ANCHORITES IN CHURCH AND CLOISTER

Recluses who dwell under the eaves of the church.—*Ancren Riwle.*
He sawe a chappel where was a recluse whiche hadde a wyndowe that she myghte see vp to the Aulter.—MALORY, *Morte d'Arthur.*

THE anchorite differed from the hermit in that he lived in stricter seclusion, and was not free to wander at will. He was not merely, as the word ἀναχωρητής signifies, withdrawn from the world : he was *inclusus,* shut up in a strait prison, whether in church, chapel, convent, or castle.

Various names were given to the enclosed person : *inclusus, inclusa, reclusus, reclusa,* and the indefinite *anachorita* are used synonomously in records. *Ancre* was of common gender in Middle English ; *anker* and *ancresse* occur later. Lucy "yᵉ ankereswoman" is mentioned in the *Hundred Rolls.* A study of the Christian names which appear in the Appendix to this volume seems to show that more women than men undertook this austere vocation. So large is their number, indeed, that for lack of space only a few typical persons can be mentioned.

I. THE ANCHORITE

1. *Adjoining Parish Churches*

The author of the *Ancren Riwle* makes a play upon the word *ancre ;* she is "anchored under the church as an anchor under a ship, to hold the ship so that neither waves nor storms may overwhelm it". Enclosed persons were usually attached to some church in order that they might derive spiritual advantages from it, and at the same time confer spiritual benefits upon the parish. Being a holy place, it was suitable for a dedicated person, and it was also a frequented spot for one who lived partly upon alms. The churchyard not only stood for a wilderness, but seemed a fitting habitation for one, as it were, dead to the world.

The most celebrated anchorite of mediaeval England was, perhaps, Wulfric, enclosed for twenty-nine years at Haselbury, a village near Crewkerne. Wulfric was born at Compton, probably Compton Martin. He became priest of Deverill near Warminster, but at that time he was more addicted to sport than to spiritual exercises. Upon his conversion, he determined to devote himself entirely to a life of contemplation and rigorous asceticism at Haselbury—"burying himself in Christ in a cell adjoining the church". Sir William FitzWalter had a great respect for his saintly neighbour ; he sent provisions to him and visited him from time to time. Wulfric numbered among his intimate friends Osbern, the village priest ; William, a lay-brother of Ford Abbey ; and Brichtric, who seems to have joined him as a disciple or attendant. During the reigns of Henry I and Stephen, he exercised a powerful influence, not only in his own neighbourhood but also at the court. The story of Wulfric as prophet and wonder-worker is related elsewhere.

Wulfric died in 1154, and was buried in his cell by the Bishop of Bath who had visited him on his death-bed. The monks of Montacute sought to obtain possession of the saint's body, but Osbern the priest interposed, and the remains were translated to the adjoining church. Miracles subsequently took place there, and the shrine became a place of pilgrimage. The north chapel is still known as "Wulfric's aisle".

Another interesting recluse was Lauretta, Countess of Leicester. Her mother and brother were amongst those persons "miserably famished" at King John's command. Her father, William de Braose, a man of singular piety, escaped, and died in an abbey in France. Lady Lauretta wedded Robert Fitz Parnell, Earl of Leicester, who, after distinguishing himself in the Crusades, died in 1204, and the widowed countess eventually retired into solitude at St. Stephen's, Hackington.

A more familiar name is that of Katherine of Ledbury. She was the daughter of John Giffard, Baron of Brimsfield, and was born in 1272. Her husband, Nicholas, Baron Audley, died in 1299, leaving her with two young sons and a daughter.[1]

---

[1] For genealogy see *Staffs. Coll.*, N.S., IX. 264.

No more is heard of the Lady Audley until 1312, when she gave away into lay hands a portion of her maternal inheritance. Since the deed is witnessed at Ledbury by the bishop and the vicar, it may be presumed that she had already taken up her abode there, or was about to be enclosed by the bishop. In 1323, "Katherine de Audele, recluse of Ledbury," was receiving £30 a year through the sheriff, and as the sum was paid out of lands which were in the custody of her husband's executor, it seems probable that she had made some arrangement about her property in order to obtain a pension.

Around these prosaic facts the following poetic legend grew up. In obedience to a vision which bade her not to rest until she came to a town where the bells should ring untouched by man, Katherine and her maid Mabel wandered from place to place, following out of Worcestershire into Herefordshire the hoof-marks of the lady's mare which had been stolen—prints still shown in the sandstone at Whelpley Brook. The expected miracle was manifested at Ledbury, and there, it may be under the shadow of the bell-tower, the Lady Katherine determined to remain. The story is familiar through Wordsworth's sonnet :—

> When human touch (as monkish books attest)
> Nor was applied nor could be, Ledbury bells
> Broke forth in concert flung a down the dells,
> And upward, high as Malvern's cloudy crest;
> Sweet tones, and caught by a noble Lady blest
> To rapture! Mabel listened at the side
> Of her loved mistress: soon the music died,
> And Catherine said, *Here I set up my rest.*
> Warned in a dream, the Wanderer long had sought
> A home that by such miracle of sound
> Must be revealed :—she heard it now, or felt
> The deep, deep joy of a confiding thought;
> And there, a saintly Anchoress, she dwelt
> Till she exchanged for heaven that happy ground.

The title " Saint " Catherine of Ledbury is a late addition to the tale, suggested, doubtless, by the dedication-name of the hospital of St. Katharine, a house founded years before the birth of Katherine de Audley.

There were also cells attached to many town churches. The foundation of some of these was so remote as to be lost in obscurity. Chester, for example, had an anchorage by the collegiate church of St. John. The tradition handed down by

Giraldus Cambrensis was, that King Harold, sorely wounded, fled from Senlac to Chester, " and lyued there holily an ankers lyf in Seint Iames celle faste by Seint Iohn his chirche, and made a gracious end ".[1]

At Oxford there were six or seven churches where recluses were dwelling between 1180 and 1280.[2] One, Matthew, was enclosed at Holywell, outside the town. It was said to have been revealed to this holy man that the church of Dorchester contained the bodies of two Saxon bishops. He heard a voice saying : *Birinus in pavimento, Bertinus retro ostium ;* and when the relics were discovered, miracles occurred—a dead man came to life, a leper was cleansed, and one learnt to speak French in three days. These startling events were duly recorded at an inquiry held by the archbishop in 1224. Soon after this, Henry III issued an order for a *reclusorium* to be made at Holywell church of which he was the patron. Another was founded at St. Budock's :—

" Intimation to R[obert Grosseteste] bishop of Lincoln that, yielding to the prayers of Alice, the bearer, who has made a vow to serve God in some solitary place, the king has granted that on the north side of the church of St. Bodhuc, Oxford, she may build herself a cell, where she may for her life serve God and the Blessed Virgin."

In the quietude of the closet, many a solitary strove to shut out the city's turmoil. Edward III gave alms to eight anchorites, as well as to three hermits, in London and the suburbs.[3] It was the same in other cities, e.g. Norwich, Lincoln, York. By comparing scattered records, it is possible to gather a few facts about some of these persons. There was, for example, a cell at St. Leonard's, Exeter. In 1397, the bishop commissioned John Dodyngton, canon of Exeter, to enclose a certain Alice in a house in the cemetery. Three years later, when the canon died, he bequeathed 40*s.* to her. That same year the bishop permitted Alice Bernard to choose a confessor with plenary powers. The rector of Little Torrington left to her 20*s.* and a book of sermons in English. Another bequest was made as late as 1430.

---

[1] Higden, *Polychron.,* J. Trevisa (Rolls S. 41), VII. 245.
[2] See Appendix. The vision of the Eynsham monk concerns a recluse, possibly at St. Thomas's.
[3] F. Devon, *Issues of Exchequer,* 395, cf. 160.

Fifteenth-century wills abound in references to persons living the solitary life. Lord Scrope bequeaths money to anchorites in twenty villages and market towns, as well as to those in and about London and York, and to any others found within three months of his death.

(2) *In Conventual Houses*

The great Benedictine communities of Crowland, Durham, Westminster, Worcester, and Sherborne had their solitaries, as had also many other monastic houses. Mottisfont Priory was founded by William Briwer, and his brother, a wonder-worker known as "the holy man in the wall," probably dwelt in the precincts of that monastery. Even the more secular hospital might be used as a place of seclusion. The Bishop of Exeter founded a cell by the chapel of St. Laurence, Crediton, and appointed Brother Nicholas as the first inmate. Alice was enclosed at the church of St. Giles in the suburbs of Hereford (1321); and clearly this was the hospital, for a will of the previous year mentions not only the anchorite of St. Giles but the brethren and sisters there. With the assent of the master and brethren of Holy Innocents' outside Lincoln, the king, as patron, permitted Elizabeth de Elm to become a recluse by the chapel of the hospital. Probably the infirm materially benefited by the presence of such persons in their precincts.

The Austin Friary at Droitwich had a cell on the south side of the choir of the conventual church. It was founded by Thomas Beauchamp, Earl of Warwick, who stipulated that the candidate nominated by the founder's heirs, should be religious and devout, of the same order as the convent, or willing to submit to the prior; and that he should not be a burden on a house which was pledged to poverty.

The White Friars and the Black Friars favoured the solitary life. The Carmelites of Norwich had two cells. Thomas Bradley (p. 163) dwelt in that next the entrance of the friary. Dame Emma, daughter of Sir Miles Stapilton, was probably enclosed in the chamber under Holy Cross chapel, set apart for women. She was buried in the church of the friary in 1442. Other Carmelite nuns took similar vows, e.g. Alice Wakleyne of Northampton, Margaret Hawten, Joanna

Catfelde of Lynn, and Agnes Gransetter of Cambridge.   Bale mentions elsewhere that Mistress Alice Wakelyn, a woman of illustrious family, died on 13 June, 1426, and was succeeded by Margaret Hawton, who died on 17 November (the year is not recorded).

Dominican friars were enclosed at Lynn, Lancaster, Newcastle, Arundel, and Canterbury; and Dominican sisters at Norwich, Bristol, and Worcester.

3. *Adjoining Chapels*

There were cells attached to chapels which were neither parochial nor directly monastic.   Henry II pensioned Geldwin, *inclusus* of St. Aedred at Winchester, and Richard, of St. Sepulchre's, Hereford.   Henry III appointed others to several royal free chapels, including those of the fortresses in London and Dover.   In 1237, he ordered the Constable of the Tower to admit Brother William to the cell by St. Peter's church in the bailly which was dedicated to St. Eustace.   Idonea de Boclaund afterwards occupied this chamber, and received the daily dole of a penny, and every year a robe.   Emma de Skepeye was enclosed by the church of St. Mary in Dover Castle (1234).   Twenty-three years later, the king, before setting sail from Dover, ordered that the customary alms (three halfpence a day) should be made to her for life.

In the tower of Bristol Castle there was a chapel and anchorage dedicated to St. Edward.   Directions were sent by Henry III for certain alterations in the fortress :—

" Block up the doors of the chapel beside our great hall there, and let a door be made in the chancel towards the *reclusorium :* in which *reclusorium* let there be made an altar in the chapel of the blessed Edward, and above that *reclusorium* in the turret let the chamber of the clerks be made ".

A chaplain, probably a recluse, was to perform masses for the soul of Alienora of Brittany, the king's cousin.

During the thirteenth, fourteenth, and fifteenth centuries, a succession of solitary women dwelt in the chapel of St. Helen by the castle at Pontefract.   They were in receipt of a pension from the lords of the town.[1]

[1] P.R.O. Duc. Lanc. Accounts (Various) Bdle. 27, No. 3; Lanc. Bk. 79.

PLATE XXVI

ANCHORAGE AT HARTLIP

Cells were frequently situated in places of thoroughfare, e.g. "in the midst of the town" at Wakefield, at the end of Frenchgate Street in Richmond, by bridges at Doncaster and Derby. Speed's plan of Kendal marks the *Ankeriche*, which tradition describes as a small beehive hut, concealed by fences from the road which encircled it.

II. THE CELL

The place of seclusion is called indifferently *domus anachoritæ, reclusorium, inclusorium, reclusagium*, and *anchoragium*. Since English sources of information are scanty on this subject, we are obliged to turn to foreign writers. Grimlaic in his *Regula Solitariorum* [1] directs that the dwelling be very small and surrounded, if possible, by an enclosed garden. Two anchorites might share a single chamber. If the recluse had disciples, they dwelt in a separate apartment and served him through the window. The cell communicated with the church; but if the inmate were a priest, he also had a consecrated oratory. A Bavarian Rule directs that the cell be of stone, 12 feet square. Through one window, towards the choir, the recluse partook of the Blessed Sacrament; through another, on the opposite side, he received his food; a third, closed with glass or horn, lighted the dwelling. [2]

In the *Ancren Riwle*, particular instructions are given concerning the windows. " Hold no conversation with any man out of a church window, but respect it for the sake of the holy sacrament which ye see therethrough." Communication was held through a parlour window, small, narrow, and always fast on every side. [3] Even when the recluse unclosed her shutter, she was hidden by a curtain—a black cloth bearing a symbolic white cross. " The black cloth also teacheth an emblem, doth less harm to the eyes, is thicker against the wind, more difficult to see through, and keeps its colour better against the wind and other things."

The house, which might consist of several apartments, often

---

[1] L. Holstenius, *Codex Reg.*, II. 464-600.

[2] Ducange, *Glossarium*, " Inclusagium ".

[3] In the Norwich Museum is preserved an old oak window frame, about 2 feet square, with iron bars. It was found in the south wall of the Cathedral (choir), and may possibly have communicated with a cell [per Mr. F. Johnson].

included an oratory in which Mass was celebrated from time
to time.   There was an austere simplicity about the building.
Abbot Aelred did not approve of covering the naked walls with
pictures and carvings, or of decking the chapel with a variety
of hangings and images : such ornaments savoured of vanity.
He decreed that the altar should have upon it only a fair white
cloth and a crucifix :—

"Now shal I shewe the how thou shalt arraye thyn oratory.
Arraye thyn autier with white lynnen clothe, the whiche bitokeneth
both chastite and symplenesse. . . . In this autere sette an ymage
of cristis passion, that thou may have mynde and se hou he sette and
spredde his armes abroad to resceyve thee and al mankynde to mercy,
if thai wil axe it.   And if it plese the, sette on that oo side an ymage
of our Lady, and a nother on that other syde of seynt John." [1]

The *Rites of Durham* contains a description (1593) of one
such chamber within the cathedral.   It was a loft, evidently a
wooden structure, close to the high altar and behind St. Cuthbert's shrine :—

"At the east end of the North Alley of the Quire, betwixt two
pillars opposite, was the goodlyest faire porch, which was called the
Anchoridge, havinge in it a marveillous faire roode, with the most
exquisite pictures of Marye and John, with an altar for a Monke to
say dayly masse ; beinge in antient time inhabited with an Anchorite.
. . . The entrance to this porch or anchoridge was upp a paire of
faire staires adjoyninge to the north dore of St. Cuthbert's Feretorie."

There was also an anchorage adjoining Chichester Cathedral.   William Bolle, rector of Aldrington, resigned his benefice,
and obtained permission to construct a cell and retire thither.   It
was agreed that after his death it should pass into the bishop's
hands.   The chamber, 29 feet long and 24 feet wide, communicated with the Lady chapel.

The anchorite attached to Sherborne Abbey dwelt in the
chapel of St. Mary le Bow on the south of the thirteenth-
century Lady chapel (now part of the School).   An inmate of
this place is mentioned in the codicil to the will of Lady Alice
West : "Also, for hit was for-yete byfore in this testament, I

---

[1] Bodl. MS. 423, f. 186, 186 *b* (cf. *Informacio*, cap. xi. in *Englische Studien*,
vii. 315-6); *Regula*, cap. xxxiv., xxxviii.

bequethe to the Reclus of Shirbourn, whos Surname is Arthour,[1] xl*s.* for to do and to preye as othere Reclus forseyd Shulleth don and preye ".

The cell at Worcester was next the cathedral on the north, between the porch and the west end. In a fifteenth-century account-book of the priory is an entry of x*s.* paid : " for brycks, lyme, and sonde, to ye repa' con of ye anckras house by ye charnel howse ".[2]

There was no rule as to the situation of such dwellings. The records are apt to be vague, as, for instance, that a religious woman abode " in a remote corner of the church ". Information is sometimes supplied incidentally, e.g. a testator of Faversham desires to be buried on the north side of the churchyard, opposite the door of the anchoress. Occasionally, however, some particulars are given. Juliana, anchoress of Worcester, dwelt at the north-west corner of the church of St. Nicholas, in an angle of the churchyard, bounded by the main street and by a side street. She petitioned for the enlargement of her courtyard, and the king, satisfied that this would not be to the nuisance of the city, granted permission to widen the court on three sides, by 7, 5, and 4 feet, respectively.[3] Situated in a busy thoroughfare (now " The Cross ") it was conspicuous to all passing to and from the Foregate.

Writing of the Norwich church of St. John Baptist, Timberhill, Blomefield says : " Anciently a recluse dwelt in a cell joining to the north side of the steeple, but it was down before the Dissolution ". The anchorage at St. Edward's was also on the north. From numerous examples it seems that the ascetic would deliberately forego the sunshine with the rest of Nature's gifts. Rare instances occur of a brighter aspect. The Westminster anchorage was on the south side of the chancel of St. Margaret's.[4] The cells at Droitwich and Polesworth

---

[1] Since going to press Canon Wordsworth sends an extract dated 1397. *Indulgencia pro Edmundo Artur, anchorita* " capelle B. Marie vocat' le Bowe infra scalare cimiterii ecclesiæ conventualis de Shireburn ". Reg. Metford, f. cxxi. *b.*

[2] The charnel vault under the courtyard, near the Deanery gate.

[3] The cells at Droitwich (p. 77), and Winterton (p. 92) had enclosures (*clausura*).

[4] Westminster MS. Extra Parcels, No. 14 [per Mr. C. Welch].

were also on the south.   That at the west end of Crewkerne church was still standing in the seventeenth century.

Although so many recluses were dwelling " under the eaves of the church," the church itself has in many cases been rebuilt, and no traces of the cell can be found.   Thus even in ancient buildings (for example, in St. Michael's and St. Peter's at St. Albans) there is no clue as to the position of the annexed chambers.   In none of the eleven fine churches described by Mr. McCall in *Richmondshire Churches* have indications of cells been found, although recluses are known to have dwelt in three of those parishes, viz. Burneston, Kirkby Wiske, and Wath.   It must not be forgotten, however, that the dwelling might stand apart in the churchyard, as at St. John's, Chester.

In several churches architectural features confirm the records.   Two cells in the south have been described by Mr. P. M. Johnston, and three in the north by Mr. J. R. Boyle.

Hartlip (Kent).—That of Hartlip (Plate XXVI), where a certain Robert was anchorite, remains at the west end of the north aisle.

Hardham (Sussex).—The same writer [1] traces the site of a chamber on the south side of the chancel, which may have been the abode of the recluse to whom the bishop bequeathed half a mark in 1253.   All that remains is a thirteenth-century squint.

Newcastle-upon-Tyne.—The vestry on the north of the church of St. John Baptist seems originally to have been an anchorite's house.   This conjecture is supported by a document, dated 1260, confirming to Christiana Umfred a place (*locum inclusionis*) in St. John's churchyard to be her habitation for life.   The original grant had been made by the bishop, prior, and convent of Carlisle (patrons of the mother-church of St. Nicholas), with the assent of the mayor and burgesses. Christiana probably witnessed the services through the cross-shaped opening shown in Plate XXVII, which is about 14 feet above the present floor.   The chamber was probably of two stories.   There is a blocked thirteenth-century window on the north.   It may be observed in passing that the cell founded in

---

[1] *Sussex Arch. Coll.*, XLII, 176-7 ; *Arch. Journ.*, LVIII, 66-8.

PLATE XXVII

ANCHORITE'S WINDOW, NEWCASTLE-UPON-TYNE

Gateshead churchyard in 1340 was replaced by a vestry, which retains the name Anchorage.

Staindrop.—Mr. Boyle describes a chamber with an ancient fire-place over the vestry of this church. At the head of the stone newel staircase is a square-headed window of three lights, the mullions of which are cut askew from east to west in order to command the high altar.

Chester-le-Street.—This church has retained what is probably the most complete anchorite's house remaining in England. It is at the west end of the church, on the north side of the tower, partly within and partly beyond the ancient walls. Two of the four rooms, one above the other, have been formed by walling off the western bay of the north aisle. This inner room is about 18 by 10 feet, whilst the two outer rooms are about 10 feet square. The recluse's upper chamber had a hagioscope commanding the altar in the south aisle ; the slit on the church side is only about 10 inches high and 1 or 2 inches wide. The west window consists of a large slab pierced with four rectangular openings and a lancet. Below the floor is a well, which is probably ancient. There appears to have been an outside stairway to the upper story of the outer room, which has a window and a slit aperture. There is no architectural clue to the date of " the ankers house," which is mentioned in the Chantry certificate of 1548. Its subsequent history is told in chapter xiv. The house contains several doors, windows, and recesses, but it has suffered under alterations, and is now used for heating apparatus and lumber. The small upper chamber, once a museum of antiquities, contains a fine sculptured Saxon cross-shaft.

York : All Saints', North Street.—At the west end of the north aisle are the supposed traces of a two-storied cell, which was inhabited by a recluse famous during the reign of Henry VI (p. 35). Both the upper and lower windows command the high altar.[1]

It may be well to mention certain supposed cells, which have not at present been authenticated by documentary evidence.

Bengeo (Herts) *and Chipping Ongar* (Essex).—These

---

[1] The lower window was carefully opened out by the Rector and Miss M. Leaf, 1909.

"ankerholds" were investigated by Mr. J. T. Micklethwaite and Mr. Dewick.[1] In both cases openings were found in the north walls, and above them holes which might have held the timbers supporting a lean-to building.   At Chipping Ongar traces of a shuttered lancet window were discovered.

Letherhead (Surrey).—The foundations of a chamber on the north side of the chancel were excavated by Mr. Johnston, and were described and illustrated in the *Surrey Archæological Collections* (XX).

Compton.—Another Surrey church has a chamber annexed to it on the south side.   A narrow window communicates with the churchyard, but the outer doorway is blocked.   The arch of the inner doorway, leading into the church, springs from the capital of the sanctuary arch.   The hagioscope, deeply splayed, is so close to the high altar as to be over the aumbry adjoining the piscina ; it is cruciform, of graceful and uncommon design.

Michaelstow (Cornwall).—On the north side of the chancel are traces of a cell.   About 4 feet 8 inches from the floor is a diamond-shaped stone, pierced with a quatrefoil aperture.[2]

Traces of the anchorage, then, may reasonably be sought near the chancel.   It might be an upper room, but a chamber in the tower or over the porch was a most unlikely abode for the recluse.   Since the term "leper's window" has become discredited, there is a tendency with some to describe any inexplicable low-side window as an "anchorite's squint".   It is well to bear in mind that even where a habitable room exists, with fire-place, seat, or book-desk, it may have been a sacristy or a priest's lodging.   There is abundant opportunity for research on this subject, and it is much to be desired that architects should follow up the clues supplied by records.

---

[1] *Arch. Journ.* XLIV, 26-9 ; XLV, 284-7, with plates.
[2] J. C. Cox, *County Churches.*

VIII. ORDER AND RULE

What sawest thou before thee when thou didst vow thyself to this manner of life?—RULE OF ST. AELRED.

Do you now ask what rule ye anchoresses should observe? Ye should by all means, with all your might and all your strength, keep well the inward rule, and for its sake the outward. . . . The outward rule may be changed and varied according to every one's state and circumstances . . . it is only a slave to help the lady to rule the heart.—ANCREN RIWLE.

THE eremitical life, it has been truly said, "was once a career, and not the abdication of all careers". Recluses were therefore set apart for their vocation, whether they were regular or secular clergy, nuns, or men and women who had as yet taken no vows. A monk might become a hermit by permission of his abbot, but he could only be admitted to the order of an anchorite by the joint consent of his superior and of the bishop. A lay person required the sanction of the bishop before taking either step.

I. HERMITS

The place of the hermit in the ecclesiastical system is hard to define. There were many kinds of solitaries—all, perhaps, of a less conventional and canonical type than other churchmen, —but all, in theory at least, recognized by the Church. Some were in close touch with a monastery. The monk Bartholomew and the lay-brother Godric were both under the ægis of the Benedictine house of Durham, the prior of which exercised the right to "create" hermits. The secular clerk naturally turned to the bishop for licence, institution, or ordination. He might be admitted to minor orders, or even to full orders if the cell were sufficiently endowed for it to be accounted a benefice. Robert of Lilbourne, for example, after being made successively acolyte, sub-deacon, and deacon, was ordained priest on the "title" of five marks a year from his patron, Robert de Hawkwell. Unlettered hermits were also licensed, for episcopal recognition was required even by civil law.   The vagrancy statute of 1388 exempts "approved hermits having letters testimonial of their ordinaries".[1]   Such approval is frequently entered in episcopal records, e.g. the Bishop of Sarum gave J. Spensar letters testimonial that he had received the habit.

The ceremony of receiving the habit was a feature in the Office of Benediction (Appendix B).   The candidate appeared before the bishop, bare-headed and barefoot, carrying on his left arm the scapular and other garments suitable to the pro-fession of a hermit.   During the service the old garments were put off, and the new ones, after being blessed, were put on with appropriate prayers.   The hermit signed a deed of pro-fession, made a vow, and received a charge as to his future manner of living.

Some English hermits belonged to a branch of Augus-tinians[2] called "the Order of St. Paul the first Hermit".   In 1431 Richard Spechysley took the following vow at Hartle-bury :—

y Rychard Spechysley sengleman not wedded promytte and solempne a wowe make to god, to hys blessed moder Marie, and all the seyntes of heuene yn presence of your reuerent Fadyr yn cryst Thomas by the grace of god busshopp of Worcestr fulle and hole purpose of chastity perpetually to be kept by me after the Rule of seynt poule yn name of the fadyr and sone and holy gost amen *et faciat heremita cruce super cedulam.*

Similar instances occur elsewhere, but chiefly within the last fifty years of hermit-life in England ; e.g. Robert Michyll and John Smith were professed before the Bishop of Ely in 1494 ; John Ferys took the vow at Norwich (1504) ; John Colebrant received the habit from the Bishop of Rochester (1509).   Geoffrey Middleton, Richard Pury, and Nicholas Heage, all of Sarum diocese, likewise joined this Order.   The Lydence Pontifical (1521) contains the special service for ad-mission into the Order of St. Paul[3] (see Appendix B).   The habit worn by its members is shown in Fig. 6.

Various Rules of Life are extant, including the following :—

[1] Statute 12 Ric. II, c. 7.
[2] The " Augustinian Hermits " or " Friars Hermits of the Order of St. Augus-tine " have nothing to do with our subject ; they were mendicants living in community.
[3] See also Exeter and York Pontificals.

(*a*) *Regula Heremitarum* (Cambridge MS.), sometimes ascribed to Richard Rolle.

Fig. 6.—Hermit of the Order of St. Paul.

(*b*) *De pauperate, statu, et vita Heremitarum* (Bodleian MS., fourteenth century).

(*c*) *Rule,* called " of Pope Celestine," a manuscript which

belonged to the House of St. Mark, Bristol.   It begins :
" Thyes are the notable rewles of the lyfe heremiticalle . . .
made by Pope Celestine ".   The preface and much of the
matter are similar to (*b*).

(*d*) *Rule*, called "of Pope Linus" (Lambeth MS., fifteenth
century, bound as fly-leaf into a Carmelite work).   It begins :
" Lyne owre holy fadyr [Pope] of Rome he ordeyned thys
rowle to all solytary men that takys the degre of an heremyte " ; and ends : " Thys is ye charge of an hermygtis
lyffe ".

(*e*) *Episcopal Charge*, or form of living (Pontifical, sixteenth century, see Appendix B).

These documents contain directions about times of labour,
eating, sleep, silence, and worship.   Obedience in the monastic
sense was not required.   " The hermit should make obedience
to God alone, because he himself is abbot, prior, and prefect
in the cloister of his heart."   To Almighty God he may, if he
so desire, vow poverty and chastity before the bishop, but not
by any man's commandment.   Minute instructions are given
as to the repetition of the Creed, Lord's Prayer, and Angelic
Salutation, at the set hours.   He was to hear Mass daily, if
possible, and to be houselled once a week.   Regulations concerning food, dress, etc., are referred to in the chapters which
follow.

Although celibacy was doubtless customary among those
professed as hermits, it was not obligatory.   It is recorded
that " John Shenton, Armett, and hys wyffe " took charge of
the ornaments of the chapel at Derby bridge (1488).   Nor is
this a mere instance of laxity of discipline.   When it was noti-
fied to Archbishop Arundel that Adam Cressevill, after taking
a hermit's vow, had married a certain Margaret, the archbishop
adjudged that the reception of such a habit did not *de jure*
bring upon any one a tacit or express profession of religion,
nor include in itself holy orders, so as to preclude a subsequent
contract of " marriage which was instituted in Paradise ".
The Adam of 1405 was, therefore, declared to be effectually
bound and held to the observance of the marriage.[1]

In theory, the solitary was canonically appointed and

---

[1] Lambeth, Reg. Arundel, Pt. I, f. 438 *b*.

placed under definite rule, but every age has its free-lances. The difficulties connected with due order and discipline were as old as sixth-century monachism. The Benedictine Rule declares that there were not only hermits trained in the monastery, but also self-appointed ones, some of whom roamed from cell to cell. Self-constituted or wandering solitaries were bound to interfere with parochial, monastic, or episcopal rights. When Archbishop Thurstan was granting a charter to the priory of Holy Trinity, York, he inserted this clause : " Let no hermit or anyone else presume to construct a chapel or oratory of any kind within the territory of that parish church, without the permission and free consent of the prior and chapter ". [1]

The Church prohibited hermits of irregular life or belief. About the year 1231 the Bishop of Lincoln excommunicated Elias, a monk notorious for excesses, and a chaplain was admitted in his place to Mirabel hermitage in Stockerston. In 1334, heresy and schism are recorded both in north and south. The Archbishop of York issued a mandate forbidding anyone to listen to the teaching of Henry de Staunton, hermit.[2] The Bishop of Exeter took proceedings against a peculiar person named William, who had set himself up as a hermit at St. David's chapel in Ashprington.[3] Two years later Ranulf, an apostate friar, being " a heretic in the habit of a hermit," was examined by theologians, and convicted of holding false doctrines ; but the prisoner was released by death.[4]

Sometimes, indeed, the habit was assumed by mere beggars :—

"William Blakeney, *shetilmaker* . . . was brought into the Guildhall . . . for that, whereas he was able to work for his food and raiment, he . . . went about there, barefooted and with long hair, under the guise of sanctity, and pretended to be a hermit, saying that he was such, and that he had made pilgrimage . . . and under colour of falsehood he had received many good things from divers people."

[1] *Cal. Doc. France*, ed. J. H. Round, 443.
[2] Dixon, ed. J. Raine, *Fasti*, I. 421.
[3] *Ex. Reg. Grandisson*, Pt. II, 751-2.
[4] *Chron. Edw. I* (Rolls, 76), I. 365.

The impostor, who had lived by fraud for six years, was condemned to the pillory (1412).[1]

The desire to be independent of authority led some persons to seek the solitary life. William Stapleton, clerk, left St. Benet's, Holme (where, as he confesses, he had often been punished for laziness), went to London, and purchased from Cardinal Wolsey a dispensation to be a hermit. The truth was, that his whole mind was set on necromancy. He used enchantments in digging for hidden treasure, and practised spirit-raising. When he returned to Norfolk and showed his licence, his friends motioned him to go about his " science " again, saying they would help him to his habit. This runaway monk was intimate with Wolsey (to whom, in 1528, his long letter is addressed), Cromwell, More, and the Duke of Norfolk. Whether he became solitary or sorcerer does not appear.[2]

Even authorized hermits were apt to upset the parochial system, if persons resorted to their chapels to the neglect of their parish church. A long-standing grievance at Hinxton was met by an agreement between the vicar, wardens, and parishioners, and William Popeley, hermit of Whytford Bridge. Tithes and dues were commuted for fixed oblations at the principal feasts, when the bridge-chaplain must, like all other parishioners, make his oblations. The vicar was to say mass yearly at St. Anne's chapel, and in return for his labour, should receive 4d. and a good dinner from the hermit.

II. ANCHORITES

Turning to the stricter order, we find that the permission of the bishop of the diocese was required before any person could be enclosed. A notable exception was Wulfric of Haselbury ; for "without any appointment of the bishop, with no solemnity of benediction, but by the authority of the Holy Spirit who dwelt within, he buried himself with Christ in a cell close to the church". A canon of St. Edmund (1233) enacted that anchorites should not be made without the bishop's special approval; and Lyndwood, commenting on this clause, observes that assistant bishops may not give the

---

[1] H. Riley, *Memorials*, 584.
[2] *L. and P. Hen. VIII*, IV (2), No. 5096 ; *Norfolk Archæology*, I, 59.

requisite licence, nor may an abbot enclose a person on his own authority.[1]

It was also necessary to obtain the consent of the incumbent and patron of the church to which the person was to be attached. Henry III permitted Celestria to be enclosed at his chapel of Kingesham (probably Kingsholm in the manor of King's Barton at Gloucester), the sheriff having signified that this would not be detrimental to the Crown. The approval of the patrons was not sought by the parishioners of St. Michael's, Bristol, and the chronicler of Tewkesbury therefore records that : " Both the townsmen of Bristol and the anchoress intruded into the cell (*reclusagium*) of St. Michael on the hill without Bristol confessed that they had acted presumptuously and contrary to justice, and sought forgiveness from Robert, the Lord Abbot ".

The prefatory note to the Sarum Office declares that no one ought to be enclosed without the will of the bishop, who was to cause the candidate to be instructed and warned how he should examine his conscience and consider his motives, whether he is setting himself to please God, or to acquire gain or the praise of man. Nor was the applicant accepted without close investigation. A commissary was appointed to inquire into the circumstances of the case, not only as to the suitability of the proposed place, but as to the person's estate, whether maiden, married, or widow, and, above all, concerning her character. Sometimes the mandate included permission to induct the candidate, should the examination prove satisfactory. The following charge was given by the Bishop of Worcester concerning Lucy, who was eagerly desirous to inhabit the cell upon St. Brandan's Hill, near Bristol :—

" John by the mercy of God Bishop etc. greeting, to our beloved son Master John de Severley, Archdeacon of Worcester, peace and blessing.

" Lucy de Newchirche has approached us many times with earnest and humble devotion, as was clear to us from her appearance and demeanour, asking to be enclosed in the hermitage of St. Brandan at Bristol in our diocese. But as we have no knowledge of the life and conversation of the said Lucy, we commit to you, in whose trustiness, diligence, and caution we have full confidence, an enquiry

---

[1] W. Lyndwood, *Provinciale*, ed. 1525, *Lib.* III, f. CLV. CLVI.

from men and women worthy of credit with regard to the conversation of this Lucy, and whether you would consider her to be of pure and praiseworthy life, and whether she excels in those notable virtues which ought to prevail in persons who give up the life of the world. And if at a day and time appointed, at your discretion and in accordance with law and reason, for her examination, you should find her to be resolutely and firmly set on the pure purpose with regard to which we have burdened your conscience in the presence of God, we commit to you our power, so far as by the divine law we can, of enclosing her, either personally or by deputy as an anchoress in the aforesaid hermitage." [1]

Since the bishop himself had been impressed by Lucy's earnestness, it is probable that she was enclosed.   Barrett cites a deed referring to land near St. Brendan's which the anchoress held.   Who the petitioner was does not appear ; but two years previously a certain Lucy de Newchurch, from the diocese of Hereford, obtained a papal indult to choose a confessor who should give her plenary remission at the hour of death.

The would-be anchoress might be some maiden "without the habit of a nun" who desired to devote herself to religion in the village where she had been brought up, as, for example, Matilda de Campden, who sought to be enclosed in the churchyard at Chipping Campden.   She might be one who, like Emma Sprenghose of Shrewsbury, "from childhood always affected, and still affects, the solitary life".   She might be already in a convent.   A nun of Stainfield, Beatrice Franke by name, petitioned the Bishop of Lincoln to be enclosed at Winterton Church ; the Abbot of Thornton, therefore, released her from her previous vows and proffered to her new vows at high mass in that church.   The anchoress might even be some matron.   A curious case is that of the vowess Emma Cheyne —"late the wife of the recluse of Bury St. Edmunds, aged sixty-eight years and professed for twenty-two years in the order of widowhood and daily persevering in honest conversation"—who dwelt at St. Peter's, Cornhill.[2]

The applicant might be one of the regular or secular clergy. William de Pershore, priest, sought permission to be enclosed in the parish of Wickwar, and he was given a dispensation to

[1] Reg. Thoresby, f. 21.
[2] Pat. 28 Hen. VI., Pt. i, m. 11.   The veiled widow may have dwelt in the anchorite's cell, without being actually enclosed.

PLATE XXVIII

ENCLOSING AN ANCHORESS

build a little house for that purpose, subject to the consent of the rector as patron of the church.   Robert Cherde, a Cistercian monk of Ford, who desired to become a solitary at Crewkerne, brought letters from his abbot, and made his petition in person before the bishop at Wells.

In certain cases it was thought advisable to fix a period of probation.   In May, 1403, the Bishop of Exeter commissioned the Abbot of Hartland and Rector of Southill to place Cecilia Moys in a house in the cemetery of Marhamchurch, assigning her until Christmas as a time of probation.

The ceremony was performed by the bishop or his deputy. The Bishop of Lichfield empowered his Suffragan, Robert *Prissinensis* (1376) to administer Holy Orders, etc., and to enclose anchorites.[1]   Episcopal prerogative might, however, be overruled by papal privilege.   Richard Gilbard, an Augustinian canon of Longleat, obtained licence " to choose and remain in any hermitage in the realm in order to lead therein a solitary life " (1399).[2]   The Mendicant Orders were free from episcopal jurisdiction.   John Toker, a Franciscan, gained permission to be enclosed, without licence of his superiors, at Buckland ; he was fifty years of age and had been a friar since he was thirteen.   Carmelite recluses were professed before the Provincial of the Order.   Again, the Abbot of St. Albans enclosed members of the community at will.   He himself celebrated the solemn mass when (at the instance of Edward IV and his queen, and "at the supplication of divers magnates dwelling in the king's household") Elizabeth Katherine Holsted was admitted to the anchorage at St. Peter's.[3]

As a general rule, however, the bishop was, by virtue of his office, the guardian of every solitary in his diocese.   The Archbishop of York made himself responsible for a religious refugee from Scotland.   The nuns of Coldstream having been dispersed (probably in 1296, when Edward I made his headquarters in their house) Beatrice de Hodesak, for this just and reasonable cause, left the nunnery by permission of the bishop and prioress.   She afterwards, with the licence of Archbishop Thomas, became an anchoress at Sprotbrough, near Doncaster, at the house adjoining St. Edmund's chapel by the bridge.   It

---

[1] *Staffs. Coll.*, N.S., VIII, 131.   [2] *Pap. Lett.*, v. 200.
[3] *Chr. S. Alb.* (Rolls, 28, Pt. VI.) ; *Registers*, II. 202.

had been founded by Lord Fitzwilliam, who provided yearly for each of the women five quarters of corn. When Beatrice settled there about the year 1300, her companion was that Sibil de Lisle who had been enclosed in 1294 by the Abbot of Kirkstall. Beatrice probably died before 1328, when the Dean of Doncaster was commissioned to enclose Joan, daughter of William of Easingwold, who desired to live with Dame Sibil.[1]

There are numerous liturgical forms for the enclosing of anchorites. The earliest extant seems to be that entitled *Ad recludendum Anchoritam*, in a fragmentary twelfth-century Pontifical.[2] Of later examples, Cambridge has several—the Clifford Pontifical (Plate XXVIII) at Corpus Christi College, the Chichele Pontifical at Trinity, the Sarum Manual at St. John's, and the Russell Pontifical in the University Library. In this chapter we draw chiefly upon three published offices, namely, those found in the Exeter Pontifical belonging to Bishop Lacy (1420-55), the York Pontifical of Archbishop Bainbridge (1508-14), and the Sarum Manual (printed in 1506).[3]

The "Order of enclosing servants or handmaidens of God," according to the Sarum Use, provided that the candidate, before being admitted to the cell, should fast and make his confession, and should keep vigil throughout the preceding night. On the morrow the bishop or his commissary made an exhortation to the people and to the one who was about to be enclosed, and the office opened with versicles and psalms. The celebrant proceeded to mass, which included special prayers. After the Gospel the *includendus*, having offered his taper to burn upon the altar, stood at the altar-step and read his profession in a clear voice. He then made the sign of the cross with a pen on the roll, and placing it upon the altar with bended knee, prayed. Next came the sprinkling and blessing of the habit, in which the newly-professed was clad. Whilst he lay prostrate before the altar, the celebrant chanted over him *Veni, Creator Spiritus*, when, Mass being finished, all, including the novice who carried his taper, moved in procession

---

[1] *Northern Reg.* (Rolls 61), 196-8 ; Raine, *Fasti*, 380 ; Reg. Romeyn, f. 46 ; Reg. Melton, f. 175.

[2] B.M. Cott. Vesp. D., xv., f. 61-5.

[3] *Liber Pontif.*, ed. R. Barnes ; *York Pontif.* (S.S. 61) ; *Sarum Man.* (S.S. 63) ; see Appendix A to this volume.

towards the cell. The bishop advanced, and, taking him by
the hand, led him to his habitation, whilst the clerks chanted
a litany. The bishop, having hallowed the altar and house,
went out and brought in the *includendus*, and after solemn
prayers and benedictions, he—now the *inclusus*—was left
alone. The bishop recited the antiphon in a loud voice,
audible, may be, in the utter silence of the cell, the door of
which had been firmly shut. After united prayer for the
solitary, the procession formed again and returned into the
church.

The Exeter Office bears a general resemblance to the foregoing. The opening rubric directs that the would-be recluse,
if a clerk, should prostrate himself barefoot in the midst of the
choir ; if a layman, he should lie outside the gate of the choir ;
if a woman, in the western part of the church, where women
are wont to worship. Having recited certain psalms and a
litany, the bishop and his ministers should come to the prostrate person, with cross, thurible, and holy water, and after
sprinkling and censing him, the bishop, with another venerable
person, should raise him up. Holding a taper in each hand,
the candidate should listen devoutly as this lection was read
from Isaiah : " Come, my people, enter thou into thy chambers,
and shut thy doors about thee : hide thyself as it were for a
little moment, until the indignation be overpast ". The Gospel
was taken from St. Luke : " Jesus entered into a certain village :
and a certain woman named Martha received him into her
house. And she had a sister called Mary, which also sat at
Jesus' feet, and heard His word," etc. Having read the form
of profession, the candidate should kneel at the altar-step,
repeating thrice : " Receive me, O Lord, according to Thy
word ". After further prayers, " let the bishop make a discourse to the people, explaining the manner and form of living
of a recluse, and let him commend the person about to be enclosed to the people that they may pray for him ". The Mass
of the Holy Spirit was now celebrated, by the *includendus* himself, if he were in holy orders, but if not, by the bishop or by
another priest. The bishop, having led the novice to the door
of the *reclusorium*, was to enter, and consecrate the whole house
by prayers, holy water, and censing. He should then go out
to the waiting person and say : " If he wishes to enter, let him

enter ". The bishop then began to perform rites which were designed to impress upon the devotee the fact that in a strict sense he was henceforth dead to the world. The office of extreme unction was performed, with the commendation of the soul, lest death should anticipate the last rites. "These things being done, let the grave be opened, entering which, let the recluse himself, or another in his name, sing : *This shall be my rest for ever*". Dust was scattered with the words : *From dust wast thou created*, etc. Before going out, the bishop made a final exhortation, and the door of the house was built up.

"We left her, as is believed, in peace and calm of spirit, in the joy of her Saviour": so it was reported of the nun Beatrice (p. 92), who almost from her youth had craved for this life.

In this solemn manner the self-dedicated person was admitted to the "order" of an anchorite, as it was termed. It was "in the order of an ancresse" that one Margery made her profession in 1521 in the church of the Blackfriars, in the following words :—

"I sister Margerie Clyute offereth and giueth myselfe to the mercie of Godd in the order of an Ancresse to lyue in his seruice after the rule of an ancresse and here in the presence of you worthy father in Godd Thomas Bishop of Lydene [1] I make myne Obedience to the worshipful father in Godd lord Ric. fitz James Byshop of London and to his successours".

This word "order" often occurs in documents, but, in the *Ancren Riwle*, recluses were warned against using the term in a limited sense : "If any ignorant person ask you of what order ye are, as ye tell me some do . . . answer and say that ye are of the order of St. James," that is to say, of those who keep themselves unspotted from the world.

The recluse's Rule of Life consisted of friendly counsel rather than rigid regulations. Several such books of instruction were written in England for English women—by an abbot, by some unknown churchman, by a layman-hermit, and by an Augustinian canon.

(*a*) *Rule of Aelred* (twelfth century).—The *Regula, Informa-*

---

[1] In 1495 the Bishop of Lydda was Suffragan to Bishop Blyth of Sarum. This Thomas Lydensis owned the Pontifical mentioned elsewhere.

PLATE XXIX

ENCLOSING AN ANCHORESS

cio, or *Institutio Inclusarum*[1] was compiled by Aelred of Rievaulx, "a man glowing with enthusiasm for the solitary life".
It is dedicated to his sister, who had long besought him for a
form of living. He says in his preface that being her brother
after the flesh and in spirit he could not refuse her request,
but he would she had asked one wiser and more experienced
than himself: "Natheles after that simple felynge that god
hath youen me I shal write to the a forme gadert out of holy
fadirs tradition". The first chapter is entitled: "How the
eremitical life was appointed". Looking back to the ancients,
many of whom dwelt alone in the wilderness, Aelred inquires
wherefore this life was undertaken. Some, he says, find it harm-
ful to live in a crowd, and profitable to be in solitude ; finding
in the world a freedom of loveliness and possibility of wandering, they think it safer to be confined within a cell. Aelred
gives wise counsel on spiritual and material matters, extracts
from which will be found in succeeding chapters. After giving
some details as to dress, he adds: "These things, dear sister,
I have written at thy request concerning the manner of outward
conduct, not on account of zeal for antiquity, but for the short-
ness of our time here on earth ; setting forth a certain form of
life adapted for weaker sisters, leaving to the stronger ones to
go forward unto fuller perfection". The humble abbot con-
cludes with a personal plea: "If any one shall have profited
by the discourse of this book, let her render back to me this
return for my labour and study: that she may intercede for
my sins with my Saviour whom I love, with my Rewarder for
whom I look, with my Judge whom I fear".

(*b*) *Ancren Riwle*[2] (thirteenth century).—The Rule bearing
this name is a handbook of devotion, conduct, and household
management. The author was familiar with Aelred's work
and quotes from it (p. 122). He was the personal friend of
those for whom he wrote—"my dear sisters, women most dear
to me". He enjoins the three-fold vow of obedience, chastity,
and constancy of abode. They must be guided by an inward

---

[1] L. Holstenius, *Codex Regularum*, III. 186-239. Also English paraphrase,
Bodl. MS., 423, f. 178-92: "Here endith the Reule of a Recluse that seynt
Alrede wrote to his suster". Another copy, Vernon MS., is transcribed by
Horstman in *Englische Studien*, ed. E. Kölbing, VII. 304-44.

[2] *Camden Soc.*, O.S. 57 (1853) contains original and translation ; latter reprinted in 1905 by Abbot Gasquet (*King's Classics*).

law—that of love which regulates the heart.   Mere outward rules might vary according to each one's estate and circumstances.   The precepts contained in the book are, he declares, written for themselves alone : other anchoresses must not say that he, by his own authority, makes new rules for them. The regulations may be changed at will for better ones : " In regard to things of this kind *that have been in use before*, it matters little ".

The question of authorship has yet to be solved.   It was formerly attributed to Richard Poer, Bishop of Salisbury (1217-29), but the evidence is insufficient.   The preface to one imperfect Latin copy, preserved at Magdalen College, Oxford, states that Bishop Simon of Ghent (1297-1315) wrote it for his sisters, anchoresses at Tarrent, but this is clearly a translation and the original English work is of considerably earlier date.   The researches of Prof. Koelbing and Dr. Thummler will doubtless contribute much to the question of date and authorship.   Their critical edition is to be published by the Early English Text Society (see note on p. 100).

The writer was a man of high ideals, a practical person, with sound judgment and clear insight.   A marked gift of sympathy is shown by his tender, delicate, and understanding instructions.   Careful thought and infinite labour were bestowed upon the work :—

"In this book read every day, when ye are at leisure—every day less or more ; for I hope that if ye read it often it will be very beneficial to you through the grace of God, or else I shall have ill employed much of my time.   God knows, it would be more agreeable to me to set out on a journey to Rome, than to begin to do it again."

(*c*) *Form of Perfect Living*[1] (fourteenth century).—This treatise was written by Richard Rolle for his friend, Dame Margaret.   It is an intimate spiritual letter rather than a set rule.   The second chapter (often found as a separate tract) deals with the solitary life, its peculiar trials and joys.   Of its mystical teaching the following is a specimen :—

"For that thou hast forsaken the solace and the joy of this world, and taken thee to solitary life . . . I trow truly that the comfort of Jesus Christ and the sweetness of His love, with the fire of

---

[1] C. Horstman, *R. Rolle*, i. 3-49.

the Holy Ghost that purges all sin, shall be in thee and with thee, leading thee and teaching thee how thou shalt think, how thou shalt pray, what thou shalt work, so that in a few years thou shalt have more delight to be by thyself and speak to thy love and thy spouse Jesus Christ, that is high in heaven, than if thou wert lady here of a thousand worlds. Men ween that we are in pain and penance : but we have more joy and very delight in a day than they have in the world all their life. They see our body, but they see not our heart, where our solace is. If they saw that, many of them would forsake all that they have, for to follow us."

(*d*) *The Scale* (or Ladder) *of Perfection*,[1] written by Walter Hilton, an Augustinian canon who died in 1396. It deals with the life of action and of contemplation, but especially with the latter. He addresses it to a woman " closid in a hous," and reminds her that the cause of her bodily enclosure is that she might thereby the better come to a " ghostly closynge ". Since her estate required of her to be contemplative, it behoved her to be right busy both night and day with travail of body and of spirit, in order to come as nigh as she might to that life.

(*e*) *Book for Recluses*[2] (fifteenth century), containing advice based upon various reasons for embracing this life, whether (1) intention of living at her own will without labour, (2) fervent repentance, (3) avoidance of sin, or (4) desire for Divine contemplation. The first counsels of the preface aim at changing the purpose of any whose first motive had been temporal solace, comfort, independence, acquisition of goods. The remainder of the book is entirely devotional. The first part contains plain teaching drawn from the Old and New Testaments. Prayer is illustrated by David and Hezekiah, Moses and Joshua, Elijah and Elisha ; repentance, by David, Peter, Mary Magdalene, and " the publican asking mercy ". The second part is a call to praise, and treats of the excellence and might and goodness of God as maker and keeper of all things. There is pathos in the suggestion made to one so straitly shut up that she might stir her heart to praise by thinking upon the merry noise of birds in their sweet song, the delight of flowers and fruits, the usefulness of beasts, which follow without fail the

[1] First printed by Wynkyn de Worde, 1494. Latest edition, 1901.
[2] B. M. Harl. 2372.

law of nature and are every year marvellously renewed to the behoof of man. But chiefly was she to meditate upon "the glorious Passion of our Lord". The third part, which is unfinished, contains sacramental teaching.

The Order and Rule have necessarily been dealt with only in outline. Details of the outer life will now be considered, whilst an account of the inner life with its trials and discipline is reserved for a subsequent chapter.

Note on the " Ancren Riwle ".

Since going to press Professor Gollancz has called my attention to a fourteenth-century version of this Rule, recently edited by Joel Pählsson (*The Recluse*, University of Lund, 1911). The original is found at Magdalene College, Cambridge (MS. Pepys, 2498). It is addressed to men and women, and several of the intimate touches of the *Ancren Riwle* are omitted, e.g. allusions to the circumstances of the three sisters (see pp. 97-8, 105-6, 109, 131, 136 of this volume). In place of the homely allusion to the scullion Slurry, the Camb. MS. preaches the patient endurance of insolence from underlings. "Our lay-brethren" and "our order" are not mentioned, but the religious of the later version include friars. The Camb. MS. inserts passages which are wanting in the Cottonian; but the full practical directions found at the end of the latter are given in briefest outline. The compiler describes himself as "him that drew it out into this language".

IX. CONCERNING THE BODY

A bird sometimes alighteth on the earth, to seek his food for the need of the flesh. . . . Even so, the pious recluse, though she fly ever so high, must at times come down to the earth in respect of her body—and eat, drink, sleep, work, speak, and hear, when it is necessary, of earthly things.—ANCREN RIWLE.

ALTHOUGH the true solitary was chiefly occupied with the affairs of the soul, either he himself or his neighbours were bound to take thought for his bodily needs. The possession of a little plot of land enabled the hermit to be more or less independent, but the anchorite could not maintain himself. The hermit's absorbing interest in his garden was even supposed to become an obstacle to his spiritual progress. In the *Hortus Deliciarum*, compiled by a German abbess in the twelfth century, the ladder to perfection is depicted in symbol, with the climbers and their respective hindrances. Among men of religion, the hermit is foremost, although his *garden* has proved a stumbling-block; whilst the anchorite is kept back by sloth, represented by a *bed*.[1]

I. FOOD

The early hermits lived a primitive life as tillers of the soil, and their food consisted of herbs, roots, grain, and fruit. Godric of Finchale used to refuse the gifts of food offered to him, and cultivated his garden as long as he was able; we read of his planting and grafting, and of his crops. He also kept cows, and in his old age, lived almost entirely upon milk. Robert of Knaresborough was another hermit-husbandman. He fared frugally, but one day he was left hungry, for robbers invaded his dwelling and stole his bread and cheese. After a time he was granted as much land as he could dig, and later, as much as he could till with one plough. He was also given two horses, two oxen, and two cows. Robert's parable was an ear of corn (p. 153); and the miracles ascribed to him are

---

[1] L. Eckenstein, *Woman under Monast.*, 246.

the miracles of a farmer. He tames the wild cow, and yokes
to his plough the stags which trample his corn :—

> Hertes full heghe of hede and horn ꞌ
> Vsed to come to Robertt corn . . .
> He wentt and wagged att them a wand
> And draffe thise dere hame wᵗ hys hand.

This legend and also that of a counterfeit cripple, who begged
a cow from St. Robert, were depicted in a window set up in
Knaresborough church in 1473.[1]

In some cases the hermit had no land to cultivate. Richard
Rolle, for example, was homeless. At first he was provided
with food and shelter by Sir John and Lady de Dalton, but
when they died, he became a wanderer, dependent upon alms.
Ill-clad and ill-shod, he suffered severely from exposure. At
times he subsisted on mouldy bread, and had but a scant
supply of water. Yet Richard did not refuse proper sustenance when it was provided. He had eaten and drunk of
the best, not for love of good food, but for nature to be sus-
tained in God's service. He would not appear unto men to
fast, but conformed himself to them with whom he dwelt,
fearing lest he should feign holiness, and win praise. He
advised the contemplative not to attempt too much fasting,
lest " for febilnes of body he myght not synge ".[2] Enemies
were therefore not slow to say that he would not abide but
where he might be delicately fed ; whilst as a matter of fact
he frequently suffered exhaustion from abstinence.

Flesh was rarely tasted by the hermit. It was lawful to
partake of it on the three great festivals, and on the four
following days ; also in time of sickness, or strenuous work—
" for grete labore past or labor for to come yf nede ax yt ".
At the commandment of the bishop or patron, he might indulge
in meat for a single day. He was directed to fast three days
in the week, and on Friday upon bread and water. He was
also required to observe seasons of abstinence, namely, forty
days before Christmas and Easter, and nine days before Whit-
sunday and Michaelmas.[3]

---

[1] Dodsworth, *Church Notes*. (Rec. S., 34), 158. The glass is said to have
been removed during the last century (? into Lincolnshire). Further information
will be welcomed by the writer.

[2] *Fire of Love* (E.E. Text S.), 25-6.

[3] Bristol City Library, MS. 6 (cf. Appendix B).

In one Rule interesting directions are given under the heading *Of provision in his cell* :—

"If a hermit dwells in a borough, town, or city, or nigh thereto, where each day he can well beg his daily food, let him before sunset distribute to Christ's poor that which remains of his food. But if he abides afar, as in a country village or a desert spot one or two miles from the abode of men, let him make provision for one week strictly from Sunday to Sunday, or he may begin on another day of the week ; and if aught remains over, let it be given to the poor forthwith, unless on some ground he can excuse himself in the sight of God, as that he is sick or weak, or that he is tending a sick man, or is busy at home with works bodily or spiritual which are well pleasing to God."[1]

This encouragement to town hermits to beg their bread was mischievous. Langland complains that there were false hermits living in idleness and ease by others' travail (p. 61-2). More than one Rule, however, devoted a clause to manual labour, and impressed the apostolic saying : "He that laboreth not, owght not to ete".

Anchorites, on the other hand, could not support themselves. There are, indeed, two chapters in Aelred's Rule (VI., XI.) to the effect that the recluse should live by the labour of her hands, or, if she were not in want, bestow the price upon the church or the poor. But if either sickness or tenderness did not allow this, let her, before she is enclosed, seek out certain persons from whom day by day she may receive food.

The bishop was careful not to license anyone unless he was satisfied that sustentation was secure and permanent ; indeed, if the solitary were in want, the burden of maintenance fell upon the bishop, as in the case of a clerk ordained without a title.[2] Archbishop Arundel granted permission for the enclosure at Broughton (Lincolnshire) of the monk John Kyngeston, "according to the appointment and disposition of certain venerable friends of his".

Maintenance was provided in money or in kind. The allowance varied according to the person's estate. During the century 1160-1260 royal pensioners were usually granted $\frac{1}{2}d$. or 1*d.* a day ; but Adam, a recluse at Gloucester, had the liberal dole of 2*d.* a day, paid out of the farm of the city.

[1] Bodl. Rawl. MS., C. 72. [2] Lyndwood, *Provinciale, Lib.* III.

The ample yearly allowance of 100s. was made to the anchoress of Iffley, who also frequently received oaks for her fire. Other donors gave smaller sums, even 1d. or 2d. a week, supplemented, perhaps, by food, fuel, or clothes. In some cases, anchoresses received a grant of corn, but this was often commuted for a money payment.

The recluse lived on simple foods, chiefly vegetarian. The rules direct that she have potage made of herbs, peas, or beans, furmity sweetened with milk, butter, or oil, and fish seasoned with apples or herbs. On Wednesday, Friday, and Saturday, Lent meals only were allowed. During Lent she might have one kind of potage daily, but on Fridays only bread and water. No flesh or lard was eaten except in great sickness. The hour of the meal was noon, but in Lent, not until after vespers.[1] Langland says that he will give alms to anchorites " that eten nought but at nones, and no more ere morrow ".[2]

The inmate of a cell which was dependent upon a monastic house usually received a corrody, or fixed allowance of food and clothing ; thus in the compotus rolls of Worcester Priory are entered the portions of bread and ale given out to two recluses. About the year 1235 it was ordained that the anchoress of St. Michael's church at St. Albans should enjoy the corrody left to the abbey by Adam the Cellarer. At Whalley the provision seems liberal. The sum of 3d. a week was paid to the three inmates of the cell, who received every week seventeen loaves such as were usually made in the monastery, and seven loaves of an inferior sort (each loaf to weigh fifty shillings sterling), with eight gallons of beer. At the feast of All Saints they were given ten large stock fish, one bushel of oatmeal, and one bushel of rye. For the lighting and warming of the house oil, turfs, and faggots were provided.

Some persons contributed towards their maintenance. Agnes Booth or Shepherd (a nun of Norton Priory) was enclosed at Pilling in Garstang, a chapelry of Cockersand. Eight years later, in 1501, the following entry occurs in the rental : " M^d yat Annes Scheperte hasse payn to James y^e

---

[1] Reg. Inclus., cap. XIX. ; Bodl. MS., 423, f. 182.
[2] Piers Plowman (E.E.T.S., 38), Text B., pass. VI., 147-8. But in summer two meals were permitted, see Ancren Riwle.

Abbott of Cokersand for her lyuing—ii^s ii^d to me & vi^s viii^d to ye Convent".

The necessaries of life were sometimes provided from the manor-house. The ladies for whom the *Ancren Riwle* was written were maintained in an unusual degree of comfort :—

"For ye take no thought for food and clothing, neither for yourselves nor for your maidens. Each of you hath from one friend all that she requireth ; nor need that maiden seek either bread, or that which is eaten with bread, further than at his hall."

The writer adds emphatically that "many others know little of this abundance, but are full often distressed with want".

The recluse was warned not to grumble at her meat and drink, were it ever so stale ; if it were actually uneatable she might ask for more palatable food, but reluctantly and tactfully ; for it were a sin to cause men to say : "This anchoress is dainty, and she asks much". Only sheer necessity should drive her to make a request : "yet humbly shew your distress to your dearest friend". If fragments could be spared from her meals, she should send them secretly to poor women and children who had laboured for her. Waste, untidiness, and neglect of household duties were forbidden. The category of faults to be confessed included these : "Dropping crumbs, or spilling ale, or letting a thing grow mouldy, or rusty, or rotten ; clothes not sewed, wet with rain, or unwashen ; a cup or a dish broken, or any thing carelessly looked after which we are using".

II. CLOTHING

In a convent it was customary, for uniformity's sake, that all should be attired alike ; "but wherever a woman liveth, or a man liveth by himself alone, be he hermit or anchorite, of outward things whereof scandal cometh not, it is not necessary to take so much care". Foolish people, supposing that the "order" consisted in kirtle or cowl, would question recluses about the colour and cut of their garments, as though religion were a matter of a wide hood, or of a black, white, or grey cowl.

As the visible sign of separation, however, a habit was essential. No man felt himself a hermit until he had assumed some distinctive dress. Even that most unconventional of solitaries, Richard Rolle, when about to flee from home, persuaded his sister to send to him in the wood two garments and his father's raincloak, whereof he fashioned a habit and hood. Putting off his own clothes, he put on his sister's white tunic. Above this he wore her grey tunic, thrusting his arms through the holes which he had left by cutting out the sleeves; and over all he drew on the cloak, " so that, in some measure, he might present a confused likeness to a hermit ". Sir John de Dalton then provided him with "garments suitable to a hermit ". Long afterwards, when he was established as a hermit, his friends removed a tattered habit, mended it, and put it on again, whilst he was in spiritual absorption.[1]

The Rules direct that the hermit's dress be according to the bishop's ordinance; it must not too closely resemble that of any order, lest it cause offence. " Let hys clothyng be humyle and not curius. . . . And yf he wyll of devosyon were next hys flesh a cylyce it ys laufull." He was to wear plain shoes without hose, or else go barefoot. In his coat or kirtle, girded with a cord, he slept, and he was at length buried in it : "and he shall be graved whan he ys ded in hys habyt as he gothe ".

The habit varied as considerably as did the office. It usually consisted of loose garments of sober hue, caught up with a cord. A wall-painting at Rampton shows a hermit with sleeved surplice, tippet, and skull-cap. Another type of dress is shown in Fig. 6.

There was no regulation dress for the anchoress. Against the winter she was to have a pilch, a thick garment made of skins; and in summer, a kirtle with a black mantle. The head-covering was not to be of fine texture or varied colour, but of a mean black. If the ladies dispensed with wimples, they should have capes and veils. Clothing was to be simple and serviceable. " Because no man seeth you, nor do ye see any man, ye may be well content with your clothes, be they white, be they black; only see that they be plain, and warm, and well-made—skins well tawed; and have as many as you need, for bed and also for back." Underclothing was to be of coarse linen or woollen material. Shoes must be thick and warm, but in summer recluses were at liberty to go barefoot.

[1] Officium, *York Breviary* (S.S., 75), App. V.

They might wear no ring, brooch, ornamented girdle, or gloves.

The male anchorite probably wore some clerical garb. Symon, of Allhallows, London Wall, is represented in the frontispiece of his book as a priest (Fig. 7).

Offerings were sometimes made to the recluse in the form of garments. Wulfric of Haselbury, scantily clad in his chilly cell, received a welcome gift from Bristol :—

"The man of God was very frequently benumbed with extreme cold, to such a degree that a certain man from the neighbourhood of Bristol, being warned by a vision, sent to him a new covering of fox-skin wherewith he should cover himself. For the Lord said to him in a vision : 'My servant Wulfric is tortured with cold, but thou, indeed, art pleasantly warm ; get up as quickly as possible and send this covering with all speed '. And so it was done."

But mantles which men might make, mice might mar. As Wulfric sat one day in his cell, he observed that his cloak had been gnawed by a mouse. "May the mouse perish which has thus presumed to damage my mantle ! " The words were no sooner uttered than, behold, the creature, starting out from the wall, fell dead at the feet of the recluse. Seized with compunction, Wulfric called the priest and humbly confessed that his thoughtless curse had slain the mouse. The priest exclaimed in reply : "Would that a like anathema might utterly exterminate all the mice of this district ! "

By a will, dating from the time of King John, a super-tunic of *bifle* was left to Dame Lucy, who was enclosed in the church-yard of Bury St. Edmunds. The anchorite of Colemans-church in London received from a canon of St. Martin's two fur garments. Geoffrey le Scrope made a substantial legacy to the anchorite of Holy Trinity, Lincoln, namely, 20s., a tunic furred with *calaber* with a double hood, and a cloak furred with *gris*. A priest of Lynn made a grim gift to the anker in the friary (1504) :—

"I beqwethe to the seid Fryer William a blak vestment and a blak clothe steynyd with an ymage of deth. And I wyll the sam cloth be set vpon my hers in the day of my buryyng. Item I beqwethe to the seid Fryer William a red cloth that lyeth on my bed." [1]

[1] *Wills, Bury St. Edmunds* (Camden S.), 105.

About the recluse's toilet a word must also be said. Some of the extreme ascetics with their unchanged haircloth-shirts seem almost to have gloried in dirt and squalor. So absorbed were they in an ideal of holiness that they ignored the practical needs of the poor body. It was well that rigid discipline included immersion in cold water. The Rules gave no encouragement to personal neglect. One directs: "Wash yourselves as often as ye please". Another quotes a saying of St. Bernard: "I haue louyd pouerte but y neuer louyd fylth".[1]

III. PROPERTY

To forsake all was the initial step of the hermit's career. The rhyming chronicler puts typical words into the mouth of Ive, the companion of Robert of Knaresborough :—

> I wyll forsake all thatt I se
> Fadyr and frend and folowe the
> Gold and goods ryches and rentt
> Towne and toure and tenement
> Playng and prosperyte
> In pouerte for to won wyth the.

But although the recluse's renunciation of the world included houses and land, fresh grants were made to him for his maintenance. St. Robert gave up his own inheritance; but, as hermits, both he and his successor, Ive, came to possess considerable property, held in trust for the relief of the poor.

The solitary was sometimes the owner, but usually the life-tenant, of the cell. He frequently granted it to some religious house, e.g. Geoffrey, hermit of Mosehude (a place not identified), granted his house there and all his possessions to the Knights Templars. Personal property he might dispose of at will. Robert, an inmate of the Cripplegate cell, London, was ministered to during the last months of his life by William de Wyntreburn, who received by the old man's will the sum of 30s., three messuages, and sundry small rents. William, hermit of Linstock, owned six cattle and a little money. He bequeathed two cows to Carlisle Cathedral, in the precincts of which he wished to be buried; another he devised to his parish church of Stanwix; the price of a fourth was to be divided amongst the priests and clerks who should conduct

---

[1] Bristol MS.; cf. Bodl. MS., "Paupertatem dilexi, sordes nunquam".

his obsequies. Twenty shillings was to be expended on the bridge over the Eden, and a few legacies were made to friends.

Hermits were, as we have seen, sometimes married men, or widowers, and family claims were not disallowed. There is a reference in the Bridlington Cartulary (*c.* 1220) to the hermit's wife, and also to their son who did homage for his father's land at Bridlington. Thomas Wylkys, of Ewelme, left 20*s.* to his daughter. Simon Cotes (p. 63), whose will is witnessed by his son, left to him all moveable goods; but his house and chapel at Westbourne, built upon ground which he had inherited, he bequeathed for the use of a successor who should carry on his work.

Whilst the hermit might own his three acres and a cow, the anchorite might not possess such things as would tend to draw the thoughts outward. Enclosed women were warned against becoming absorbed in household cares. There are women, says Aelred, who are busy gathering worldly goods, cattle and wool, and in multiplying pence and shillings. They arrange food for their beasts, and at the year's end they reckon their number and price; then follow buying and selling, which lead to covetousness and avarice.[1] The *Ancren Riwle* is still more explicit :—

"Ye shall not possess any beast, my dear sisters, except only a cat. An anchoress that hath cattle appeareth as Martha was, a better housewife than anchoress; nor can she in any wise be Mary, with peacefulness of heart. For then she must think of the cow's fodder, and of the herdsman's hire, flatter the heyward, defend herself when her cattle is shut up in the pinfold, and moreover pay the damage. Christ knoweth, it is an odious thing when people in the town complain of anchoresses' cattle. If, however, any one must needs have a cow, let her take care that she neither annoy nor harm any one, and that her own thoughts be not fixed thereon."

Trading is condemned: "an anchoress that is a buyer and seller, selleth her soul to the chapman of hell". She was forbidden to gather alms in order to give away.

The alms of visitors or passers-by were dropped into a box placed near the cell; Langland says that "at ancres there a box hangeth". Hoccleve refers (*c.* 1411) to this popular form of largesse :—

[1] Bodl. MS., 423, f. 178.

To every chirche and recluse of the toune
Bad hem eeke of golde geue a quantite.[1]

The hermits and anchorites of Lynn were regularly assisted
from the funds of the Trinity Gild. Among the expenses in-
curred at John Paston's burial in 1466 was an alms of 40*d.* to
the *ancors* of Carrow by Norwich. Small annuities were sometimes provided. In the schedule of charges incumbent on St.
Alban's Abbey in keeping the anniversary of Humphrey, Duke
of Gloucester, occurs this entry : " Item to a ankres at Sent
Petur chirch, a nother at Sent Mich. the seid day, yerly, to
euerych xx*d.*". Alms were frequently bestowed upon these
religious women of St. Albans.[2] When the prioress of St.
Mary de Pré was paying certain estate-charges, she set aside
a few pence by way of charity (1487-9) : " Item spente at the
ankers of Seint Petres whan I sawe the fermours indentures of
Bemond iiij*d.*". When passing through the town in 1502
Elizabeth of York gave 3*s.* 4*d.* to the anchoress of St.
Peter's, and the following year, 26*s.* 8*d.* to the anchoress of
St. Michael's.

During the fifteenth century, alms were so liberally bestowed
that money became a snare. A Harleian MS. (2372) of that
period shows that the anchoress was tempted to live in comfort, to receive poor folks and pilgrims, and to support needy
cousins :—

" Some Recluses in these dayes [dwell] nat in wildernesses but in
the citees that they may there receyue large almes wher of thei may
holde greet meynee [i.e. company] and helpe and promote more
largely her kyn and her freendes than thei myghte in othir estat and
lyue more delicatly than thei were likly haue doon in seculer plyt."

lthough the *Ancren Riwle* speaks disparagingly of " rich
anchoresses that are tillers of the ground, or have fixed rents,"
the recluse did, for the sake of maintenance, retain houses and
lands and receive rent for them. Not infrequently she made
over her property to a religious house, accepting in lieu thereof
a definite allowance for life ; thus the abbey of Oseney made
yearly payments to Childlove, anchoress of Faringdon. Margaret, of St. Edward's, Norwich, issued charters, sealed with
her own seal, whereby she conceded land to Langley Abbey,

---

[1] *Piers Plowman* (E.E.T.S.) B., xv. 208 ; *Reg. of Princes* (E.E.T.S.), 156.
[2] Dugd., II. 202 n. ; III. 360 ; for bequests see *Herts Genealogist*, I., II.

and the abbot in return granted her 6s. a year.[1]   If such agree-
ments were not kept, a plea might be sent to the itinerant
justices, or a petition lodged in chancery.   The case of Cecily,
recluse of St. James's, Colchester, is entered on the Assize
Roll (1272) ; the abbot of St. Osyth's, who had not fulfilled
his promise to pay her an annual rent of five quarters of wheat,
undertook to do so, and to pay arrears.   Aline of Wigan fell
on evil days.   Her benefactor, Sir Robert Holand, being involved in the rebellion of 1321-2, forfeited his property ; hence
" la povre recluse " lacked the sum of 30d. which he had
granted annually for her sustenance.   Aline, unable to obtain
her allowance from John Travers or John de Lancastre, who
had charge of the forfeited lands, at length appealed to the
King for restitution.   The law recognized the right of enclosed
persons to hold property, if need be, and to defend it.[2]   The
learned judge Littleton, writing in the time of Edward IV,
declares that albeit the recluse could not leave his cell to appear in court—" for this kind of Order always dwells separate
and apart from civil life "—yet he could appear by attorney,
on the principle that " inability suspends the operation of the
law ".[3]

If the solitary fell into a condition of helplessness, the
bishop constituted himself her guardian.   When Dame Joan
of Blyth was weak and poverty-stricken, Archbishop Wichwane took her under his protection, and arranged for the
administration of her affairs, lest she should suffer loss.   " She
is now fallen into sickness, so that she scarcely possesses things
needful for her bodily welfare, and has been obliged to give up
those lawful occupations in which she formerly spent her
time."   The archbishop deputed the vicar to look after his
poor parishioner and her household, directing " that in all
things both with regard to persons and goods, while she
survives or when she is taken away from our midst, they
be kept in all honesty and always treated with discretion,
as we will that an account shall be required of you concerning
the matter ".

---

[1] B.M. Add. ch. 14558, etc.
[2] Cf. case of W. Lucas, who appealed in Chancery for repayment of loan,
C. Welch, *Churchwardens' Accounts of Allhallows*, xxx., xxxi.
[3] Coke, Littleton's *Institutes*, ed. Butler, II.

Although goods and chattels could be disposed of at will, they seem usually to have been given for pious purposes. Robert, the anchorite of Hartlip, gave a silver chalice to the cathedral church of Rochester. Two enclosed monks of Westminster Abbey caused it to be enriched with paintings.[1] Brother John Myrymouth spent 26s. 8d. upon an altar-piece for St. Benedict's chapel. The more famous Brother John London provided a painting above the altar of St. John Baptist; he is also named among the benefactors of Syon monastery. Dame Agnes Vertesance, of St. Michael's church at St. Albans, bestowed upon the shrine of St. Alban a gold ring.[2] An inventory of the goods of Allhallows, London Wall (1501) includes this item : " A grett paxe with iij Images of sylver by the gyfftt off the Anker ". Successive recluses were liberal donors to the fabric fund. The sum of 4s. 6½d. was paid by " the ankyr Syr Symon of the gaynes of a stande of ale whiche he gave to the cherche ". On another occasion he gave 9s. 3d., " the gyft of dyuersse men and women of ther dewocion at dyuersse tymys ". When a new aisle was being built, he lent 32s., and gave 32s., besides supplying the scaffolding.[3]

The treasures of the cell were usually of a devotional character, consisting of sacred vessels, rosaries, and relics. A set of beads (*i Par Pater Noster Geinsid de gete*) was left to the anchorite of Westminster by Lord Scrope ; another, of *mestylden gauded with Calsedonys* was given by a Norwich citizen to the anker of the White Friars. The relics of the parish church at Tavistock included " a little cross of silver, the gift of John Armytt in which is a piece of the holy cross " ; and there the anniversary of the donor, John the hermit, was kept.

The possessions of the solitary might, however, be given to friends, or even sold. Sir Brian Stapelton owned a silver basin with an image of Our Lady in alabaster which had belonged to the anker of Hampole.[4] Another testator (John de Dodyngton, canon of Exeter and rector of Crewkerne) mentions in his will " a cup with a cover, formerly the property of one Stephen, a recluse " (1400).[5] Thomas Coke, the

[1] Stanley, *Memorials*, ed. 1868, p. 609.   [2] B.M. Cott. Nero D., 7, f. 137.
[3] Welch, *Churchwardens' Accounts*, 52, 56-9, 68.
[4] *Test. Ebor.* (S.S. 4), I. 199.   [5] *Ex. Reg. Stafford*, 379.

TOMB OF ROGER AND SIGAR, HERMITS

(BY TRADITION)

anchorite-priest, dwelling in Kexby chapel, sold a missal and a great portifer to Sir Thomas Ughtred, who agreed that the priest should have them in his keeping during his lifetime.

After the death of Margaret, anchoress of Richmond, a dispute arose respecting the disposal of her property (1490). It was settled that, after her debts were paid and the anchorage (which belonged to the burgesses) repaired, the remainder of her goods should go to the Grey Friars, from whom she had received the habit; whilst the effects of her successor were to pass to Easby Abbey. In some cases the enclosed person was able to make a will, witness that of Katherine Dytton, of St. Albans (1437).[1]

IV. BURIAL

In early days it was customary for the cell to become the tomb of its tenant, whether hermit or anchorite. We read in the lives of Bartholomew, Godric, and Robert how each was buried in his oratory in a tomb prepared by himself, which had for years served as a solemn reminder of the end.

Sometimes, however, the solitary was buried elsewhere. Tynemouth Priory claimed the body of Henry of Coquet. When Roger of Markyate died, his body was borne to St. Alban's Abbey and was placed with honour " in an arched tomb built into the south wall of the church, hard by the choir of the brethren ". In the same spot Sigar of Northaw was also buried. When Henry III visited St. Albans in 1257, he gave offerings at various shrines, including rich cloths for that of these famous monks.[2] Over the recess of their traditional tomb (Plate XXX) is the inscription:—

Vir domini uerus iacet hic Heremita Ro.   s
Et sub eo clarus meritis Heremita Sigari.

Human remains have frequently been fou 1 on the sites of hermitages. In the Hermitage Field at 'arporley, the plough turned up a stone coffin containing a skeleton. Local tradition tells of a burial-ground at Oath Farm, in or near a field called Chapel Five Acres. In 1328 the sick recluse of Oath petitioned that when he died he might not be buried

---

[1] Somerset House, Reg. " Stoneham," f. 31 b.
[2] *Gest. Abb.* I., 101, 105, 184 ; *J. Amund.*, I., 433.

in his cell *as the custom was*, but in Aller churchyard or else-where.

During the fifteenth century it seems to have become usual to bury the hermit in his parish church or in any other cemetery that he willed. One of the hermits of Newbridge in Ickburgh desired to be interred in Munford church porch, another at the Chapel-in-the-Fields, Norwich. Robert Leake of Blythburgh was buried before the font. There is at Wellingham a monu-mental brass inscribed *Hic iacet enim Thomas Leeke Heremita ;* this is clearly the memorial of Thomas Leek who at the be-ginning of the sixteenth century was hermit of Weasenham, close to Wellingham.

In the case of the enclosed person, the tomb was sometimes prepared before his admission to the cell, and lay ever open to his gaze (p. 96). The same custom prevailed when the *Ancren Riwle* was written. The anchoress was bidden not only to meditate upon death but actually to scrape up earth every day out of the pit. " She . . . hath her death always, in a manner, before her eyes." At the close of the fourteenth century, one of the Westminster recluses was buried in the oratory adjoining his chamber, in a leaden coffin with iron clasps. The keeper of Westminster Palace suborned a plumber of the convent, who, after flinging the mortal remains into the well in the cloister-cemetery, removed the coveted chest to the palace. Divine retribution fell on both partakers in this act of sacrilege.

Few churches have preserved monuments of the solitaries who dwelt under their shadow. The tradition that Lady Lauretta was buried at Hackington church under the large stone on the altar steps is recorded by Hasted. There is at St. John's, Lewes, the curious memorial of Magnus the Dane.[1] The inscription (which is supposed to date from the thirteenth century) is built into the wall on fifteen stones arranged in a double semi-circle.

CLAUDITUR HIC MILES, DANORUM REGIA PROLES;
MANGNUS NOMEN EI, MANGNÆ NOTA PROGENEI :
DEPONENS MANGNUM, SE MORIBUS INDUIT AGNUM,
PREPETE PRO VITA, FIT PARVULUS ARNACORITA

which may be rendered : " Here is enclosed a soldier of the

[1] M. A. Lower, *Hist. of Sussex*, II. 25.

royal race of Denmark, whose name Magnus bespeaks his noble lineage : laying aside his high estate, he assumes the demeanour of a lamb, and exchanges a life of ambition for that of a lowly anchorite ".

In Lower Quinton church (Gloucestershire) is the tomb of Joan, Lady Clopton, who (from the use of the word *clauditur* in her monumental inscription) is supposed to have been enclosed there after the death of Sir William Clopton. The fine brass lies on an altar tomb at the east end of the south aisle. The costume shows the veiled head-dress with the *barbe*, the sign of widowhood. In the chancel of Faversham church is the brass of William Thornbury, the vicar, who is said to have been preparing to become a recluse in 1472. The meaning of the inscription is obscure, but it seems probable that he retired to live in solitude in his " chapel and parvise situated in the corner of the churchyard," described in his will.[1]

The year 1846 saw the death of two recluses at Allhallows, London Wall. The sum of 6s. 8d. was paid by the church-wardens " ffor the Berynge of the nue Ancker, that is to say, for the grete Bell for his knyll ".

[1] See *Arch. Cant.* XI. 26-9, plate, p. 27.

X. TRIAL AND TEMPTATION

Lord, for Thy great pain have mercy on my little pain.—MARGERY KEMPE OF LYNN.

He said not: "Thou shalt not be tempested, thou shalt not be travailed, thou shalt not be afflicted," but He said: "Thou shalt not be overcome".—JULIAN OF NORWICH.

THERE are times when the human heart longs to escape from the overwhelming evil and sorrow of the world. The Psalmist yearned for the wings of the dove that he might escape from the tempest and wander far off and remain in the wilderness. Obeying this impulse, world-weary souls have oftentimes fled to some remote spot as to a place of refuge.

The hermits have been stigmatized as weak and morbid persons who sought retirement in order to avoid the struggles of life; but, in truth, the very object of the true solitary when he set his face toward the wilderness was to enter into fierce conflict with the tempter. "The fiend tempteth much those who lead a solitary life, for envy that he beareth them: but he is there always overcome. For our Lord himself standeth by them in the fight, and emboldeneth them to resist strongly, and giveth them of his strength."

The desert, then, was a place for combat and conquest—not "a retreat for the feeble, but a training-place for the strong".[1] So terrible was the warfare, that raw recruits were not permitted to engage in it; they had first to prove themselves disciplined soldiers of Christ. St. Benedict, himself an anchorite, ordains thus in his Rule :—

"The second kind [of monks] are the hermits, that is, settlers in the wilds, who, not in the first fervour of religious life, but after probation in the monastery, have learned by the help and experience of others to fight against the devil, and going forth well armed from the

---

[1] Farrar, *Saintly Workers*, 51.

PLATE XXXI

HERMIT TEMPTED BY THE DEVIL

ranks of their brethren to the single-handed combat of the wilderness, are able without the support of others to fight by the strength of their own arm and the help of God against the vices of the devils and their evil thoughts."

The same ideal of spiritual warfare inspired the recluse in England. Cuthbert, even in the monastery, would withdraw to the most secluded spot, there to contend with the invisible adversary ; and, when he went to Farne, he ousted " that wicked enemy with all his followers ". Nearly seven centuries later, another Northumbrian hermit retired to Norham, that there, apart from the turmoil of men, he could fight with the old enemy. Indeed, the reality of the personality of the devil was so strong to the minds of men like Cuthbert, Guthlac, Roger, Godric, Robert, and Richard, that they seemed themselves—like Anthony of Egypt—to have actual conflicts with demons, whose insults and attacks are described at length in the lives of these saints.

The inexperienced solitary was warned against the snares of the devil :—

" Account no vision that ye may see, waking or sleeping, or in a dream, to be anything but an illusion, for it is one of his stratagems. He hath often thus deceived wise men of holy and pious life, as him . . . whom he made to believe that he was an angel, and of his own father that he was the devil, and made him kill his father."

The allusion here is to the popular allegory of *The Pilgrim*. The tempter " full of fetheres bryght and clere " went to a certain hermit in the desert, bidding him beware of Satan who would assail him on the morrow in the likeness of his father. Thus counselled, " this innocent, this sely man." started up anon, and took a knife and slew the old man (Plate XXXI).[1]

Richard the hermit warns his solitary friend Margaret against the quaint and subtle temptations of the fiend. He relates the story of an anchoress to whom the evil one often came in the form of a good angel, saying that he was come to take her to heaven. Overjoyed, she told this to her shrift-father, who, doubting the vision, counselled her to bid the angel show her the Blessed Virgin. At her request, he showed her the fairest woman that might be ; but when she knelt and

[1] Lydgate's translation.   B.M. Cotton. Tiberius A., VII. f. 56, 90.

said *Ave Maria,* the fair figure vanished. Richard himself
was specially anxious to help recluses and others who were
vexed by evil spirits. He was once summoned to a lady's
death-bed, whence, by means of prayer and holy water, he
ejected a multitude of horrid demons.[1] The mediaeval belief in
dæmonology was of a highly superstitious character, and the
terror of death was enhanced by the thought that devils and
angels were wrestling for the departing soul.

The apparition sometimes assumed human shape. To
Robert of Knaresborough, much tried with "imps and war-
lows," the devil appeared as a lad gaping and grinning at him;
but the sturdy saint took his staff and beat "Sir Gerrard"
soundly.[2] To the sick Emma, he seemed to take the form of
a physician, who desired to touch her person and prescribe a
cure; but the holy woman exorcised him by the sacred spell
Verbum caro factum est.[3]

The subjection of the body was the lifelong labour of
recluses. The seriousness of the struggle is shown by the
extreme measures devised by way of training. Wulfric, for
example, "used to mortify his members with much fasting,
and bring them under control by toil of vigils, so that his flesh
scarcely hung on his bones". He and certain other cham-
pions of the ascetic life, were clad not only in spiritual but
material armour. Night and day the iron habergeon pressed
the rough hair-shirt upon the emaciated frame. When Wulfric, having worn out one penitential suit, obtained a new one
from Sir William FitzWalter, its length impeded his kneeling.
The knight offered to send the coat of mail to London to be
shortened, but the anchorite bade him in God's name take a
pair of shears and cut it. Whilst he hesitated, thinking the
good man mad, Wulfric brought shears out of the house, and,
having drawn a thread through the rings of the chain-armour
to mark where it should be cut, he placed it in the window
before the knight, saying: "Be steadfast, and fear not. I go
to pray to my Lord about this matter; meanwhile do you set
about it confidently." The two warriors were now busily occu-

---

[1] C. Horstman, *R. Rolle,* i. 12, 13; *Officium,* col. 798-9.
[2] Godric also had nicknames for his tormentors, viz., Carcaueresard, Corin-
brand.
[3] *Lanercost Chr.* (Maitland Club), 185.

pied, the one in praying, the other in cutting. Their work prospered, and the iron seemed like a linen texture. Amazed, Sir William fell at Wulfric's feet, but he raised him and bade him tell no man. Such things, however, cannot be hid, and the fame of the wonder-worker traversed the whole realm. " From that time the man of God, without any shears, with his own weak fingers, but with no less faith, distributed rings of the coat of mail to heal the diseases of all who asked it of him in charity." Godric wore the *lorica* for fifty years. Indeed, he wore out three in succession, the metal rings of which were treasured as relics.

Another ascetic practice was that of standing in cold water for hours, sometimes throughout the night. Godric often stood in a hollowed rock in the icy waters of the Wear, or descended into a tub sunk in the floor of his oratory. Such being likewise Wulfric's habit, it is not surprising to learn that he was wont to suffer torture with the cold (p. 107).

Nor was the anchoress less ready to endure almost inconceivable misery. Christina was shut into the corner of a hut, huddled up on the bare floor. The door was so fastened that she could not herself open it, and she was released once a day, at dusk :—

" Here the handmaiden of Christ sat crouching on the hard cold stone. . . . Oh, what discomfort she there endured from heat and cold, hunger and thirst, and daily fasting! The place was too narrow for her to wear the clothing needful for cold weather, whilst in the heat this close-fitting closet allowed her no refreshment."

The description of physical agony is too painful to repeat, and " to all these sufferings were added many and terrible diseases ". Roger, her spiritual father, was remarkable for his asceticism. William of Malmesbury says that he led an austere life, " seldom heard of in our times " (*c.* 1125). He had been on pilgrimage to the Holy Sepulchre, where he resolved upon a life of sacrifice and self-abnegation. The ardent receptive nature of his young disciple led her to emulate his austerities. After she had endured much suffering for over four years, a vision of comfort was vouchsafed to her. One fairer than the sons of men appeared, bringing a golden cross. He bade her take up this cross, as all must needs do who would fain go to Jerusalem; but He promised that she should not bear it long. When Christina told this vision to Roger, he wept for joy, saying in the vulgar tongue: "Rejoice with me, *Myn gode Sonendayes doghter* (that is, my good daughter of the Lord's day) for your tribulation will shortly be ended" : and so it came to pass.

Roger, Christina, and Wulfric, Godric and Bartholomew, all lived in the twelfth century. When the *Ancren Riwle* was compiled (early in the thirteenth century, as is supposed) there were still persons performing similar penances :—

"I know a man who weareth at the same time both a heavy cuirass and haircloth, bound with iron about the middle too, and his arms with broad and thick bands, so that to bear the sweat of it is severe suffering; he fasteth, he watcheth, he laboureth, and, Christ knoweth, he complaineth and saith that it doth not oppress him, and often asketh me to teach him something wherewith he might give his body pain . . . I know also a woman of like mind who suffereth little less. And what remaineth but to thank God for the strength that He giveth them?"

Although the compiler of the Rule could not but admire their courage, he did not commend their practice as a pattern for other recluses. Those who have not physical strength to fast, keep vigil, endure cold, and such other hardships, as many can bear and many cannot, may very well be excused, and please God with less. He forbids the misguided self-torture practised by the great ascetics :—

"Wear no iron, nor haircloth, nor hedgehog-skins; and do not beat yourselves therewith, nor with a scourge of leather thongs, nor leaded; and do not with holly nor with briars cause yourselves to bleed without leave of your confessor; and do not, at one time, use too many flagellations."

Their food had seemed to him less than was fitting, and he bids them fast no day upon bread and water without permission. For the devil craftily suits the temptation to the nature of the recluse; knowing, therefore, that he cannot make this one sin through gluttony, "he incites her to so much abstinence that she is rendered the less able to endure fatigue in the service of God, and leads so hard a life, and so torments her body that her soul dieth". The night's rest must not be neglected; "in bed, as far as you can, neither do anything nor think, but sleep". Foolhardiness concerning health is sternly condemned. "Sickness is a fire which is patiently to be endured—sickness which God sends; but not that which some catch through their own folly."

Richard the hermit also writes against self-neglect. With him it was a matter of personal experience, he having frequently been so exhausted by abstinence as to suffer excruciating headache. The tempter, he says, sometimes entices thus: "Eat little, drink less, reck not of sleep, wear the hair and the habergeon, so that there be none that pass thee in penance". This so enfeebles them that they cannot love God as they should. He reckons it no virtue but a sin to withhold necessaries from the body. The young anchoress should eat and drink, better or worse, as it comes; when she is proved, and knows herself and God better than she did, she may take to more abstinence.

The ascetics sought to discipline themselves until all the desires or shrinkings of nature were changed. Thus Margery Kempe so dwelt upon the thought of Christ's Passion that all pain was transformed "in the sight of the soul". She saw Christ in every sufferer and "she had great mourning and sorrowing that she might not kiss the leper when she met them in the way, for the love of our Lord: which was all contrary to her disposition in the years of her youth and prosperity, for then she abhorred them most". She even desired pain for herself, but it was revealed to her that inward communion was better than any outward observance: "Daughter, if thou wear the habergeon or the hair, fasting bread and water, and if thou saidest every day a thousand Pater Nosters, thou shalt not please me so well as thou dost when thou art in silence, and suffereth Me to speak in thy soul".[1]

It was for strict, self-controlled recluses of this kind, who were inclined to excessive penance, that both the *Ancren Riwle* and *Form of Living* were written. There were others, however, who considered comfort and health overmuch and raised objections to discipline. "My dear sir," one of them is heard to say, "is it wisdom now for a man or woman thus to afflict

[1] *Treatise of Contemplation*, ed. E. G. Gardner, see p. 178.

themselves?" But the writer of the Rule replies that Christ's followers must surely imitate Him in suffering; and he quotes from the earlier Rule to enforce the lesson that not without bodily discipline can purity be maintained :—

"Let not any one handle herself too gently, lest she deceive herself. She will not be able, for her life, to keep herself pure, nor to maintain herself aright in chastity without two things, as St. Ailred wrote to his sister. The one is, giving pain to the flesh by fasting, by watching, by flagellations, by wearing coarse garments, by a hard bed, with sickness, with much labour. The other thing is the moral qualities of the heart, as devotion, compassion, mercy, pity, charity, humility, and other virtues of this kind. . . . Yet many anchoresses, more is the harm, are of such fleshly wisdom, and so exceedingly afraid lest their head ache, and lest their body should be too much enfeebled, and are so careful of their health, that the spirit is weakened and sickeneth in sin."

One fault to which solitary women were prone was that of sitting too long at the parlour window. "Wherefore, my dear sisters, love your windows as little as possible; and see that they be small,—the parlour's smallest and narrowest." Within the shutter was a heavy curtain bearing on both sides "the white cross appropriate to white and unstained maiden purity, which requires much pains well to preserve". Convent-bred or sheltered in her own home, the inexperienced inmate of the cell found herself exposed to new temptations. The extreme monotony made her yearn for diversion and excitement; hence the warnings of Aelred (*Cap*. VI.). Danger might arise from that old woman, who, hoping for alms, comes as a messenger, and whispers soft words in her ears. Bad women will come as well as good. Settling down before the window they utter a few pious phrases and then pass to secular matters and even weave love-tales : thus they drive away from the recluse almost all sleep. Bearing in mind that she was an anchoress, "a woman in whom such confidence is put," she was to keep a strict watch over herself, lest she should bring reproach upon her holy calling: "for who can with more facility commit wickedness than the false recluse?" Constant vigilance was needed. "Surely our foe, the warrior of hell, shoots, as I ween, more bolts at one anchoress than at seventy and seven secular ladies." Hers was by no means one great renunciation followed by years of freedom from tribulation, as was pointed out by her sympathetic spiritual guide:—

"An anchoress thinks that she shall be most strongly tempted in the first twelve months . . . and when, after many years, she feels them so strong, she is greatly amazed, and is afraid lest God may have quite forgotten her, and cast her off. Nay! it is not so. In the first years, it is nothing but ball-play."

For the young and feeble are spared at first, and drawn out of this world gently and with subtlety; thus are they gradually taught to fight and to suffer want.

Secret faults, such as spiritual pride and a desire for praise, were to be shunned:—

"For the sorcerer would fain cajole you, if he might, and with flattery render you perverse, if ye were less gentle and docile. There is much talk of you, how gentle women ye are; for your goodness and nobleness of mind beloved of many; . . . having, in the bloom of your youth, forsaken all the pleasures of the world and become anchoresses."

Richard Rolle alludes to the temptation of ostentatious piety: "Men that come to thee, they love thee, for they see thy great abstinence . . . but I may not love thee so lightly for aught that I see thee do without". The prefatory note to the Sarum Office strikes a note of warning against self-satisfaction, lest at the outset the person to be enclosed should imagine that he was being separated on account of merit, but rather, lest he should infect his fellow-men. He must consider himself as it were condemned for sin and committed to a solitary cell as to a prison.

The much-tried anchoress was inclined to low spirits. She was therefore reminded that the Lord would sometimes withdraw Himself for her good—like some fond mother who hides from her darling, and waits until he calls *Dame ! Dame !* when she leaps forth laughing and kisses away his tears.

"When two persons are carrying a burden, and one of them letteth it go, he that holdeth it up may then feel how it weigheth. Even so, dear sister, while God beareth thy temptation along with thee, thou never knowest how heavy it is, and therefore, upon some occasion, he leaveth thee alone, that thou mayest understand thine own feebleness, and call for his aid, and cry aloud for him. If he delay too long, hold it up well in the meantime, though it distress thee sore."

Some of the sicknesses and sins of the solitary life were intimately connected. Indolence, languor, apathy, despondency —all arising from accidie, a besetting sin of the cloister—were not unknown to the recluse. Doubtless, her mind became morbid and her nerves overwrought by the unintermittent strain of existence under conditions so unnatural ; this resulted in peevishness, and she was obliged to confess to having grumbled and having been of gloomy countenance. She was therefore counselled never to be idle, but to work, read, or pray, and be always doing something from which good may come.

A tender leniency and strong commonsense are shown by the writer of the *Ancren Riwle* with regard to illness. Remedies might be used, but over-anxiety was to be avoided, both because it was displeasing to God, and because " we often dread a bodily disease before it come ". In times of physical weakness, enclosed women ought to do nothing that might be irksome, but rather talk with their maidens, and divert themselves together with instructive tales : " Ye may often do so when ye feel dispirited, or are grieved about some worldly matter, or sick. Thus wisely take care of yourselves . . . when ye feel any sickness, for it is great folly, for the sake of one day, to lose ten or twelve." Prudence was based on the highest motives. They were so to rest that long thereafter they might labour the more vigorously in God's service. The infirm person was to shorten her devotions. " Whoso is very ill, let her be free from the whole service, and take her sickness not only patiently, but right gladly, and all is hers that holy church readeth or singeth."

To learn to suffer, and to suffer well, was one of the chief ambitions of the anchoress. Matilda, who was enclosed for sixteen years at Wareham, was a signal example of unmurmuring patience. This stoical woman would not tolerate complaining in the cell, and when her handmaiden Gertrude (afterwards her successor) was suffering agonies with toothache, Matilda told her that she herself had uttered no word or groan even when her jaw had been in such a state of disease that it seemed to be breaking away.[1]

---

[1] B.M. Cott. Faust. B. IV (Vita S. Wulfrici), II. f. 97.

In a life of untold hardship, the recluse must surely have fallen a ready prey to disease.   One was unable to occupy herself on account of failing eyesight, whilst another was a prisoner in herself through deafness.   Indeed, when we read of the ill-health of Joan of Blyth (p. 111), of the paralytic seizures and consequent loss of speech suffered by Margaret Kirkby (p. 139), and of Dame Julian's severe attack of sickness, we cannot but marvel that frail women were able thus to endure want and weakness.   For this illness Julian had longed and had definitely prayed, though she afterwards confessed: "If I had wist what pain it would be, I had been loth to have prayed".   She lay for several days in a helpless condition, and on the fourth night received the last rites of the Church. During the succeeding three days she seemed to be at the point of death.   Some minute details of the illness are recorded, as though they were fresh in the writer's mind.   "The persons that were with me beheld me, and wet my temples ; and my heart began to comfort."   Once, indeed, her mother, believing her to be dead, lifted her hand to close her eyes. When the priest came, with his acolyte, Julian was unable to speak, but fixed her gaze upon the crucifix which he set before her.   Then sight began to fail, and it was dark about her and murky, as it had been night, save in the image of the cross. Julian seemed to see and actually to share Christ's sufferings, and sank exhausted.   But, suddenly, all the pain was taken away from her.   "I was brought to great rest and peace, without sickness of body or dread of conscience."   Through this experience she gained a firmer faith : "then saw I well, with the faith that I felt, that there was nothing betwixt the cross and heaven that might have distressed me".

At the time of her illness, which occurred in 1373, Julian was "thirty winters old and a half".   She was still living in 1413, when she would be in her seventy-second year.[1]   "I saw," she says in her *Revelations*, "that the age of every man shall be made known in heaven. . . . And specially the age of them that willingly and freely offer their youth unto God, passingly is rewarded and wonderfully is thanked".

[1] Blomefield seems to have read the date in the MS. as mccccxlij.   The true reading is mccccxiij.   See Mr. Harford's introduction to *Comfortable Words*, p. 7; also Mr. Edmund Gardner's article on Dame Julian in the *Catholic Cyclopedia*.

The hermit's venerable aspect was proverbial. It was not merely that hardship produced a premature appearance of great age, but the rigour of his life seems actually to have preserved his health and promoted longevity. Hermits of England carried on the traditions of those of Egypt, where Paul had died at the age of 113 years, and was buried by Anthony, who was already ninety. Despite " frosts and fasts, hard lodging and thin weeds," the solitary "overpassed his days," until he was indeed, as pictured by Shakespeare, " a withered hermit, five-score winters worn ".

Shortly before the Norman Conquest, three ancient anchorites were dwelling at Evesham ; Basing had been in seclusion seventy-two years, but Ælfwin and Wulsi no less than seventy-five years. There were also three aged ascetics in the twelfth century. Wulfric lived to be " full of days·". Bartholomew enjoyed good health throughout almost the whole of his sojourn of forty-two years at Farne :—

" He was so strong and in such full possession of his powers that his face was always cheerful and full of the beauty of bright colour, so that even when he was following a course of the sharpest fasting, and neglected all care of his body, any one would think that in all respects he fared delicately ".

Bartholomew retained all his faculties to the end, but in his last days he suffered from an internal abscess, hæmorrhage, and heart disease. Turning to Godric, " the athlete of Christ," who passed sixty years at Finchale, we marvel, with Charles Kingsley, "not only at the man's iron strength of will, but at the iron strength of constitution which could support such hardship, in such a climate, for a single year ".[1] The weather-beaten old sailor-hermit was bedridden for nearly eight years, and unable even to turn on his side without help.

How pathetic, and yet how striking, a picture the venerable solitary presented ! In his earlier days the famous anchorite of Westminster had been the counsellor of kings (p. 154) :—

" He had reached the extremity of age allowed to man, even, it was said, his hundredth year. For sixty years he had been immured. Those who conversed with him (but of late his discourse was wild)

[1] *The Hermits*, 311.

PLATE XXXII

saw through an iron grating a long, bent figure, with white hair and white beard reaching to his waist. His face was like the face of some corpse which had escaped corruption—so thin, so white, so sunken it was ; but for the gleaming of his eyes one would have thought him the figure of Death as he is painted in the cloister of Paul's." [1]

The chronicler also gives an impression of the spiritual strength of the veteran. " Formerly he would recount engagements with devils . . . but of late the devils being routed, he was left to his meditations . . . and for the last year or two his soul being rapt, his voice spoke only words uncertain." [2]

From first to last, as we have seen, the mystic was waging war with demons. To strive to dwell in thought solely upon the invisible was a severe strain upon the mind. Some of his fightings and fears were the result of self-repression and shattered nerves ; some apparitions were hallucinations or feverish dreams. Nevertheless, the indomitable will of these men and women command admiration. We see in them not feebleness but fortitude. They lived a life of unflinching sacrifice—a life typified by the nakedness of the cell with its dominating crucifix (Plate XXXII). Voluntarily they stripped themselves of the natural joys of life. Patiently they persevered in hardness of living and unremitting moral effort. Contemporary writers witness to the reality of their discipline. Langland says :—[3]

> To preyere and to penaunce · putten heom monye,
> For loue of vr lord · liueden ful harde,
> In Hope for to haue · Heuen-riche blisse ;
> As Ancres and Hermytes · that holdeth hem in heore Celles.

And the ascetics themselves testify that they found a rich recompense in thus faithfully performing in what they conceived to be their duty. " Full swete melody makis mery the solitary man," says the hermit of Hampole. " In the end after long toil, He giveth them sweet rest, here, I say, in this world, before they go to heaven ; and then the rest seemeth so good after the labour." So writes, out of her own experience, the anchoress of Norwich.

---

[1] This description may be compared with Sven Hedin's affecting account of a Tibetan lama, who died, within living memory, after being immured for sixty-nine years.

[2] Given on the authority of Sir W. Besant, see p. 155, n.

[3] *Piers Plowman* (E.E.T.S. 28), Text A. Prol., 25-8.

XI. HUMAN INTERCOURSE

Let him never be alone, if he can conveniently have with him a companion
or servant.—*De Vita Heremitarum.*

So ready and so buxom be thou in will for to speak with thine even-cristen
when he cometh to thee; for thou knowst not what he is, nor why he cometh,
nor what need he hath of thee, nor thou of him, till thou hast assayed.—W.
HILTON, *How an Anchoress shall behave Her.*

I. COMPANIONSHIP IN THE CELL

THE "solitary" was not condemned to a self-centred
and self-sufficing life of utter separation and silence. Companionship was permitted, and even
encouraged, on the ground that to live entirely apart from
human converse was positively dangerous to the soul. "He
thinks himself to be, that which he is not; for this, indeed, is
wont to happen to him who has not with him one who can
test his work." The Rules therefore impress the advisability
of fellowship with another of like mind and purpose. That of
Grimlaic has a clause (*Cap.* XVII.) directing that never less than
two or three be solitaries together. Although enclosed in
single cells, they could communicate through the window, and
stir up one another in the service of God.

Guthlac formed one of a group of recluses who were in
touch with one another. They included Tatwine (p. 14) and
Ecgberht, Cissa, and the clerks Beccel and Wilfrid. When a
man became renowned for sanctity, others desired to dwell near
him and emulate his manner of life. Thus around Roger were
gathered five hermits and an anchoress (pp. 21-2). In cases
of failing health, the services of a young disciple were sought.
Godric joined an aged monk at Wolsingham. Entering the
hermit's cave, he received the unexpected salutation, "Welcome, Brother Godric!" to which—though as yet they were
strangers—he replied: "How dost thou fare, Father Aelric?"

They lived together for two years, and when Aelric became
feeble, Godric waited on him and carried him about, and at
length, fetched a priest to administer the last rites. At
Finchale Godric in his turn was served by a young nephew ;
and in his old age he had a priest living with him. In the
same way, Lucian the priest ministered to Ernald the hermit
at Loughborough in Wychwood Forest.

Robert of Knaresborough was joined by Ive and by several
servants, who shared his labours. The story of Ive seems to
show that even in the " solitary " life, two were better than
one, for the strong would lift up his fellow. One day Ive
attempted to return to the world which he had renounced.
In passing through the forest, however, he broke his leg with
the bough of a tree, and fell into a ditch, where he sat crying " alas ! alas ! waloway ! "   Robert, supernaturally aware of
what had happened, hastened thither, and not without mirth at
his friend's plight, pointed the moral : " No man, having put
his hand to the plough and looking back, is fit for the kingdom of God ". Robert then blessed his leg and bade him
stand. The two hermits returned to Knaresborough, and
continued to live together until Robert's death, when Ive
received his last benediction and became his successor.

Brethren, however, did not always dwell together in unity.
The solitaries of Farne and Coquet had their trials in the way
of uncongenial companionship. Arriving at Farne, Bartholomew found the cell already occupied. Aelwin was much
annoyed, and would fain have cast out the intruder ; he endeavoured to excite him to anger, but Bartholomew would not
sin with his lips, and bore with patience Aelwin's perpetual
nagging. When Aelwin perceived that persecution availed
nought, he retired and left Bartholomew alone. Bartholomew
himself had afterwards to suffer a like trial. The new-comer
was Prior Thomas, who, having been deposed from his office
at Durham, was seeking seclusion. During years of solitude
Bartholomew had acquired certain habits which unfitted him
for society ; these he gave up, even changing his hair-shirt out
of consideration for his companion. But there were limits to
his complaisance. He was not prepared to linger over the
pleasures of the table, such as they were, and Thomas, who
enjoyed a hearty meal, made painful insinuations, questioning

9

his motive in withdrawing so hastily. In such close quarters, familiarity without true fellowship became intolerable, and Bartholomew at length retired to the monastery of Durham. After he had remained there for a whole year, he was persuaded that it was his duty to return to the island. Perhaps a little social intercourse had done good to the lonely monk, whilst an interval of unbroken solitude may have refreshed the harassed ex-prior, worn out with governing a large community. At all events, it proved on Bartholomew's return that a transformation had taken place, and henceforth the two men lived " in complete tranquillity both of tongue and soul ".

A similar story is told of the relations between Henry the hermit and the keeper of the island of Coquet, with whom he had constant dealings, though probably they did not dwell together. This monk did not cease to attack Henry daily with harsh and opprobrious words ; but at length, admiring his immense humility and holiness, he fell at his feet with tears, entreating forgiveness. Henry raised him from the ground with joy of heart, and the two men became united in the bond of spiritual friendship.

But friction did not always end in fellowship, as is shown by another Northumbrian tale. A certain Gilbert de Niddendale associated with a hermit called Seman de Botelesham. The latter was attacked by his companion, who beat him and left him on the moor for dead, taking away his clothes and a penny. Gilbert fled, but was seized by an official and taken prisoner for the robbery. In the meantime the hermit had recovered, and the King's servant caused him to behead with his own hands his former comrade, such being the custom in that wild border country when a man was caught red-handed.

Nor did the enclosed person necessarily live alone. Wulfric, for example, seems to have had the company of Brichtric (p. 74). Richard le Coupe of Swepestone, priest, and Geoffrey Richard, layman, dwelt together in London in the churchyard of St. Lawrence, Jewry (1367).[1] Ela, the niece of Walter, Bishop of Norwich, had companions at Massingham. Margaret and Alice were anchoresses at St. Olave's, Norwich. Isabel and Olive lived together at Fordham. Those for whom the *Ancren*

---

[1] *Reg. Wykeham* (Hants Rec. S.), II. 122-3.

Riwle was written were three sisters—" of one father and of one mother ".

Recluses had to avoid the pettiness, suspicion, and ill-temper which a narrow life might foster. The above-mentioned Rule comments thus upon the ungenerous person who is not willing to share her good things: "See, now, how different are the envious from our Lord! The anchoress who refused to lend a book to another had turned her eyes of faith very far from Him." A spirit of unity was to be cultivated: "Let your dear faces be always turned to each other with kind affection, a cheerful countenance, and gentle courtesy". One must never heed a rumour whispered about another by the devil's messenger, who would separate them by anger or envy. Nevertheless, one sister should warn another sweetly and affectionately of anything that she does wrong, if she knows it with certainty; but the person who bears such a message must repeat it often before she go out to deliver it, that she may not report it otherwise, nor patch anything more upon it. The other sister should receive such admonition humbly and readily. Should any resentment be caused, none ought to receive the Blessed Sacrament, nor even behold it, lest they should look with anger towards Him who came down to earth to make peace. A peacemaker's blessing is offered to the one who restores peace by taking the blame upon herself, although the other might be more in fault. These passages seem to show that the individuals composing the little community were living to some extent a separate life.

It was customary for the enclosed person to have servants. Loretta, Countess of Leicester (an elderly widow, p. 74) had a serving-man who was granted exemption from being put on juries, etc., during her lifetime. Katherine, anchoress of St. Michael's church at St. Albans, was attended by a certain Joan Gerard, and also by Philip Gerard (1424, 1433). The enclosed lady usually had a confidential companion. Christina of Markyate had her maid Doet; nor is the faithful Mabel unremembered in the story of Katherine of Ledbury (p. 75). The recluse's attendant held a responsible post. Cecile, handmaid of the anchorite at St. Chad's chapel, Chester, appeared (probably to represent her mistress) as plaintiff in the Court of Piepoudre against several persons. If she were a suitable person, she might even succeed her mistress.   Already familiar with the life, she might in turn be professed as an anchoress. An instance occurs early in the twelfth century at Wareham (p. 124).   Agnes Vertesance who, in 1424, was one of the companions of Katherine Dytton of St. Albans, became her successor ; she died in 1478, having spent at least fifty-four years in that cell by St. Michael's church.[1]

Aelred describes the qualifications and duties of the waiting-women :—

"First chese an honest anxient womman in lyvynge, no jangler, ne royler aboute, noo chider, noo tidynges teller, but such oon, that may have witnesse of hir good conversacyon and honesty.   Hir charge shal be to kepe thyn houshold and thy lyflod, to close thy dores, and to resceyue that shuld be resceyved, and to voide that shuld be avoided.   Under hir governaile shuld she have a yonger womman of age, to bere gretter charges, in fettynge of wode and water, and sethynge, and greithynge of mete and drynke.   And that she be ouerloked under gret awe."[2]

The *Ancren Riwle* ordained that the elder woman, who went out on business, should be very plain, whilst the younger one should generally stay within doors.   The chapter "Of Domestic Matters" contains "the rule concerning your maids," which was to be read to them every week until they knew it well.   It was imperative that they should be well looked after : "for ye may be much benefited by them, and, on the other hand, made worse".   There was a danger lest through them the lady might hear gossip : "for people say of anchoresses that almost every one hath an old woman to feed her ears".   It was, indeed, a common saying that "From mill and from market, from smithy and from ancre-house, men bring tidings ".   When upon some errand, the women were to behave with propriety, and never linger or converse ; even their attire should be such that it might be easily seen to what life they were dedicated. Should they meet with annoyance when fetching their food, they must take it meekly : "be glad in your heart if ye suffer insolence from Slurry, the cook's boy, who washeth dishes in the kitchen ".   The maidens were to be considerate :—

[1] B.M. Cotton. Nero. D. vii. f. 137.
[2] Bodl. MS. 423 f. 179.

PLATE XXXIII

RECLUSE MINISTERS TO WOUNDED KNIGHTS

SIR PERCEVAL VISITS A CELL

THE RECLUSE IN ROMANCE

"Let them, by all means, forbear to vex their mistress ; and whenever they do so, let them before they either eat or drink make obeisance on their knees . . . and say *Mea culpa ;* and accept the penance that she layeth on them, bowing low. And let not the anchoress ever again thereafter upbraid her with the same fault, when vexed, except she soon afterwards fall into the same, but drive it entirely out of her heart."

The mistress, on her part, was to be affectionate and gentle, and seldom stern. " It is right that they should both fear and love you ; but that there should be always more of love than of fear. Thus it shall go well."

II. INTERCOURSE WITH THE WORLD

Having considered the question of daily companionship, we turn to that of communication with the world outside. There was a great diversity of practice according to the character and circumstances of the individual. His love for silent contemplation might grow with the exercise of it, and his life shrink into ever narrower isolation ; or, full of human interests, he might be constrained to social service by some pressing call. St. Cuthbert, as we have seen, passed through both these stages. It is significant that the island of Farne had two buildings— the cell and the guest-hall. Pilgrims and sailors alike found shelter in the house of hospitality by the seashore. Long after the days of St. Cuthbert, many persons crossed to Farne to receive the help of Bartholomew, or of Aelric. Bartholomew was equally ready for solitude or service. His bright, outspoken, sympathetic manner attracted people. Many were drawn to him by the report of his holiness, to whom he gave advice and consolation :—

"Troubled therefore by the throngs and crowds, and fearing lest their esteem should lead him into vanity, he proposed to be enclosed, so that in proportion as he cut himself off from the cares and gossip of men, he should grow nearer to God. But . . . he continued even to the end content with that measure of quiet which he had at first, following that word of wisdom of the apostle, who, when he had a desire to depart and be with Christ, thought it needful for the welfare of many to remain in the flesh, choosing in his loving soul not that which was better for himself but for others."

Godric of Finchale was an austere reserved man, and held no intercourse with strangers unless they had been recommended by the Prior of Durham.   In the early years of his retirement he maintained strict silence, even to the extent of using a code of signs for purposes of communication ; but he abandoned this practice.   He was dutiful and affectionate to his family, several of whom followed him to Finchale ; namely, his mother, who died there, his brother, and his nephew.   His sister Burchwene lived the solitary life in a cell hard by his own, but falling ill she was nursed until her death in a hospital at Durham.   He was kindly to his servants, and was venerated by those who visited him.   Godric's visitors were usually admitted to his little church, dedicated to St. John Baptist ; only a privileged few were ever allowed to enter his inner dwelling-place with its oratory of the Blessed Virgin. His friends included Aelred, the saintly Abbot of Rievaulx, Robert of Newminster, Cuthbert, Prior of Guisborough, William, Bishop of Durham ; and his biographers, Prior German and the monk Reginald.

The genial, generous Robert of Knaresborough was ever surrounded by a crowd of poor pensioners and pilgrims, for which he built a guest-house near his cell :—

> Heghe and lawe vnto hym hyed
> In faith for to be edified.

Richard of Hampole, too, was of a sociable disposition. When first the youth comes before us, at a crisis of his life, he was indeed silent.   During the dinner to which he was bidden after his first sermon (p. 161) "he was such a perfect keeper of silence that no word proceeded out of his mouth ".   When asked by Sir John de Dalton [1] whether he were indeed the son of his familiar friend, William Rolle, Richard, fearing lest he should be hindered in his purpose, replied, "Perchance I am "; but he was afterwards prevailed upon to talk with his host.   Friendliness was, however, his leading characteristic : he would be all things to all men if he might thereby save

---

[1] A certain John de Dalton (*militis, armiger*) and Margery his wife, of Kirkby Misperton, are mentioned in 1371, when their son, John, was dealing with the property (Final Concords of Lands, 44 Edw. III) Bodl. MS. Dodsworth, i. f. 505.   R. Rolle's birthplace was Thornton, probably Thornton le Dale, between Pickering and Kirkby Misperton.

some.   It was his custom to go in and out of houses, and even to eat and drink with the people.   His wanderings were so habitual that his biographer makes a kind of apology for him—lest he should be confounded with those roving hermits who were in ill-repute—and explains that he moved about in order better to edify the people.   Richard confesses that he was wont to go from place to place, and maintains that there is no harm in leaving the cell with good reason : " Cellis forsoth to leue for cause resonable, to harmetis is not ill, and eft, if it accorde, to the same to turn agayn ".   Some of the old fathers had done so, though they suffered man's " grutching " for it.   But Richard himself speaks of " rynnars aboute, that ar sclaunderes of hermyts ".[1]   Langland, too, would give alms to some ancres and heremytes—" but Robert renne aboute shall nought have of mine ".[2]   According to more than one Rule, the hermit ought not to go often about the country for his errands, but should send a servant, if he should have one, because by unlawful wandering or straying he might lose devotion by negligence.

Whilst the hermit might leave his dwelling and mix with men, the anchorite abode always in one place, and conversed only with those who came to his window.   Some considered it wrong for the enclosed person even to extend a hand out of the window for the purposes of healing.   Wechelen, the Welsh recluse of Llowes, was advised by Cistercian monks not to put forth his hand to cure the blind, lame, and sick who resorted to him ; but he was persuaded by the famous archdeacon of Brecknock to make use of his healing touch.[3]   Wulfric is said to have exercised a similar power (p. 152).

Although recluses were permitted to speak at discretion, they bore the reputation of being taciturn ; " little will they speak ".   A sixteenth-century critic refers to the iron grating through which they peep " when they will vouchsafe to speak with any man at whose hand they hope for advantage ".   Silence, however, was by no means a thing to be condemned in one supposed to be dead to the world.   Many are the counsels how a recluse should speak, and when.   Only at

[1] *Officium*, col. 792-3 ; *Fire of Love* (E.E.T.S. 106), 32, 35.
[2] *Piers Plowman* (E.E.T.S. 38), Text B, pass. VI. l. 150.
[3] Giraldus Cambr., *Opera* (Rolls, 21) I, 92.

stated hours was she permitted to talk with visitors, and even with her fellow-inmates.   In Lent she must be silent altogether, or if that were impossible, speak seldom, with her confessor and her maidens only, unless some reverend person should come from afar.

The anchoress was expected to confine her very thoughts within the cell.   It was not enough to keep her body and limbs within walls whilst her mind and senses were frittered away by wandering thoughts, wasted with care and weariness, even stirred up by unworthy desires; or her tongue, maybe, ran idly to and fro the livelong day through streets and cities, market-places and fairs.[1]   She was therefore shielded from everything that could engross her mind or excite her emotions. She was not to become a teacher, almoner of the poor, or guardian of church property.   Aelred strictly forbids access to children, condemning a practice which he touchingly describes:—

" Let not boys or girls approach thee.   There are some recluses who undertake the teaching of girls and turn their cell into a school. She sits at the window and they settle down in the porch.   She watches them one by one, and according as each behaves, now she is angry, now she laughs, now she threatens, now she beats them, now she coaxes them, now she kisses them, now calls a weeping child to come nearer to be beaten, she strokes her face, she draws up her head, and eagerly embracing her, calls her now daughter, now darling." [2]

The *Ancren Riwle* permits to the solitary woman at least a link with child-life.   " Her maiden may, however, teach any little girl concerning whom it might be doubtful whether she should learn among boys, but an anchoress ought to give her thoughts to God only."

Aelred says moreover : " Let not the poor cry out around the cell, nor orphans weep, nor widow lament ".   If she ask how this can be prevented, he replies, that she must sit still, keep silence, and restrain herself until they depart worn out, perceiving that they will receive nothing.   " Thou mayest exclaim that this is cruel : but if thou hast aught besides food and clothing, thou art not a nun."   Prayer and pity she ought to give, but not alms.

[1] Aelred, *Cap.* ii.   [2] *Ibid. Cap.* vi.

The canon formulated by St. Richard of Chichester (1246) ordains not only that recluses should have narrow and suitable windows, and avoid communication with persons concerning whom sinister suspicions might arise, but forbids that they be entrusted with the charge of vestments.[1] A similar warning occurs in the *Ancren Riwle* against the use of the cell as a depository of goods: " neither receive under your care the church vestments, nor the chalice . . . for oftentimes much harm has come of such caretaking ".

The recluse's one regular visitor was her father-confessor. If the cell were dependent upon some monastery, the abbot would appoint to that office. A secular chaplain nominated by the abbot said mass for the recluse of Whalley and her two servants.[2] When Emma Stapilton was professed as a Carmelite anchoress, the Provincial appointed as her advisers and protectors the prior and subprior of Norwich and three others of that convent.[3] Not infrequently the recluse held the bishop's licence to select her own ghostly counsellor. The name of Alice, anchoress of Hereford, occurs amongst those to whom papal indults were granted to choose confessors, who should give them, being penitent, plenary remission at the hour of death.[4] It was a matter of great importance what manner of person was sent to her, or summoned by her. The Rules direct that the shrift-father be a priest of good life, prudent, and not young—" not young of wit, nor yet foolish old men ". Without his direction, the recluse was advised to speak with no visitors, except a bishop, or abbot, or prior of high character, and even then, it should be in the presence of some other person. She was bidden never to allow messengers to run to and from between her and any man under colour of charity or spiritual friendship, neither should she receive or send gifts and letters without leave. She was warned to accept "not so much as a race of ginger " from any man whom she distrusted.

In conversation with visitors, the anchoress was to exercise restraint and discretion :—

[1] Wilkins, *Concilia*, I, 693.
[2] Towneley's MS. Transcripts from Monastic Cart., p. 151, penes W. Farrar.
[3] B.M. Harl., 1819, f. 197* [per Rev. B. Zimmerman].
[4] Pap. Lett., III. 504.

"When you have to go to your parlour window, learn from your maid who it is that is come ; for it may be some one whom you ought to shun. . . . Say first, *Confiteor*, and then *Benedicite*, which he ought to say ; hear his words and sit quite still, that when he parteth from you, he may not know either good or evil of you. . . . Some one is so learned and of such wise speech, that she would have him to know it, who sits and talks to him and gives him word for word, and becomes a preceptor who should be an anchoress, and teaches him who is come to teach her ; and would, by her own account, soon be celebrated and known among the wise. Known she is well ; for, from the very circumstance that she thinketh herself to be reputed wise, he understands that she is a fool. . . . For, at last, when he is gone away, he will say, ' This anchoress is a great talker '."

Many a recluse was perplexed because she could not pre-vent worldly people from coming and telling tales, sometimes of vanity. One woman confided her difficulty to a friend, probably Walter Hilton, who wrote a letter advising her how she should conduct herself. He tells her that intercourse ought to be a help, not a hindrance. Although she ought not to go out of the house to seek occasion to do deeds of mercy, she should love her fellow-Christians, and be ready to help them ; she must "speke gudely, gladly, and mekely to thaim all ". Even should she be called away from her devotions to the visitor, let her not think that in so doing she is leaving God for the sake of any man. "Methinks not so in this case," declares the writer, "for if thou be wise, thou shalt not leave God but thou shalt find Him and have Him and see Him in thine even-Christian as well as in prayer—but in another manner thou shalt have Him." Discretion was of course needful. If a man came to tell some trouble, suffer him to ease his heart. When he is done, comfort him gladly and charitably, but soon break off ; should he then fall into idle tales of other men's deeds, discourage him by answering shortly, and he will soon take his leave. If a man of holy church come, hear him in a lowly, reverent manner, but do not attempt to get to know him. It falls not to thee to reprove any for his faults ; when possible, however, profit him spiritually, if he will take it. " And of all othir thyngs kepe silence als mykel as thou may." [1]

---

[1] Hilton's *Scale of Perfection*. The tract " How an ancre should have her " is also found in MSS. ascribed to R. Rolle, see Horstman, i. 106-7.

But in the excitement of receiving a great visitor, the anchoress did not always keep silence. The celebrated prior, called St. John of Bridlington, went to see over the property of the monastery in Richmondshire, and took this opportunity of visiting a certain recluse. The story, which occurs in detail in the saint's life, is thus quaintly told by Fuller :—

"Going to view their lands in Richmondshire, he gave a visit to a woman lately turnd an Ancorist, and renowned for her holiness ; she told him, that now her vision was out, who the night before dreamt that an Eagle flew about her house with a label in his bill, wherein was written *Jesus is my love ;* [1] 'and you,' saith she, 'are the person who so honour him in your heart, that no earthly thing can distract you'. To whom our John returned : ' I came hither to hear from you some saving and savoury discourse, but seeing you begin with such idle talk, farewell ; ' and so waved any further converse." [2]

The anchoress seldom received visitors within her cell. Margaret Kirkby, the devoted disciple of Richard the hermit, lived at Ainderby in Richmondshire, twelve miles from the place where Richard was then dwelling. Receiving word that she was suffering from a terrible disease, and had been now speechless for thirteen days, he came to see her. He does not seem to have entered her house, however, in spite of their close friendship. Much comforted by the sight of her teacher, Dame Margaret fell asleep at the window, and leaned upon him. She was seized with a convulsion and seemed to desire to break open the window ; then she suddenly awoke, having recovered her power of speech. With fervent devotion she immediately burst forth in these words : *Gloria tibi Domine*, and the Blessed Richard went on, *Qui natus est de Virgine*, and so forth. Then he said : " Now speech is restored to thee, use it like a woman who talks sensibly ".[3]

The subject of hospitality is dealt with by Aelred, who sets forth " that a Recluse shulde not haue to do of hospitalyte anempst Religious gestes, for it longeth not to hir ".[4] Guests

---

[1] A popular religious watchword ; chalices, seals, etc., were engraved *Jhesus est amor meus.*

[2] Fuller's *Worthies*, ed. 1662, *Yorks*, p. 193 ; also *Nov. Leg.*, Life of St. John of B.

[3] *Officium*, col. 801.   [4] Bodl. MS. 423, f. 192.

were occasionally admitted within the anchorite's house, but
they rarely entered the inner chamber of seclusion, or stayed
the night.   According to the *Ancren Riwle*, the maid ought to
receive and entertain the visitors with glad cheer ; and the
recluse should have leave to open her window once or twice,
to make signs of gladness at seeing her friends.   She was not
to eat with them, for " there are anchoresses who make their
meals with their friends outside the convent," but that is too
much friendship, she being quite dead to the world.   Sir John
de Beauchamp made a petition to the Pope in 1363 that his
wife Elizabeth might visit her mother, an enclosed Minoress,
accompanied by six fit persons.   The request was granted,
but Elizabeth was forbidden to eat or spend the night with her
mother.[1]   Without open and manifest cause, secular persons
were on no account to stay in the houses of anchorites.[2]
Nor were men to be received as guests : " Let no man sleep
within your walls.   If great necessity should cause your house
to be used, have with you a woman of unspotted life day and
night."

The Franciscan Chronicle of Lanercost tells how some
such occasion of necessity once arose at a cell six miles from
Shrewsbury.   It was in the year 1296, on the eve of St. Francis, to whose Order belonged the nun who was enclosed by
the parish church of the village.   This pious woman, Emma by
name, was accustomed to receive visits from holy men, and on
the vigil of the saint she admitted two Minorite friars to hospitality.   At midnight she rose from her bed, called her handmaid, and bade her bring a lamp for early worship.   The lamp
was twice set upon the altar of the oratory, but was as often
extinguished by a gust of wind, the place being at the same
moment brightened by rays coming through the window of
the oratory of St. John Baptist which was next the church.
This light " surpassing the radiance of the sun, beautified with
a heavenly lustre the features of her maidens, who lay in a
distant part of the house, notwithstanding that the maidens
themselves were weeping because of the abundance of the
celestial illumination ".   A vision of saints was then manifested.
The Blessed Virgin bade the anchoress rouse her slumbering

[1] *Pap. Reg.* (Petitions), I. 457.   [2] Lyndwood, *Provinciale*.

guests that they might see the wondrous light wherewith that dwelling had been purified. Desiring to know the source of this light, one of the friars looked through the window of the church, and saw what seemed to be a torch burning before the image of the Blessed Baptist, the herald of Eternal Light.

III. CONSTANCY OF ABODE

The recluse might never leave her cell "except only by necessity and fear of death, obedience to her bishop or superior". There is one recorded instance of an anchoress refusing to abandon her dwelling even to save her life. This horrible event took place when William the Conqueror sacked Mantes in 1087. The woman enclosed at St. Mary's church remained therein and was burnt to death :—

> An auncre godes spouse
> That nolde vor no thing fle out of hire house.[1]

The word immured is sometimes applied to the solitary in the sense that he never left his four walls ; but he was seldom walled in or sealed up with no means of egress. Grimlaic's rule, indeed, directs that the bishop seal the door with his ring after performing the solemn act of induction, the chamber being unfastened only in time of sickness. Sometimes even in mediaeval England the entrance was actually blocked up. A petition was made to the bishop by Thomas, a Franciscan brother enclosed in the hermitage of Oath in Aller. Since the time of his enclosing no one had visited him, or seen how ill he was, and he therefore entreated that a door might be made in his dwelling so that some one might come and hear his confession. The vicar of Muchelney (four miles away) was therefore charged to make a door and keep the key for his visits to Thomas and his companion. Again, when Bishop Grandisson of Exeter gave permission for Beatrice of Colyford to be enclosed at the chapel of St. Kalixtus in Colyford, he directed the Abbot of Newenham "to shut her up in the cell or house aforesaid, and, when she is enclosed, block up the door of her house and do all other things which are fitting and convenient in this case". The Exeter Office certainly implies the building up of

[1] Wm. Malm. *Gest. Reg.* (Rolls, 90), ii. 336 ; *Chr. Robert of Glos.* (Rolls, 86) ii. 562.

the entrance.   According to the Sarum Use the door was to be
" firmly closed from the outside ".   Doors and locks are mentioned in other documents.   When the Abbot of Thornton,
on behalf of the Bishop of Lincoln, set apart Beatrice Franke
at Winterton, he described it as " shutting her up in a certain
house and enclosure . . . and securing the door of the same
with bars, bolts, and keys ".

The recluse, according to civil law, " is so mured or shut
up that he is always alone and remains in his enclosure and
can never come out of his place ".[1]   It was a matter of conscience rather than of keys.   In some cases the inmate was
able to quit the cell if she chose ; the anchoress who should
go to the play in the churchyard does not escape censure in
the *Ancren Riwle.*

In the life of Wulfric it is recorded that on one memorable
occasion he did leave his chamber to enter the adjoining church.
This deliberate act of self-mortification evidently created a profound impression.   On the feast of Pentecost, in the face of all
his neighbours, this sensitive saint openly denounced himself
on account of the evil thoughts by which he had been assailed
the night before :—

" When morning was come and all the congregation were assembled, he came forth in public from his cell and opening his mouth
spoke this speech against himself. ' Thus,' said he, ' it has happened
to this miserable Wulfric, that on this most holy night my sins have
pressed upon me, so that my enemy has led me, an unhappy one,
astray.   I confess my sin to God and to you.   I pray for pardon
from God through your intercession.' . . . So this bold follower of
humility did not spare in any degree his own shame, or the respect of
those who stood round, nor, lastly, the reputation for holiness which
spread far and wide.   When he had said these things, he returned to
his cell."

The enclosed person remained in the same spot for life
unless a change of domicile became necessary.   The reason
for removal is not recorded in the case of Simon, who was
translated in 1222 from Lichfield to Dunstable where, six
years later, he died.   In the case of Margaret de Kirkby, permission to change her abode was sought in order to obtain

---

[1] Coke, Littleton's *Institutes.*

facilities for worship. Archbishop Thoresby therefore issued a commission (January, 1356-7) to the abbots of Jervaulx and Eggleston to transfer Margaret from Layton to " a place near the parish church of Aynderby, where, according to the desire expressed in her petition, she may see and hear the solemn sacrament of the Lord's altar, which in her present place of enclosure she is unable to do, and to dispense her from her vow of dwelling perpetually at Laton ". It is related in the life of Richard the hermit that after he died (as is supposed, in 1349 [1]), the anchoress, Dame Margaret Kirkby, transferred herself (*se transtulit*) from Ainderby to Hampole. Whilst her spiritual father lived, his presence had caused her to recover from illness. She therefore sought to dwell near his place of burial : and never thereafter was she oppressed with that horrible sickness.

Another left under compulsion, exchanging her stone walls for a veritable prison. Matilda, enclosed in the churchyard of St. Peter's, Leicester, was cited as one " infected with the pestiferous contagion of heretics and Lollards ". Examining Matilda, Archbishop Courteney found her not to answer plainly and directly, but sophistically and subtilely ; whereupon he commanded the abbot that the door of her cell should be opened, and the inmate put in custody. On his return to Leicester, she answered his questions humbly, and retracted any unorthodox opinions which she might have held. Wherefore the archbishop placed her again in her *reclusorium*. Lest the anchoress should suffer from a loss of prestige, the archbishop issued a mandate *pro anachorita reducta ad viam veritatis*, setting forth that she had confessed her errors and was penitent, and offering indulgence to those who should come to her aid with gifts by way of charity. Possibly the *Matilda* of 1388 is the *nostre bienaimé Maude Wardesale Ankores recluse en leglise de saint pierre* who in 1400 received six marks a year from the Duchy of Lancaster.[2]

In cases of necessity or expediency, a dispensation for de-

[1] The dates present difficulties, it is true. There was some connexion between the East Layton cell and Hampole, for in 1348 Margaret la Boteler, nun of Hampole, was enclosed there. Possibly she was Margaret la Boteler of Kirkby.

[2] P.R.O. Duchy of Lanc. Misc. Bks. 15, f. 11.

parture could be obtained from the bishop or from the pope. In 1402, a Dominican friar of Arundel sought to quit his cell in the friary, pleading its inconvenience and the extreme poverty of the community. About the same time (1401), a woman at Pontefract obtained permission to change her dwelling-place. This Emma was a privileged person and enjoyed a liberty unknown to most.

"To Emma Scherman, of the diocese of York. Indult to her— who formerly took a vow of a recluse and has had herself for many years enclosed in a cell in the place of Pontefract, with a little garden contiguous thereto for the sake of taking fresh air—on account of the tumults and clamours of the people in the said place, to have there another cell with a like garden, and to leave her cell yearly for the purpose of visiting churches and other pious places, and of gaining the indulgences granted there, without requiring licence of the diocesan or other."

When the monastery of Syon by Sheen was founded, several solitaries left their dwellings and entered the community. Margaret, an anchoress dwelling near Bodmin, obtained her bishop's consent to migrate thither, and to join the Order of St. Bridget. Matilda Newton, a nun of Barking, was appointed to rule this house, but difficulties arose, and she was not elected abbess. In 1417 she returned to Barking as a recluse. The accounts of the earliest father-confessors are somewhat confusing. According to the foundation charter (1415), it seems that Brother William Alnwyk was appointed by Henry V as first father-confessor of Syon. John of Amundesham records that William Alnwyk, a recluse monk of Westminster, together with others, presided over the care of the women; [1] " but in the course of a year, worn out by weariness and old age, he returned to the cell whence he had gone forth ". Another priest, Thomas Fyschbourn, who had been an anchorite by St. German's chapel at St. Albans, succeeded him as confessor-general at Syon. He died in 1428, and his obit was kept yearly, for he, as counsellor and confessor of Henry V, had promoted the King's benevolence towards that house.

There was one particular sphere of labour for which it was commonly accounted justifiable to abandon the solitary life.

---

[1] St. Bridget's own confessor had been a hermit.

" They maye by no meanes bee suffered to come oute of their houses excepte it bee to take a streighter and an harder life uppon them, which is to be a bishop." [1] Elsewhere we have seen how St. Cuthbert and others were drawn from solitude to undertake arduous posts of responsibility and care. In continental history, there is the notable instance of Pietro Morone, the aged peasant, taken from his cave at Sulmona to become pope (1294). An English copy of the Rule ascribed to St. Celestine refers to him as a hermit chosen for his holiness to be pope, who afterwards returned to the wilderness again. [2] To Dante this act of resignation may have been *il gran refuto*, but the anchorite felt himself under a moral obligation to return ultimately to the life to which he had been dedicated by solemn vows. In truth, the simple solitary was rarely fitted for strenuous social work, though he might on occasion emerge from his solitude as a counsellor, and even a leader, of men.

[1] Thos. Becon, *Reliques of Rome*, ed. 1563, f. 54.
[2] Bristol City Library MS. 6.

XII. PROPHETS AND COUNSELLORS

The prophets that have been before me and before thee of old prophesied . . . of war, and of evil, and of pestilence.—Book of the Prophet Jeremiah.

Forsooth, John Baptist, prince of hermits after Christ . . . chose the solitary life.—RICHARD ROLLE, *Fire of Love.*

THE hermits and anchorites of England occupied an independent position somewhat akin to that of the Hebrew seer. Whereas monks living in community looked back to "the sons of the prophets" as the first cœnobites, the recluse regarded himself as the follower of Elijah and of John the Baptist. It was therefore his vocation to read the signs of the times, to declare, to preach, and, it may be, to predict. If, then, the solitary had a striking personality, if he were a man with force of character, or possessed the mysterious power begotten of deep personal holiness, he was to his generation the servant of God to whom secrets were revealed. To the simple people who sought him, his counsel seemed to come as a voice from heaven.

The first authentic record of an anchorite in Britain (603) illustrates this oracular office. When the bishops and monks of the British Church heard of Augustine's arrival, they were face to face with a hard problem. They therefore visited a solitary sage before attending a second conference with the strangers :—

"They that were to go to the aforesaid council, repaired first to a certain holy and discreet man, who was wont to lead an eremitical life among them, consulting with him, whether they ought, at the preaching of Augustine, to forsake their traditions. He answered : 'If he is a man of God, follow him'. 'How shall we prove that?' said they. He replied, 'Our Lord saith, Take my yoke upon you, and learn of Me, for I am meek and lowly in heart; if, therefore, this Augustine be meek and lowly of heart, it is to be believed that

146

PLATE XXXIV

HERMIT EXHORTS SIR LANCELOT

THE BURIAL OF SIR GALAHAD

THE HERMIT AND THE KNIGHTS

he has taken upon him the yoke of Christ, and offers the same to you to take upon yourselves. But, if he be stern and haughty, it is plain that he is not of God, nor are we to regard his words.' They again asked: 'And how shall we discern even this?' 'Do you contrive,' said the anchorite, 'that he may first arrive with his company at the place where the synod is to be held; and if at your approach he shall rise up to you, hear him submissively, being assured that he is the servant of Christ; but if he shall despise you, and not rise up to you, whereas you are more in number, let him also be despised by you.'"

When they arrived at the synod, Augustine remained seated, which circumstance augured ill for the cause of unity. At once they charged him with pride, and endeavoured to contradict all he said.[1]

In those primitive times, the recluse was the regular religious teacher. Maildubh, the Irishman who settled among the Christian Britons at Malmesbury (c. 637), gathered round him a school whence missionaries went forth to the pagan Saxons; and it was Maildubh the hermit who taught Aldhelm the bishop.

In the realm of romance, the solitary is a teacher, expounder of visions, confessor, counsellor, healer, and host. In the Celtic legends, especially in the *Quest of the Holy Grail*, there is ever a cell in the background. When a joust takes place, a recluse is at hand to intervene (Plate XXXIII a). Sir Perceval, hoping for tidings of a certain knight, knocks at the recluse's little window (Plate XXXIII b). On hearing his name, she commands the gates to be opened, for she is his aunt; she tells him of his mother's death, and gives him counsel. On Good Friday Sir Lancelot goes barefoot into the Forest Perilous and confesses to a hermit. He even stays three days in a cell, receiving exhortation (Plate XXXIV a). Again, when sorely wounded, he is nursed by the knight-hermit and good leech, Sir Baudewin. When Gawayne is granted harbour at a hermitage, the good man insists on knowing how it stands betwixt his guest and God. Gawayne and Ector repair to the holy Nacyen, who, in teaching them, shows an intimate knowledge of the Round Table. Galahad, Bors, Lionel, and other knights-errant might often be found at the hermitage. After the burial of Sir Gal-

---

[1] Bede, *Eccles. Hist.*, ed. Stevenson, 358.

ahad, at which a hermit assists (Plate XXXIV b), Sir Perceval takes a religious habit, and so lives until his death. The solitary is always some noble knight of fame who has forsaken great possessions.[1]

Returning to Bede and the chroniclers, we find amongst the Saxon saints many renowned counsellors, men like Cuthbert and Guthlac, endowed with intellectual gifts, rare insight, and a wisdom born of experience and meditation. It was remembered of Cuthbert that, even before he entered upon the solitary life, he spoke so beautifully and had such a bright angelic countenance that no man durst conceal from him the most hidden secrets of his heart, but confessed his guilt, believing that it could not be hidden from him. Guthlac also had a winning personality and a powerful influence. He was sought by men of every condition, and, from the King to the least of his subjects, none left the young monk of Crowland uncomforted or uninspired. Among the illustrations on the fine Harley roll is one entitled: "Guthlac consoles the exile king Ethelbald (Plate XXXV)". The King is represented as gazing intently at the hermit, who is in the act of exhortation, with one hand uplifted, and clasping in the other the holy book. The saint is declaring that he has made intercession for Ethelbald, predicting that he will be restored to his kingdom, and encouraging him to wait patiently.

The same rôle is attributed to St. Neot. A Saxon homily declares that King Alfred often came to this holy man about his soul's need, and relates that Neot reproved and exhorted him with foreknowledge. Neot's later biographers, indeed, represent him as pronouncing judgment upon his royal kinsman for pride, tyranny, and licentiousness ; but there is no occasion to quote what Dr. Plummer with righteous indignation calls " wretched tales which besmirch the fair fame of our hero king in order to exalt a phantom saint ". Without giving credence to legends which are inconsistent with historical fact, we may believe that Neot was a friend and adviser of the King, and a faithful pastor of the people. He cheered the sad and turned aside the wrath of those who had been burning with anger. The homily relates that he preached

[1] *La Queste de S. Graal*, ed. Furnivall (Roxburghe Club) ; Malory's *Le Morte Darthur* (Caxton, 1485), ed. H. O. Sommer, etc.

PLATE XXXV

A HERMIT·COUNSELLOR

to all men the true faith, and to those who confessed and renounced their sins, he declared the goodness and mercy of God.

Among the less-known saints, few are more interesting than
Wulsi, who became the oracle of Crowland during a critical
time (p. 37). When he removed to the west of England,
he was still an influential counsellor. Knowing how to speak
a word in season, he was able to induce St. Wulstan to accept
the bishopric of Worcester :—

"Since, then, Wulstan the man of God could not be led to consent, although he had been asked by many men of the religious life
and worshipful persons, at length, having been sharply rebuked for
his disobedience by Wulsi the recluse, a man of God who had lived
the solitary life for more than forty years, and being terribly warned
by a divine oracle, he was compelled to consent with great sorrow of
heart ".[1]

Again, like some dreamer of old, Wulsi had a vision which led
to the re-foundation of Westminster Abbey (p. 38 and Plate
XIV). The departing seer (like Edward the Confessor, whose
last utterances showed premonitory instinct) predicted evil
times, though he hoped that he might "be found a lying
prophet".

From the cell there went forth now and again warnings of
impending misfortune. Godric, for example, who showed
many tokens of possessing clairvoyant powers, discerned "the
spirit of famine". The devastating dearth of 1258 was pre-
saged, it was said, in a vision seen by the anchoress dwelling
at St. Peter's church at St. Albans—"a most holy recluse,
who was accustomed to see not simply dreams but heavenly
signs of the future". One of her visions was that of a venerable man ascending the tower of the church, turning towards
the town and pronouncing repeatedly the dire message : *Woe,
woe, woe, to all the inhabiters of the earth !*

"And soon, in the same year, on account of the failure of the
crops, the herds also died, and so great a famine ensued that in the
city of London 15,000 souls perished of hunger. In various by-ways,
indeed, folk fell down and died miserably. And so great was their
number that the grave-diggers for very weariness threw many bodies
in a heap into a single pit."

[1] M. Paris, *Chron. Maj.* (Rolls, 57) ii. 39-40.

The neighbourhood of St. Albans had formerly been famed for the spirit of prophecy manifested by Roger the hermit and Christina the recluse. The chronicler declares that Roger, " the friend of God," taught Christina almost incredible things of the secrets of heaven, for his body alone seemed to remain on earth, his soul conversing with the invisible.   Christina's super-natural faculty consisted in thought-reading, presentiments, and the power of seeing what took place at a distance.   She was regarded with awe as a prophetess—for did not an angel in the form of a bird alight in her bosom, foreshowing her things ?   The discrimination of her counsels caused her to be frequently sought by the abbot himself, even in political mat-ters, as, for example, when he was sent as ambassador from King Stephen to the Pope.

William of Malmesbury speaks of the " ambiguous oracle " pronounced by Roger, who was believed to have anticipated the fate of Robert Bloet, Bishop of Lincoln.   This prelate, a man of dissolute life, demanded of Christina's protector why he harboured a maiden who, having forsaken her suitor for the sake of celibacy, had sought refuge with him.   When the her-mit gave a fitting reply, the bishop broke out : " Bold and insolent is your answer ; your cowl alone sustains you ".   To which Roger retorted ominously : " Despise the cowl as you will, a day will come when you will sorely wish to have one, and words shall be wanting to you in which to ask for it ". Roger's words were remembered when, without a moment's warning, Bishop Robert died of apoplexy.[1]

The dark saying was sufficiently vague, and its half-enig-matical language might have admitted of many interpretations. Wulfric of Haselbury, however, predicted events with astound-ing clearness.   He claimed to speak in the name of the Lord, and was highly esteemed as a prophet.   When he heard that Henry I was arranging for his departure to foreign lands, he said : " He will go, indeed, but he will not return ; and even if he should return, he will not be either sound or whole ". Hearing this, the King was wroth with the seer, and sent to inquire whether he were indeed the author of these words. Wulfric replied : " If I said them, I am not sorry, because I

---

[1] *Gest. Pontif.* (Rolls, 52), p. xvi.

have not spoken from myself". King Henry departed, and when his death took place, the anchorite intimated it to Sir William Fitzwalter : " Yesterday the King died ; do you take counsel what you will do ". Then the knight, being amazed, commanded him to be silent. " It is easy enough for me to be silent," said the priest, " but it will happen on the morrow that all men will speak it openly ; and so it fell out. On another occasion Wulfric predicted that King Stephen was about to be led away captive, but would be set free. Some time before Stephen's accession, the recluse had saluted him as the future king ; and he subsequently announced to the young Prince of Anjou that he would reign in succession.

Godric uttered predictions of a similar nature. The following story, accurate in detail, is too long to relate fully. About March, 1170, a knight from the court visited Godric and sought his blessing. As his visitor turned to go, the hermit sent a message to Henry II in which he referred to his own approaching death and also mentioned "the young King ". Before long, the import of the mysterious allusion became plain. The old sailor-saint did indeed—to use his own words —"pass the borders of the Great Sea," and a month later the King's son Henry was crowned, on account of unforeseen political circumstances.[1]

Such oracles were frequently given unasked, but persons used also to inquire of the recluse, as warriors of old resorted to seer or prophetess. When he was in the Holy Land, Richard Cœur de Lion went by night to consult the hermit of St. Samuel, who predicted that Jerusalem would not be taken by him.[2]

Nor was it unusual for the solitary to act as spiritual adviser to those who visited him. No voice carried more weight than did the voice crying repentance in the wilderness. To Coquet Island, near the Northumbrian coast, came many from distant parts to converse with Henry the hermit. Their secrets he made perfectly clear, as though his bodily eyes could look into hidden things. When a monk of Tynemouth came to him, he bade the man beware and keep sober, and told him both the place and hour when he had been disgracefully

[1] *Vita*, pp. 302-4.   [2] M. Paris, *Chron. Maj.* (Rolls, 57), II. 386-7.

drunk. Bartholomew of Farne exercised a strong and abiding influence alike on rich and poor, on wild border barons and rough sailors. The chronicler Gaufridus describes him thus :—

"Jovial also was he in his talk, and yet was he grieved by sin. Whenever they came before him, he used fearlessly to convict the pride of those rich men the report of whose cruelty reached him. So grave was his countenance and so reverend his mien that many of them, moved by his words, set themselves earnestly to leave off oppression of the poor, to keep their hands from unlawful gain, and to atone for their sins by alms. He had compassion on the poor and the sick, persuading them to bear life patiently."

Even the proud and passionate Norman Kings were open to influence when brought face to face with an outspoken man of God. Henry I came to Wulfric a suppliant; Stephen left him a penitent.

"A certain great prince [1] of the household of King Henry said when he heard of the fame of Wulfric : ' The king would do well if he sent to the cell of this scoffer to take possession of his property, because it is impossible that one to whom so many resort should not have laid up much treasure'. And while the words were yet in his mouth, behold, he fell throttled to the earth, with his mouth twisted back right to his ear, and wallowed foaming. The king having heard of it, went when opportunity offered, to the cell of the servant of God; and commending himself earnestly to his prayers, told all things, and made supplication for his knight. ' I do not,' said he, ' lay this sin to his charge, and I am present here to do whatever I ought to do.' Then one of those who stood by, taking the hand of Wulfric, laid it on the face of the sick man, and immediately his mouth returned to its place, and becoming sound in mind, he spoke aright, glorifying God."

Wulfric not only admonished Count Stephen as to his future conduct, but afterwards chode him because he had ruled ill, and the whole peace of England had been disturbed. After much wholesome exhortation, Wulfric added that, unless Stephen were penitent, his throne could never be established. "When the king heard these things he began to weep copiously and to make confession from the bottom of his heart, and he turned his cheek to the prophet to be smitten and spat upon."

[1] Drogo de Munci.

Robert of Knaresborough boldly spoke his mind to King John. When the king and his retinue arrived at the hermitage, Robert was prostrate before the altar, and would not leave his devotions, although aware of their presence. At length Sir Brian de Lisle roused him, saying : " Brother Robert, rise quickly : lo ! the king is here who would speak with thee ". The hermit arose, and having picked up from the ground an ear of corn, he held it towards King John, and said : " If thou be king, do thou create such a thing as this " : and when the king could make no reply, he added : " There is no King but one, that is God ". Certain of the bystanders regarded the hermit's conduct as madness, but one replied that Robert was indeed wiser than they, since he was the servant of God in whom is all wisdom. Even the unbelieving despot was duly, if momentarily, impressed by the good man's boldness. Before Robert, says the rhyming chronicler, tyrants trembled, beasts and birds bowed, and fiends fled.

It was not unknown for recluses to use their influence as protectors or mediators. The Countess Loretta, anchoress of Hackington, was one of the chief promoters of the Franciscan Order when the friars first arrived at Canterbury. Thomas of Eccleston says that she " cherished them in all things, as a mother her sons ". Through her influence, some nuns of Canterbury gained privileges, and a certain man obtained pardon for manslaughter. Henry III, yielding to the entreaty of Nicholas, the monk of Westminster, released a man from outlawry, and also issued a writ providing for the mainten-ance of another man.[1]

Westminster Abbey had a succession of anchorite-con-fessors. One of these was the chosen counsellor of Richard II during Wat Tyler's insurrection (1381) :—

" The same day the king went . . . toward Westminster, attended on by the number of 200 persons, to visit Saint Edward's shrine, and to see if the Commons had done any mischiefe there. . . . After which he spake with the Anchore, to whom he confessed himselfe." [2]

He was consulted on important political matters ; nor was he altogether free from suspicion of disloyalty by encouraging

---

[1] A. G. Little, in *Coll. d'Etudes*, vii. 25-6 ; Patent Rolls (various).
[2] J. Stow, *Chron. of Eng.*, ed. 1631, p. 288.

rebels. He was said to have acted as adviser to Thomas, Earl of Warwick, one of the Lords Appellant (1397). Accused of treason, the aged nobleman pleaded that he had been led away by the Duke of Gloucester and the Earl of Arundel—" trustyng also in the holynes and wisdoum of the Abbot of Saint Albones, and of the Recluse of Westmynstre, that saide it was lawfulle that he dede ".[1] It was perhaps from this same man that Henry V received serious impressions at the time of his accession (1413), as related by Thomas of Elmham, afterwards his chaplain :—

" After he had spent the day in wailing and groaning, so soon as the shades of night covered the earth, the weeping prince, taking advantage of the darkness, secretly visited a certain recluse of holy life at Westminster ; and laying bare to him the secret sins of his whole life, was washed in the laver of true repentance ".[2]

The Abbey archives may yet prove whether these various monks can be identified as one and the same. Sir John London was enclosed before 1389 and lived until 1429. About the year 1415, however, another priest was enclosed there, William Alnwyk by name, who was appointed by Henry V to a burdensome ecclesiastical office, but shortly returned to his cell (p. 144). With one or the other the king had monetary transactions, perhaps by way of alms, for the Issue Roll of the Exchequer (1420) notes £4 as " paid by the hands of a certain recluse within the monastery of Westminster ".

John the anchorite of Westminster was remembered in the will of the noted conspirator, Lord Scrope of Masham (1415), who bequeathed him the rosary which he used, and a considerable sum of money. One of such exalted virtue was believed to have superabundant grace, and a high value was set upon his intercessions. This is confirmed by the curious *Revelation respecting Purgatory*,[3] in which the spirit of the nun Margaret is represented as appearing to her friend on earth requesting prayers and masses :—

" And also sende to thi fadir the recluse of Westemynster, and byd hym synge twa messis of saynt Petir for me, and saye fyve dayes for

---

[1] *Eng. Chron.* (Camden S., 1856), p. 11.   [2] A. J. Church, *Henry V*, 44-5.
[3] Lincoln, MS. Thornton, in Horstman's *R. Rolle*, I. 384-5.

me this psalme Miserere mei deus and this ympne Veni creator spiritus and so forthe, in the manere a-bowne sayde. And bydde him warne dane Perse Cowme [1] that he saye two messis of the haly gaste for me."

This vision is dated 1422. Seven years later the Chronicle of St. Albans announces the death of Master John, the monk of Westminster, " prominent as a hermit enclosed there during forty years ".[2] An undated manuscript, said to be in the Westminster archives, seems to refer to this event, which caused a sensation in the community :—

" After the singing of Mattins, on the morning of St. Thomas' or Mumping Day, when the Brethren began the Lauds for the dead, it was whispered abroad that the Abbey Ankret was dead at last. Brother Innocent . . . sang the news in my ear when we turned to the Altar for the *Gloria :* ' Dead is our holy Ankret ; he is dead ; he died at midnight ; the Abbot confessed him ; he is dead ' ".

In so great veneration was the old man held, that, even when his mind was failing, his incoherent utterances were treasured in the monastery : " his discourse consisted of pious ejaculations, some of which have been written down by the *cancellarius* ".[3]

Claiming to know the Divine will by special revelation, the recluse often exercised an important influence both in public and private affairs. When the young Henry VI became King, an anchoress of York (Dame Emma Rawghton) declared that it had been shown to her by Our Lady that he ought to be crowned in France as well as in England, and also that no person was better fitted to be his guardian than Richard Beauchamp, Earl of Warwick.[4] The Earl turned to this holy woman for advice in his private affairs, as described in chapter III.

Whilst the secluded anchorite was the passive counsellor of individuals, the hermit might be an active leader among the people, closely associated with reform—sometimes, indeed,

---

[1] Brother Peter Combe, a benefactor of the abbey (see Stanley, *Memorials*, ed. 1868, p. 609).
[2] Jn. Amund, *Ann.* (Rolls, 28, v.), I. 33.
[3] W. Besant, *Westminster*, ed. 1897, pp. 102-10.
[4] *Pageants of Ric. Beauchamp* (Roxburghe Club), Pageant XLVII.

with revolution—whether moral, social, or political. The most notable example is that of the preaching of the first Crusade by Peter the Hermit (1096), whose cry *Dieu le veut* rang throughout Christendom. A tragic fate, however, often awaited the religious fanatic or political firebrand. The ruthless persecution of the Jews in 1190, was in York incited by a hermit. This militant priest, a Premonstratensian canon, would go early in the morning " to offer the unbloody sacrifice," and then walk forth to his bloody work. Clad in a white habit, the hermit led his fellow-Christians against " the enemies of Christ,"—the terrified Jews shut up in the castle, and he assisted the mob in placing engines for the siege. Advancing incautiously too near the wall, he was crushed by a great stone which was cast down upon him ; and it was thought that since he was the only one of the besiegers to be slain, it showed the guilt of one in that profession or order taking part in such wanton work.[1]

There was danger, too, when hermits, persuaded that they spoke as true prophets, but sometimes (in Hebrew phrase) as " lying prophets, who spoke a vision of their own heart," stood before Kings as messengers of judgment to come. The tale of Peter the Wise (called, of Pontefract, and also, of Wakefield), the troubler of King John, is related in the *Chronicle of Barnwall*,[2] written some fourteen years after the occurrence.

"There was a certain man of Wakefield, Peter by name. This simple, rustic man, living upon bread and water, was esteemed by the people as predicting future things. He foretold that the rule of King John would not last beyond the next Ascensiontide, inasmuch as it had been revealed to him in a vision that John the king would reign fourteen years. . . . Being asked whether he would die or be driven out or resign, he answered also, as they say, that he did not know : this thing only he did know, that he would not reign beyond that time, neither he nor any one of his own family in his stead, but one whom it should please God to appoint. This thing did not escape the king, and it seemed first of all that they laughed at the man as an idiot and not sound in his head. But it came to pass that, as the man was a wanderer and told the story everywhere, he was taken by the king's favourites and shut up in prison. This saying

[1] Wm. Newb., *Hist. Angl.* (Rolls, 82), I. 316-8.
[2] In Walter of Coventry's *Mem.* (Rolls, 58) II. 208-12.

spread far and wide and his name became very famous, so that he who before was known to few and despised, from the time of his imprisonment was considered a man of note and everywhere spoken about.   Daily, as is the custom of people, lies were added to lies ; daily they attributed to him new things, and everybody developing some lie out of his own heart, asserted that Peter had said it."

We learn from Matthew Paris [1] that the hermit staked his life on the certain truth of his prediction, saying : " If I be found guilty of falsehood, thou mayest do with me as thou wilt " ; to whom King John replied : " Be it according to thy word ". The King then committed him to William de Harecurt to guard him in close confinement at Corfe, until it were proved how the matter would end.

In the meantime, the King of France, urged on by the Pope, prepared to invade England, and on 15 May, 1213, John did homage to the legate, agreeing to hold his realm as tributary to the Pope.   Several causes contributed to his submission, the chief being his forebodings at the approach of the ominous festival—" afraid that he would lose with his life his kingdom, both of this world and of the world to come ".   When the day came, the King, with his bishops and rulers, were in high spirits, and those who had given credence to Peter thought that after all he was half-witted, and deceived by his own simpleness. It was represented to the King, however, to what an extent the man had troubled the country, sowed discord, and stirred up the King's enemies ; for his words had incited the French to invade England.   The passion of the King was thus kindled, and he commanded Peter to be hanged on a gibbet in the face of the sun ; and not he alone, but also his son, " who "—says the Barnwall chronicler—" being considered equally guilty was alike hung, lest by chance he also should have been a partaker, or even the author, of his father's prophecy ".

For an account of the final interview and of the hermit's last impassioned harangue, we must turn to the pages of a Scottish chronicler :— [2]

" King John, perceiving in himself that the day appointed by Peter as aforesaid had passed away, and that no bodily ailment had

[1] *Chron. Maj.* (Rolls, 57), II. 535-47.
[2] J. Fordun, *Scotichron.*, ed. 1759, II. 7, 8.

come upon him, called Peter, whom he caused to be brought forth from prison, a false prophet. Who boldly resisted the king to his face, affirming that he was telling the truth, and he stated that the king himself was not reigning at that time, since . . . he had subjected the rule of his kingdom to the power of another. When then Peter was convicted by such judgment as this, and was condemned to be hanged, he said in a loud voice to the king, That it was natural he should feel that he must rage against the Church and her members, since from the time when he was born he proceeded, forsooth, from the devil; but that he might not at last return to him, in abounding love he himself had besought the pity of the Most High. 'This one nature,' said he, 'I tell thee—thou who art not a king of men, but the dregs and a cross of all—is common both to thee and to thy relative the devil, whose work it is to lay traps, to prepare stumbling-blocks, to dig pitfalls, to make things a ruin, to stir up bodies from the depths of their evil souls, that they should not be saved ; to hate virtues, to love vices, to sow errors, to nourish strifes, to disturb the peace, to scatter true love, to profane humanity, and strain to the uttermost all that is divine.' When he had finished his short speech, the king was angry and commanded that his life should end by hanging from the nearest tree."

Matthew Paris gives a slightly different version of the execution, and tells us what the people thought of it. John commanded that Peter, who was bound with chains in Corfe Castle, should be tied to the tails of horses, and dragged over the plains to Wareham, and there hanged, together with his son. "It seemed to many an unworthy thing that he should be punished by so cruel a death for speaking the truth. For if those things which are written above are considered acutely, it will be proved that he had spoken no falsehood."

Richard II, Henry IV, and Henry V were confronted by hermits heralding judgment. William Norham delivered his message first to the Archbishop of Canterbury, who had been wrongfully appointed on the banishment of Thomas Arundel :—

"In Lent [1399], a certain hermit called William Norham came to Archbishop Roger Walden saying that he was sent to him on behalf of One whom it was not safe to disobey; to impress upon him to resign the archbishopric which he held unjustly, and to advise the king that he should amend his life and that he should recall others whom he had exiled unjustly . . . else would there certainly come upon both of them, king and archbishop alike, in a short time, such terrible and new things that both the ears of every one that heard it should tingle."

Offended at the man's message, the archbishop suspended him from the celebration of Mass, and imprisoned him for a season. He afterwards sent him to King Richard, who desired nothing less than to hear words of correction, which things the prophet proceeded to speak. Coming into the royal presence, he declared that he was sent from God to warn the King to lead a better life. Richard, thinking lightly of the matter and despising the poverty and lowliness of his appearance, said : " If indeed thou art so close a servant of God, go and run on thy feet upon the water, that we may have certainty that thou art a true messenger of God ". To whom the hermit replied : " I am not like such great saints as those who do miracles of this sort, nor may I go of my own will upon the water ; but this I boldly affirm that unless thou dost obey my warnings, there will shortly come upon thee such terrible new things as thou hast never read of or seen ". Richard, displeased at the man's freedom of speech, ordered him to be taken to the Tower of London. There he was kept until he saw his prophecy fulfilled, and the King led captive in his stead.[1]

For some time we hear nothing of William Norham. The new King, however, being regarded by not a few of his subjects as a usurper, was not likely to escape ill-omened oracles, and at his coronation many a shrewd man said openly that the third heir should be uncrowned. The soothsayer bided his time. At length, believing in his mission, and encouraged by the speedy fulfilment of his former predictions, the bold priest followed Henry IV after the Battle of Shrewsbury (1403). "That same hermit who foretold disaster to King Richard came to the King and told him many secret things which were unknown to him. Whom the King commanded to be beheaded, which was also done."[2] Much consternation was caused by his fate :—

" At this time a certain hermit who had predicted many future things to King Richard, when he had set himself to prophesy to the

[1] Chr. S. Alb., *Ann. Ric. II* (Rolls, 28, III.), 231-2.
[2] *Eulog. Hist.* (Rolls, 9), III. 397.

new king, and when he inveighed with too little prudence against him, having been convicted of speaking falsehood, he was beheaded at York; whose flesh a prickly hair-shirt had scraped; whose feet no shoes had covered for many years—except, perhaps, when he celebrated mass—although he had gone to Rome and returned; whose lips had tasted absolutely no flesh for a long while: nevertheless, he died the death." [1]

Although in the *Scotichronicon* a veil of secrecy shrouds the " White Hermit of England," we may conclude that he was none other than William Norham :—

"To this Henry there came a certain holy man who was called the White Hermit of England, saying that he had been taught by the Holy Trinity, and that he saw in spirit a reception room prepared for him, aflame with the fire of hell and attended by devils, in which after death he should be placed unless he should resign the crown of the realm which was not meet for him. To whom the king replied : ' If, indeed, I should renounce it, who will succeed me ? ' ' After thee,' quoth the hermit, 'a devil, and after a devil, a saint, and after a saint, a sword, and after a sword, a nobody.' ' Since then,' said Robert de Waterton, a counsellor of the king, 'thou art so dear to God that His secrets are thus open to thee, it is fitting that thou shouldst speedily be sent to him.' By whose counsel, and that of others who agreed with him, the king immediately commanded that his head should be smitten off. Who afterwards blazed forth in manifold miracles." [2]

Henry V was confronted during his last campaign by a French hermit, who appeared whilst the King was before Dreux, and represented to him the great ills he had brought upon Christendom by his unjust ambition in usurping the kingdom of France. The hermit threatened him in God's name with awful punishment if he did not desist from his enterprise. It seemed to Henry but an idle dream, a mere suggestion of the Dauphin's followers ; but the French chronicler tells us how the blow followed close upon the threat. Smitten with a strange incurable disease, he grew gradually worse, and was brought to Vincennes, where he died.[3] The tale is related in Southey's ballad *Henry V and the Hermit of Dreux :—*

---

[1] Chr. S. Alb., *Ann. Hen. IV*, 372-3.
[2] W. Bower, in Fordun's *Scotichron. lib.*, xv., c. IX.
[3] Mezeray, *Abregé Chron.*, ed. 1688, III. 213.

> He pass'd unquestion'd through the camp,
>   Their heads the soldiers bent
> In silent reverence, or begg'd
>   A blessing as he went;
> And so the Hermit pass'd along
>   And reached the royal tent.

The prophecies of one John the Hermit about the issue of the war with France had sufficient influence to cause them to be discussed in the Privy Council in 1439.[1]

Certain hermit-preachers now claim attention. Richard of Hampole, social reformer, evangelist, and writer, was one of the most remarkable men of mediaeval England. Of his prophetic utterances, threatening the land with famine, plague, inundation, and war, Thomas Fuller says shrewdly that these predictions " if hitting, were heeded, if missing, not marked ". It is, however, rather as a preacher and writer than as a prophet that Richard Rolle made his influence felt. Passing in and out amongst the people, like another St. Francis of Assisi, he appealed to them personally in a persuasive manner, and converted many to God. At the outset of his eremitical career, he delivered at a village church in Yorkshire a discourse which deeply affected the congregation :—

" Moreover, he entered the same church a second time, and putting on a surplice without any mandate, he sang with the others mattins and the office of the mass. But when in the mass the gospel was to be read, having before asked the priest's blessing, he went into the pulpit of preaching and made to the people a sermon of wonderful edification, so much so that a great number of the congregation were by his preaching so seized with compunction that they could not restrain their tears, and they all said that they had not themselves heard aforetime a sermon of such excellence and efficacy." [2]

The young prophet, however, was often without honour. He had enemies, persecutors, and slanderers, and even by friends he was misunderstood. Some thought him demented ; others misinterpreted his converse with the rich, and despite his rigorous abstinence, accused him of being a glutton and a wine-bibber.

---

[1] Nicolas, *Acts of P.C.*, v. 352-3 ; the visions of St. Bridget concerning international policy, were also discussed. In 1396 the mission of Robert l'Hermite to England had resulted in peace, and in Richard II's marriage with Isabella of France (Froissart, *Chron.*, bk. iv, c, 66).

[2] *Officium*, col. 791-2.

Churchmen maintained that he could not preach, and school-men ridiculed his writings. As a reformer, Richard the hermit seemed to fail, nevertheless he became the beloved master of a chosen few to whom he expounded the word of God. Speaking or writing, he was a man with a message. " He re-discovered Love, the principle of Christ. He re-installed feeling, the spring of life, which had been obliterated in the reign of scholasticism. He re-opened the inner eye of man, teaching contemplation in solitude, an unworldly life in abnegation, in chastity and charity." [1]

After this preacher of righteousness arose another social reformer, the eccentric priest, William of Swinderby. Both these men were swayed by fervent emotions, impatient of authority, eager to reform the world in their own way ; but whilst Richard was an apostle of love, and inspired people to live a higher life, William was a fanatic, and estranged his hearers by his violence of speech. Richard was able to draw women as disciples and instil into them his teaching of love and purity ; William inveighed so loudly against their sins that the women of Leicester threatened to drive him out with stones.

"There was in those days at Leicester, a certain priest, hight William of Swynderby, whom they commonly called William the hermit, because, for a long time, he had lived the hermitical life there ; they received him into a certain chamber within the church, because of the holiness they believed to be in him, and they procured for him victuals and a pension, after the manner of other priests." [2]

After returning to ordinary life for a season, he was received into Leicester abbey. He afterwards dwelt at the chapel of St. John Baptist in a wood outside the town.[3] Followers resorted thither, for William was an earnest teacher, preaching " by the desire of the people that were hungry and thirsty after God's word ". He made bitter enemies, however, by his fierce attacks upon the Church and upon ecclesiastics. In 1382, he

---

[1] C. Horstman, *R. Rolle*, p. xxxiv.

[2] Twysden's *Script. X* (Knighton), II. 2665 ; Knighton, *Chron.* (Rolls, 64), II. 189-98.

[3] A bequest was made in 1382 to W. de S., chaplain of St. John's chapel (*Linc. Wills*, 31). It was situated " near a leper-house," i.e. probably St. John's hospital. Nichols figures the remains of the " chapel of St. John set at the town's end " (*Leic.* I, pt. II., pl. XXIII., facing p. 302).

was inhibited by the Bishop of Lincoln, who forbade him to preach in any church, chapel, or churchyard in the diocese ; but the hermit evaded the order by preaching on the highway. Cited to Lincoln and convicted of heresy, he was, however, set free through the influence of John of Gaunt, and was restored to the bosom of the Church on condition that he publicly confessed at Lincoln and Leicester the falsity of his preaching.

The popularity of the Lollard leader having waned, he was left in solitude at his chapel. He fled to Coventry and preached in those parts for about a year, until he was driven away. He took refuge in the diocese of Hereford, but again met with persecution. The bishop denounced him as a child of wickedness, who had been running about in sundry places, presuming to preach—" a teacher of pernicious doctrine and a horrible seducer among the people ". William denied many of the accusations brought against him, and appealed to the King and Council, but in vain. The last we hear of the hermit-heretic is that in 1392 the King (at the instance of the Archbishop and the Bishop of Hereford) issued a commission to find and arrest " a certain fellow named William Swinderby pretending himself to be a chaplain," and his companion, who would not revoke the errors of which they had been convicted, and were in hiding in Wales.

Another zealous mission-preacher was the anchorite friar, Thomas Scrope (or Bradley), who, about the year 1425, left his cell and went forth into the world for a season. Leading a life of almost incredible austerity, he preached diligently to the people by word and by example. Clad in sackcloth, with a girdle of iron fetters, Brother Thomas went into the streets of Norwich : " And he used to cry out that the new Jerusalem, the bride of the Lamb, would shortly come down from heaven, and that she should immediately be prepared for her Spouse. And he added, that with great joy he saw her in the spirit." This extravagant conduct was not approved by the strictly orthodox, and the Provincial of the Carmelites wrote a protest to the brethren at Norwich, in which he referred to this matter as a scandal to the Church, causing schism and disturbance, and bringing discredit upon those Orders. At length, fearing for himself " this generation of vipers," he returned to his cell.[1] In 1441 Pope Eugenius IV granted to Thomas Bradley, anchorite of Norwich, an indult to choose a secular or regular priest as confessor.[2] He was afterwards dispensed from his vows and nominated Bishop of Dromore (1450).[3] He afterwards held certain Norfolk livings, and acted as suffragan bishop. In old age he returned to the mission-work of his younger days. Walking barefoot, the venerable bishop went about every Friday in the country parts of the diocese, into villages and into the fields, teaching the Ten Commandments of the Divine Law. He used also to give away all his goods to the poor. He died in 1491, aged wellnigh 100 years.

Whilst some of these preachers were pious and patriotic, others were mere pretenders. The troubled reign of Henry VI produced several adventurers disguised in this way. The *Coventry Leet Book* records the notable visit, in 1424, of one "callyd John Grace, heremyte," who, saying that he had a licence to preach and had been at Lichfield, Birmingham, and Walsall, preached for five days in the Little Park at Coventry, and created considerable disturbance. Men said he had been a monk, after that a friar, and then, a recluse. He declared himself to be a wonder-worker as well as "a gracyous man in sayng, and a hooly lyuer". The King's council afterwards ordered his arrest as "a certain false prophet calling himself John Grace," accused of sedition and of attempting to overthrow the Catholic faith, especially by his preaching in Coventry and the neighbourhood.[4]

In Kent, an agitator nicknamed "Bluebeard," who posed as a hermit, started the insurrection generally known as Jack Cade's Rebellion (1450). The man was a fuller, Thomas Cheyny by name. Fabyan says that the commons "made of themself capitaynes, and named them Bleweberde and other counterfayte names". The execution of the ringleader created

---

[1] Bale says he was enclosed fourteen years (Harl. MS., 3838, f. 107), but elsewhere he says twenty years.

[2] Pap. Lett., IX. 241.

[3] Irish sees often gave titles to suffragans. Rev. B. Zimmerman, historian of the Carmelite Order, questions whether Scrope took possession of his see, but (1) he has a letter of the Provincial, Nicholas Kenton, commending Scrope, Bishop-elect of Dromore (formerly an anchorite of Norwich) to the bishops and nobles of Ireland. (2) Scrope suggested R. Mysin as his successor ; Mysin was nominated 1457.

[4] E.E. Text S. (O.S., 134), I, 96-7 ; Pat. 3 Hen. VI, pt. I, m. 17 *d*.

such indignation that the men employed about it were in-jeopardy. The sheriffs of London afterwards requested remuneration for carrying out the writ whereby they were directed " to send and delyver the heed of oon Thomas Cheyny feyning him silf an heremite cleped Blewberd atteynt of high treson " to the mayor and bailiffs of Canterbury, and to exhibit remains elsewhere. The corpses of traitors included that of " Jack Cade " himself, but the chief charges were involved by the carriage of Cheyny's body, " for and by cause that unneth any persones durste nor wolde take upon ham the caridge of the seyd hed and quarters for doute of her lyves ". The city documents of Canterbury record the event, and add that the head was placed over the Westgate. When confirming the liberties of the citizens in 1453, Henry VI commended their fidelity in the arrest of the traitor " who called himself Blewberd the hermit ".[1]

The hermit's garb was a favourite disguise. When Perkin Warbeck was taken as a prisoner to the Tower (1497), he was followed by one of his accomplices, " clad in armittes abyt," bound hand and foot.[2]

Religious malcontents played their part in the political crisis of Henry VIII's reign. In 1535, Hugh Lathbury, hermit, was imprisoned at Bristol, for saying that he trusted Queen Katherine should thereafter be queen again.[3] Three years later, the hermit of Chesterfield was seized on the report of passionate words about the Pope being deprived of authority, because he would not approve the King's marriage with Anne Boleyne. He raised, moreover, the burning question of that year of sacrilege : " If a man will pluck down or tear the King's arms, he shall be hanged, drawn, and quartered ; what shall he do to them that doth pluck down churches and images, being but a mortal man as we be ? " This rash orator was brought before the nearest justice to be examined, and was afterwards sent to Thomas Cromwell.[4]

Even the secluded anchorite was not free from dangerous discussion. The Dominican recluse of Canterbury, Christopher

[1] *Acts of Privy Council*, VI. 107-9 ; *Hist. MSS. Com.*, R. IX. 140, 167, 168.
[2] C. L. Kingsford, *Chr. of London*, 221.
[3] L. and P., *Hen. VIII*, VIII. p. 308 ; IX. p. 48.
[4] *Ibid.* XIII. (1), p. 501.

Warener, had been visited "because he was a prisoner" by Elizabeth Barton, the "holy maid of Kent" (p. 187).   Cromwell tried to get the friar to incriminate the nun ; but he would only say that he was never of counsel with her, never saw her in a trance, nor heard her say aught against the King, except that should the marriage go forward, it would turn to great trouble.   The matter, said the anchorite, was a hindrance to his contemplation—a view of the case that would hardly disquiet the State officials.[1]

A sixteenth-century writer, Thomas Becon, who was adverse to everything monastic, complains that, whereas anchorites professed to be followers of Judith, they did not resemble her :—

"Judith, when Tyme required, came out of her Closet to do good unto other.   Our Recluses never come out of their Lobbeies, sincke or swimme the People.   Judith put herself in Jeopardy for to do good to the commune Countrey.   Our Recluses are unprofitable Cloddes of the Earth, doing good to no Man."[2]

It has, however, been shown in the earlier part of this chapter, that it proved possible to retire from the world without losing touch with men, and that to live in solitude was not to be without a sphere of influence, or a power of service. We now pass on to consider those recluses whose counsels were delivered chiefly in their writings, which were widely circulated and were valued by succeeding generations.

[1] L. and P., *Hen. VIII*, vi, 1333, 1336, 1381.
[2] T. Becon, *Reliques of Rome*, 53-4.

XIII. LITERARY RECLUSES

The solitary, therefore, ought to be learned, not one who needs to be taught; also he ought to be wise and learned in the Divine law, that he may know whence he may bring forth things new and old.—GRIMLAIC, *Regula Solitariorum* (ninth century).

THE solitary, from St. Jerome onwards, has usually been depicted in art as a student, holding a book. There is a tradition that a British recluse (*Eremita Brytannus*), living in the time of Ina, King of Wessex, collected the history of his country, and especially the deeds of King Arthur.[1] It is not unlikely that the story itself was handed down by one of those hermits who are represented as playing so important a part among the Knights of the Holy Quest.

The historian Gildas is said to have been a hermit (p. 10). His *Liber de Excidio Britanniæ* was written about the year 560, and from this book Bede drew in the earlier chapters of his history. Alcuin describes Gildas as "the wisest of the Britons," and the epithet "the Wise" passed into common use. He seems to have acquired his learning in Gaul, and he afterwards became a teacher in Wales. Gildas also wrote a book of the *Four Gospels*, wrought in gold and silver, which was held in great estimation.[2]

We owe the famous *Lindisfarne Gospels* in part to Aethelwald, who succeeded Cuthbert in his island-hermitage (chapter I.), and to Billfrith, another priest who lived the solitary life. The Latin inscription declares that "Eadfrith, Aethilwald, Billfrith, and Aldred have wrought and adorned this book of the Gospels for God and St. Cuthbert". There is a further note in Saxon characters about the work of the goldsmith: "And Billfrith the anchorite, he wrought the metal work of

[1] Bale, *Script.*, ed. 1557, pt. 2, 31, cent. x., No. XXI.
[2] *Mon. Hist. Brit.*, I. 6; *Nov. Leg.*, I. 469.

the ornaments on the outside thereof, and decked it with gold and gems, overlaid also with silver, unalloyed metal ". When, during a voyage, this precious volume accidentally fell overboard, its miraculous recovery was attributed to the merits of St. Cuthbert and of the makers of the manuscript, namely, Bishop Eadfrid, the venerable Aethilwald, and also of the hermit Billfrith, "whose skill in craftsmanship had executed the splendid work, for he was one of the first artists of his day ". The names of these two men, Oediluald and Billfrith, recur in the list of benefactors of the church of Durham.[1]

Plegmund, "a religious man, well instructed in sacred lore," and renowned for his wisdom, lived as a hermit before he was summoned to assist King Alfred (p. 16). It has, indeed, been supposed that the transcription of the *Anglo-Saxon Chronicle*, and possibly a part of the composition itself, was his work, and this work he may have done during his years of seclusion. He was one of the four men of learning who were always about the Court, and were ready night and day to read before the King when he had aught of leisure. In Alfred's preface to his translation of Gregory's *Pastoral Care*, he acknowledges the assistance of Plegmund, Asser, and others, who had expounded to him the author's meaning :—

" I began, among other various and manifold troubles of this kingdom, to translate into English the book which is called in Latin Pastoralis, and in English Shepherd's Book, sometimes word by word and sometimes according to the sense, as I had learned it from Plegmund my archbishop, and Asser my bishop, and Grimbold my mass-priest, and John my mass-priest. And when I had learnt it as I could best understand it, and as I could most clearly interpret it, I translated it into English, and I will send a copy to every bishopric in my kingdom."

The manuscript addressed to Plegmund himself is preserved in the British Museum. This hermit-archbishop is described by a later chronicler as "a right noble man of letters ".[2]

Dunstan, a more famous ecclesiastic, statesman, and scholar, once lived in seclusion within the precincts of Glastonbury Abbey, in a cell attached to the ancient church of St.

---

[1] *Lindisfarne Gospels*, (S.S., 48), 174; *Liber Vitæ* (S.S., 13), 9; *Vita S. Cuthberti.*

[2] *Pastoral Care* (E.E.T.S. Orig. Ser., 50), p. 7; *Dict. Nat. Biog.*, etc.

Mary. The eleventh-century chronicler, Osbern, visited this cell or den, which he describes as being more like a tomb than a human habitation. It seems incredible that it measured only 5 feet by 2½ feet. In this narrow dwelling the gifted young solitary studied the Scriptures, transcribed and illuminated manuscripts, and even, so it is said, practised various arts, such as casting bells and making organs. Several books and a musical composition have been attributed to Dunstan, but, as Bishop Stubbs points out, not a single literary monument survives: "he has left, beyond a few lines of writing, the endorsement of a charter, and the prayer put into the mouth of a kneeling figure in an illumination, no writings whatever". In due course the anchorite became Abbot of Glastonbury, and finally Archbishop of Canterbury.[1]

Passing on to the Norman period, we find that the student was still found in the cell. The literary Herbert de Losinga, first Bishop of Norwich (1095-1119) wrote to his well-beloved Guy (Wido), the anchorite, commending his manner of life, and giving him counsel in a deferential manner. In the course of the letter he alludes to Guy's studious habits :—

" Thou reclinest in the company of the Prophets and Apostles, and thy soul is refreshed and gladdened by the meat and drink of heavenly doctrine. Nor are modern authors who serve up the heavenly banquet wanting to thee; thou hast an abundance of them, proportioned to the ardour of thy zeal for study and thy diligence in reading."

Perhaps the cultured bishop envied his friend these uninterrupted opportunities for study and contemplation ; for, even as he writes, his colleagues call him away to the workshop of the world, so that he closes with the brief but earnest request : " Lend me, a sinner, the hand of your prayers to lift me up ".[2]

The solitary, however, was not of necessity a monk with a monastic education : he was sometimes an illiterate layman. A curious illustration of this general lack of learning is furnished by the story of the Welsh pilgrim, Wechelen. At the Holy Sepulchre Wechelen vowed to lead the solitary life, and on his return he was enclosed at Llowes in Radnor. He wit-

[1] *Memorials of St. Dunstan* (Rolls, 63), p. cix, 83-4.
[2] Goulburn and Symonds, *Herbert de Losinga*, i. 279.

nessed the services in the adjoining church, but, knowing no Latin, he could comprehend little of their meaning. He therefore besought the Lord with tears to vouchsafe him a knowledge of the Latin tongue. One day, exhausted and hungry, he fell asleep, and on awaking, beheld on his altar a loaf, which he blessed and ate. That evening for the first time he understood what was being read at vespers. On the morrow, after mass, he called the priest to come to the window with his missal ; and as the priest read the gospel of the day, the anchorite expounded the meaning correctly in his native tongue, after which they conversed in Latin. " And from that day to this," said Wechelen to Giraldus, " I have continued to speak it." " But," he added naïvely, " the Lord, who gave me the Latin tongue, did not give me the Latin syntax, but only so far as to understand others and be understood by them." For Wechelen spoke without regard to case, mood, or tense. Thus, when he desired to express that he had been on pilgrimage, he would say : " *Ego ire Hierosoliman et visitare sepulchrum Domini mei ; et quando redire, ego ponere me in hoc carcere pro amore Domini mei qui mori pro me* ". Although not skilled in Latinity, the anchorite of Llowes was the friend and adviser of the learned archdeacon of Brecknock, who, before retiring to a life of study, went to seek his approval and blessing. Giraldus besought Wechelen to pray for him that he might understand the Holy Scriptures. " Och ! och ! " cried the unlettered recluse, grasping the scholar's hand, " say not *understand*, but *keep :* vain, vain is it to understand the word of God, and keep it not." [1]

Godric of Finchale was to a great extent self-taught. As a young pedlar, his only lore was the Paternoster and Creed. Bent on acquiring religious knowledge, he frequented the churches of Carlisle, until some kinsman gave him a book, which he set himself to learn fully. This book was the valued " Psalter of St. Jerome," which he carried about with him and read continually. For a while he acted as doorkeeper in the church of St. Giles at Durham ; afterwards he resorted to the cathedral church of St. Mary, where he picked up some psalms and hymns from the school-children. He is said to have

[1] Gir. Camb. *Op.* (Rolls, 21), I, 89, 90, Pref. liv., lv.

composed an English hymn.[1] It is possible that the simple hermit was at heart a poet like Cædmon, and that as he knelt in worship, some songs in the mother-tongue rose to his lips. The hymn to the Blessed Virgin and the story of its supernatural origin were recorded by Reginald of Durham and Roger of Wendover. One day—so we are told—when Godric was praying before the altar of the Blessed Virgin, she appeared to him and placed her hands upon his head. She then sang, and taught him to sing, a metrical prayer which he afterwards imprinted firmly in his memory.

> Seinte Marie, clane virgine,
> Moder Jesu Christ Nazarene,
> Onfo, scild, help thin Godrich,
> On fang, bring heali widh the in Godesrich.
> Seinte Marie, Christes bour,
> Meidenes clenhed, moderes flour,
> Delivere mine sennen, regne in min mod,
> Bringe me to blisse wit thi selfe God.

These verses he was bidden to use whenever he was fearful of being overcome by pain, sorrow, or temptation. He seems also to have written a song to St. Nicholas, the patron-saint of his seafaring years, the words and music of which are preserved.[2]

The literary recluses of mediaeval England include Simon Stock, the hymn-writer, and Thomas Scrope, the historian ; Geoffrey, the grammarian, and George Ripley, the alchemist ; Margery Kempe and Julian, the mystics ; Richard Rolle, composer of poetry and prose, and Symon, compiler of a manual of meditations.

The early life of St. Simon Stock is a tangled web of legend. He is said to have died at a great age in 1265, but the earliest notice containing his name and a few particulars dates from about the year 1425 ; nor is it until the end of the fifteenth century that stories are related of his wonderful infancy, of his ascetic boyhood spent in the " stock " of a tree, or of the visions which sent the young solitary first to study at Oxford and then to join the Carmelites upon their arrival in England.

---

[1] The *Vita*, pp. 203-4, says that he was thoroughly instructed only in his mother-tongue. His comprehension of French on one occasion was regarded as a miraculous gift of tongues.

[2] Wendover, *Flor. Hist.* (Rolls, 84), II. 72-3 ; *Vita S. Godrici*, 288, *Dict. Nat. Biog.* ; Ritson, *Bibl. Poet.*, 4.

All that is certain is that he did become General of the Order
in 1247. The prose writings of Simon Stock have been lost.
They included *Letters*, and *Canones*, the latter probably the
acts of the General Chapter of 1259. Simon is believed to
have been the author of the rhymed antiphons *Flos Carmeli*
and *Ave Stella Matutina*, which are found in the Carmelite
breviary. The fine poem *Alma Redemptoris Mater*, sometimes
attributed to him, is much older.[1]

The learned Carmelite Order produced during the fifteenth
century two notable scholarly recluses. Thomas Scrope, a
White Friar of Norwich—the preacher referred to in the last
chapter—was a student from his youth. His *Sermones de
decem præceptis* contain the substance of his teachings. He
wrote an account of his mission as legate to Rhodes, and also
books entitled *Compendium historiarum et iurium, De sectarum
introitu ad Angliam*. His principal works were upon the Carmelite Order.[2]

George or Gregory Ripley seems to have been an anchorite
of the Carmelites. Some consider that there were two men of
this name,—a canon of Bridlington who wrote upon natural
philosophy and occult science, and a friar of Boston, who wrote
religious poetry and biography. Since George Ripley compiled lives of St. Botulph and St. John of Bridlington, it is not
unlikely that he had been associated with Boston and Bridlington. In the absence of proof to the contrary, it is per-
missible to follow Bale in identifying the alchemist with the
anchorite. Bale says that George Ripley was at first a canon
of Bridlington. From his youth he had been interested in
exploring " wonderful effects and mysterious workings ". In
order to acquire knowledge, he travelled in foreign parts, and
dwelt several years in Italy. He studied the ancient philosophers and mathematicians, Plato, Aristotle, Hermas, Bacon,
and others. On his return, he obtained a dispensation from
choir service for purposes of study, and eventually became a
recluse. He wrote a work called *The Castle with Twelve
Gates*, treating of calcination, solution, congelation, and

---

[1] Per Rev. B. Zimmerman.

[2] Bale, *Script.*, 629-30; cent. viii., No. LIV; *Bibl. Carm.*, ed. 1752, II. 829;
Dict. Nat. Biog.; Lambeth MS., 192, contains English translation of the so-called
" Johannes XLIV," probably Scrope's work [per Rev. B. Zimmerman].

similar phenomena. His *Medulla Alchimiæ* was widely
studied. After his death he was regarded as a necromancer
and magician.

The first English-Latin dictionary was compiled in 1440
by a Dominican of Lynn, Geoffrey, " the Grammarian ". It is
true that a note in one copy of an early edition declares that :
" the name of the compiler of this book is Brother Richard
Fraunces,[1] enclosed within four walls for Christ's sake," but
this statement is at variance with other authorities. Another
copy is inscribed : " The author of this work was Geoffrey,
called *Grammaticus*, friar of the Order of St. Dominic ".[2] The
writer introduces himself as a recluse of the Friars Preachers
of Bishop's Lynn, ignorant and unskilled, more fit to learn than
to teach, but desirous of helping young students. He calls
his work " a store-house of poor clerks," *Promptorium Parvulorum*, or more correctly, *Promptuarium Parvulorum Cleri-
corum*, and confesses that it is but a brief compendium of
earlier grammarians. " The author describes with simple earnestness in his *Preambulum* the troubles of aspiring scholars,
who, amidst the prevalent barbarism of his times, thirsted for
knowledge like harts for the water-brooks, and in vain sought
for guides." He desires his book to be a mirror wherein
should be clearly reflected the meaning of English and Latin
words :—

"I humbly with prayers entreat all pedagogues, teachers, and
masters, that when they have examined this little work, they will
approve what may by God's assistance have been rightly written, and
will piously correct and emend what is written ill or erringly ; since
humble grammarians and boys may look on this short volume as on
a mirror, and find freely and immediately the common words which
belong to the Latin tongue ".

Looking into this mirror, we see the following words indicative
of the solitary life :—

ANKYR (recluse), *Anachorita*.
ERMYTAGE, *Her(e)mitorium*.
ERMYTE (eremyte), *Heremita*.
RECLUSE (or ankyr), *supra*, *Anachorita*.

[1] A bequest was made to . . . *ardo Fraunseys Anachorite confessori meo* by
John L'Estrange of Hunstanton (1436) ; Reg. Surflet, f. 206.
[2] A note in an early edition (Lincoln Cath. Muniments) has caused some to
suppose that his name was Geoffrey Starkey (*Dict. Nat. Biog.*).

The dictionary was printed by Pynson in 1499, and afterwards by Wynkyn de Worde.[1]   The compilation of a Latin-English dictionary, entitled *Medulla Grammatice,* has been ascribed to Geoffrey.   He is also supposed to have written a book of hymns, and treatises on the writings of John de Garlandia and other authors.

To the works of Richard Rolle of Hampole frequent allusion has already been made.   He went to the University of Oxford " where, when he had made great progress in study, he desired more fully and more deeply to be instructed in the theological doctrines of Holy Scripture, rather than in physics or in the teaching of secular science ".[2]   The young hermit was no profound scholar, but he was well read.   His facility of expression was remarkable.   It was reported, indeed, that he could exhort and write on different themes at the same time. He was once writing in his cell when guests arrived who begged him to offer them a word of edification.   He did so : " yet in no way did this make him cease from writing for two hours continuously, but, with the same speed as before, he continued to write ".   He wrote hastily, when possessed with his subject, and his style is unpolished, disconnected, ejaculatory, sometimes even incoherent ; but his originality and vivacity caused his work to live.   " His strength lies in his lyric fervour, in the truth of his feeling, in the depth of his inner life, in graphic descriptiveness, in happy illustration from nature, life, his own experience ; . . . he excels in terse sentences, epigrammatically pointed and full of antithesis, which often convey truths far in advance of his time and of almost modern impress." [3]

No attempt can be made here to discuss the writings of Richard of Hampole.   Prof. Horstman has made many of them accessible, and it is understood that Miss H. E. Allen is about to publish the result of her exhaustive researches into his works and those of his followers.   The *Melum* (or *Melos Contemplativorum*) deals with the glory of the saints, and especially of solitaries.   Vehement and sweeping denunciation

[1] *Promptorium Parv.*, ed. Way (Camden S., 1843, 1851, 1865) ; also ed. A. L. Mayhew (E.E.T.S., 1908, E. Ser., 102).

[2] " Officium de S. Ricardo," in *York Breviary*, ii., App. V (Surtees S., 75), trans. D. Harford.

[3] C. Horstman, *R. Rolle*, ii. p. xix.

of abuses stamp it as the work of a youthful reformer, who feels bitterly towards all authority. The *Incendium Amoris* [1] also treats of the contemplative life, but it is devotional rather than controversial, and is mellowed and mature in tone. The writer shows a self-restraint ; and his impassioned love is no less strong, though more serene. So greatly was this work appreciated that it was afterwards (1435) turned into English at the request of Dame Margaret Heslyngton, a recluse—" to the askynge of thi desyre, Systre Margarete," says the translator, Richard Misyn, who is variously described as hermit and as prior of the Carmelites of Lincoln. [2]

The *Incendium Amoris* (like the *Melum*) contains some personal notes. It was written in early manhood, when the experiences set forth in it were fresh in his memory. The writer describes the stages of his inner life—the sinful follies of his youth, the penitence and "lyfe-chaunging," the temptations and self-discipline that followed thereupon, the gradual development of the soul, and its phases of rapture. Nearly three years after his conversion, Richard was sitting in a chapel, delighting in meditation, when he suddenly experienced a strange sensation of the burning heat of spiritual love. Some months later, as he sat in the same chapel singing his evening psalms, he heard the sound of chanting above him and himself burst into ecstatic song (see Frontispiece). Earnestly desiring to kindle in all manner of folk the same unquenchable love, he makes it the subject of a book, offered not to philosophers and divines "lappyd in questions infenyte, bot unto boystus and untaght, more besy to con lufe god then many thinges to knawe".

Richard Rolle was a voluminous writer, and his works, transcribed into other than his native northern dialect, were scattered far and wide. The possessions of Lord Scrope, named in his will (1415) included the *Incendium Amoris* and also "an exposition on *Judica me Deus* which Richard the hermit composed and wrote." The monastery of Syon, which possessed many of his books, treasured a *Melum*, written with his own hand. [3] He is reputed to have written Meditations on

---

[1] A critical edition of the Latin texts is being prepared by Miss M. Deanesly.

[2] *Fire of Love* (E.E.T.S., Orig. Ser., 106), p. 104 ; facsimile, facing p. 103.

[3] M. Bateson, *Syon Library*, 102 ; see also H. E. Allen, *Athenæum*, 23 Aug., 1913.

the Passion, and Treatises on the Ten Commandments, on the Paternoster, and on Prayer, besides paraphrases and expositions of Scripture in English. The *Pricke of Conscience*, which has long been attributed to him,[1] contains counsels to the soul upon life, death, and judgment. In a church at York (All Saints', North Street) is a window depicting the end of the world (Plate XXXVI). Below each panel is a couplet from this poem. The representations of fire and flood, earthquake and falling stars, of the rending of tombs and coming together of bones, are quaint but vivid, and they follow the author's description of the last fifteen days.[2]

The compiler of the *Officium de S. Ricardo* describes the influence of Richard Rolle as a devotional writer :—

"Admirable, indeed, and very useful, were the occupations of this holy man—in holy exhortations by which he converted a very great number to God ; in his mellifluous writings and treatises and little books composed for the edification of his fellow-Christians, which should all re-echo the sweetest harmony in the hearts of the devout."

Richard of Hampole excelled in books of instruction and devotion composed for religious persons, and particularly for solitaries. A careful scribe who collected his works cites the source from which his text of the *Judica me Deus* is derived. It was copied from a book in the possession of a hermit whom he had visited at Christmastide in 1409 : *Ricardus heremita dixit in libro quem habuit heremita de Tanfeld.*[3] The *Commentary on the Psalter* was written at the request of Margaret Kirkby, the recluse of Ainderby. To the same lady, his " dear disciple," was dedicated the letter of sympathetic advice, called the *Form of Perfect Living* (p. 98), which became a popular tract. He bids her, however, not to covet books overmuch : " hold love in heart and in work, and thou hast all that we may say or write ".

Mention must be made of a work occurring in whole or in part in many manuscripts, which sometimes purports to be a

---

[1] Since going to press, my attention has been called to the valuable monograph by Miss Allen on *The Authorship of the " Prick of Conscience "*. She does not consider R. Rolle to be the author, or even the translator, of this poem.

[2] See *An Old York Church : All Hallows in North Street.*

[3] Bodl. MS. 861, f. 102. Also Trin. Coll., Dublin, MS. A. 6, 9 [per Miss M. Deanesly].

PLATE XXXVI

"PRICK OF CONSCIENCE" WINDOW, YORK

"boke maad of Rycharde hampole heremyte to an Ankeresse".[1] It contains ninety-one chapters, and that numbered eighty-three is entitled : "How an anker schal haue [behave] hyr to hem that comen to hir". The work is none other than Hilton's treatise upon the contemplative life, called *The Scale of Perfection* (p. 99).

Walter Hilton was an Austin canon of Thurgarton, and died in 1396. The following account of one "Walter the recluse," which occurs in a catalogue of "English Learned Men that were Augustin Friers," may possibly refer to Walter Hilton, although the otherwise unknown friar is said to have flourished in 1280, a century before the Augustinian canon :—

"Walter the Recluse, educated among, and afterwards became one of the Eremites of St. Augustine, and being already sufficiently instructed in Secular Learning, he apply'd himself to Divinity, and became a great Proficient in both Heads, being put to teach others, he succeeded so well, that many of his Scholars became notable Doctors. But whilst he liv'd Recluse from Human Conversation, being much addicted to Solitary Life, he wrote *Pious Meditations : Of a Solitary Life: Of the Contempt of the World.*"[2]

The works of Richard Rolle and Walter Hilton were much appreciated by anchoresses, who were often well-educated women. The ladies for whom the *Ancren Riwle* had been written were bidden to read books of devotion in English or French. Reading was encouraged as a relief and help to the oppressed spirit :—

"Often, dear sisters, ye ought to pray less, that ye may read more. Reading is good prayer. Reading teacheth how, and for what, we ought to pray; and prayer afterwards obtaineth it. In reading, when the heart feels delight, devotion ariseth, and that is worth many prayers. St. Jerome saith, *Let holy reading be always in thy hand. Sleep may fall upon thee as thou lookest thereon, and the sacred page meet thy drooping face ;* and thus long and intently must thou read. Everything, however, may be overdone. Moderation is always best."

[1] Bodl. MS., Laud, 602. In another MS. (in private hands) R. is credited with the authorship.

[2] J. Stevens, Continuation of Dugd. *Monast.* II. 216. Tanner cites B.M. Cott. Faust. B. VI. as *Pious Contemplations of Walter Hylton, anchorite.* This manuscript, falsely ascribed to W. H., deals with solitary saints, and contains the paintings reproduced in Frontispiece and Plate VI.

12

We owe to an anchoress of Lynn a fragmentary mystical work, and to an anchoress of Norwich, one of the finest contributions to sacred literature. About Margery Kempe nothing is known but what we can glean from the treatise upon contemplation "taken out of the boke of Margerie Kempe of Lynn". Of this fragment no manuscript is known. One copy alone has been traced, a tiny quarto of eight pages, printed by Wynkyn de Worde about 1501, preserved in the University Library, Cambridge. This was reprinted with slight variations by H. Pepwell in 1521,[1] and he appended this note : " Here endeth a short treatise of a devout ancress called Margery Kempe of Lynn". In the dialogues between her soul and God, she reveals herself as a zealous self-disciplined woman, eager to suffer more for His sake, but restrained from undue asceticism and outward observances by her realization of His desire for her love alone. We learn how she overcame her loathing of lepers (p. 121); with what sympathy she regarded suffering even in animals ; how earnestly she desired that there should be more priests in Lynn to conduct God's worship ; how she agonized in prayer for men and women of evil life, and also " for all Jews and Saracens, and all heathen people, that they should come to Christian faith". During the fourteenth and fifteenth centuries, there were several anchorages in Lynn (see Appendix), but which was the abode of Margery the mystic is so far unknown.

Even of Dame Julian of Norwich we know comparatively little, but happily her record of religious experience is complete. The *Revelations of Divine Love* describe with considerable skill and power certain "shewings" vouchsafed to her during the severe illness of which mention has already been made. Two distinct versions of this work are found.[2] Mr. Harford has recently edited the shorter and simpler one which he considers to be the original. The more elaborate version (which has eighty-six chapters instead of twenty-five) omits some trifling details of the illness, but is in every other respect considerably fuller. Julian herself tells us that almost twenty

---

[1] Reissued in *Cell of Self-Knowledge*, ed. E. G. Gardner, XIX. pp. 51-9.

[2] *Comfortable Words for Christ's Lovers*, ed. Dundas Harford [Amherst MS., B.M. Addit. 37790]; *Revelations of Divine Love*, ed. Grace Warrack [B.M. Sloane 2449].

years after the time of the showing, she was still deriving instruction from it, and was gradually learning its meaning.

The Amherst MS. is inscribed with these words :—

" Here is a vision, showed by the goodness of God to a devout woman, and her name is Julian, that is recluse at Norwich, and yet is on life, anno domini mccccxiij. In the which vision are full many comfortable words, and greatly stirring to all that desire to be Christ's lovers."

Julian was an anchoress at St. Julian's, Norwich, a church which was under Carrow nunnery. She was a humble woman, with no opinion of the intellectual and spiritual gifts, which caused a later writer to describe her as *theodidacta, profunda, ecstatica*. She calls herself " a simple creature, unlettered ".

" God forbid that ye should say, or take it so, that I am a teacher, for I mean not so—no, I meant never so. For I am a woman unlearned, feeble, and frail ; but I know well this that I say I have it of the showing of Him that is Sovereign Teacher. But truly charity stirs me to tell you it. For I would God were known, and my even-Christians sped, as I would be myself, to the more hating of sin and loving of God. But, because I am a woman, should I therefore leave [it alone], that I should not tell you the goodness of God, since I saw in the same time that it is His will that it be known ? Then shall ye soon forget me that am a wretch, and do so that I let you not, and behold Jesus that is Teacher of all." [1]

The central scene of the Vision is Christ's Passion—in the light of which Julian ever after interprets all the mystery of life. The problems of the existence of evil and pain had long weighed upon her pure, compassionate spirit : " Thus, in my folly, afore this time often I wondered why by the great foreseeing wisdom of God the beginning of sin was not letted : for then, methought, all should have been well ". She was shown that sin was permitted because it was " behovable " : and that " all manner of thing shall be well ". Still was her heart troubled : " Ah, how might all be well, for the great hurt that is come, by sin, to the creature ? " Then did Christ make clear to her that all sin and suffering should surely be turned to profit by virtue of His Passion.

[1] *Comfortable Words*, p. 41-2.

Dame Julian reveals the secret " beholdings " and " be-seechings " of her own soul.   Now she unfolds high aspirations :
"God, of Thy Goodness, give me Thyself . . . and if I ask any thing that is less, ever me wanteth ".   Now she utters the agonized longing of her heart, and asks relief in her intense yearning for the welfare of a friend's soul : " I desired to learn assuredly as to a certain creature that I loved, if it should con-tinue in good living, which I hoped by the grace of God was begun ".   This human thirst for fuller knowledge was not to be satisfied, nevertheless she was taught not to be greatly dis-tressed for any manner of thing : " for all shall be well ".   Her-self secure in love and strong in faith, she explains faith thus –
"It is nought else but a right understanding, with true belief, and sure trust, of our being : that we are in God, and God in us, whom we see not ".

As to the full meaning of the revelation, Julian expressly tells us that it only dawned upon her gradually as she medi-tated upon this, the supreme experience of her life :—

" And from that time that it was shewed, I desired oftentimes to learn what was our Lord's meaning.   And fifteen years after, and more, I was answered in ghostly understanding, saying thus : *Wouldst thou learn thy Lord's meaning in this thing?   Learn it well : Love was His meaning.   Who shewed it thee ?   Love.   What shewed He thee ?   Love.   Wherefore shewed it He ?   For Love.   Hold thee therein and thou shalt learn and know more in the same.   But thou shalt never know nor learn therein other thing without end.*   Thus was I learned that Love was our Lord's meaning." [1]

Symon " the Anker of London Wall " was enclosed at the city church of Allhallows.   " Sir Symon " or " Master Anker " is frequently mentioned in the churchwardens' accounts.   He was the compiler of *The Fruyte of Redempcyon*,[2] an English manual containing meditations on the life of Christ, with ap-propriate prayers and thanksgivings.   The woodcut reproduced in the text (Fig. 7) is from this work : within a church, a priest (doubtless intended for the author) kneels at the feet of Christ. The book is introduced by Symon to his readers thus :—

---

[1] *Revelations*, chap. LXXXVI.
[2] Printed by W. de Worde, 1514, 1530, 1532.   Reprinted in facsimile by **Mr.** Welch in *Churchwardens' Accounts of Allhallows*.

" Here foloweth prayers and full deuoute contemplacyons with thankynges of all the benefytes gyuen to mankynde, and specyally in the werke of our redempcyon, of the incarnacyon and passyon of cryste, called the fruyte of redempcyon.   And fyrst it putteth a prayer to moue the mynde of man to laude god."

FIG. 7.—Symon " the Anker of London Wall ".

What the pious priest saw " with the inward eye of his mind," that he set down for the help of the others, knowing that there were few books of devotion in the vulgar tongue.   One example will suffice to indicate the manner of his teaching.   A short meditation " Of the oblacyon of the thre holy kynges," closes with this prayer : " Benygne Jesu I praye ye to sende me grace spyrytually to offre these gyftes to the.   The pure golde of perfite loue.   The swete encens of deuoute prayer. And the clene myrre of mortyfycacyon of my frayle flesshe." In the postscript the anchorite adds a personal touch, and pleads for the prayers of such as had derived benefit from his work :—

" O all ye seruauntes of god vnto whose handes this deuoute lytell treatyse shall come, yf ye fynde swetnesse or deuocyon in Jhesu cryste therby, laude ye god therfore, and of your charyte praye for the Anker of London wall wretched Symon, that to the honour of Jhesu cryst and of the virgyn his moder Mary hath compyled this mater in englysshe for your ghostly conforte that vnderstande no latyn.

Deo gracias."

The book was put forth with the approval of the Bishop of London, Richard Fitzjames (1506-22), who stated that he had himself studiously read it, and recommended it to all true servants of Christ—" to theyr great consolacyon and ghostly conforte, and to the merytes of the deuoute fader compounder of the same ".

Here then, at the eve of the Reformation, we leave Symon, the last of our literary recluses, a simple student of the Scriptures.

XIV. THE SIXTEENTH CENTURY

Ther was an Ancres with hom I had not a lytyll besynes to have her grauntt to cum owte, but owte she is.—Commissioners' Report, Worcester.

There ys a chappell . . . which in tyme past hath ben an hermitage, wherein a pore impotent man, sometyme heremyte thereof, doth dwel not able to pay the rent.—Chantry Survey, Tadcaster.

ALTHOUGH in the sixteenth century recluses were not so numerous as formerly, they were still to be found in many churches and religious houses ; e.g. at Wakefield, York, Lincoln, Norwich, London (Bishopsgate), Westminster, and other places. Elizabeth, queen of Henry VII, made gifts to women enclosed at St. Albans and at Gloucester ; Katherine of Aragon gave alms to the anchoress of Stamford and to the anchorite of Marlborough ; and the pensioners of Henry VIII included " ancres ".[1] Many other instances are found in wills. A Somerset testator (1523) leaves : " To the Ancresse of Crookehorne, 40*d.* and a pair of shetes. To the Ermytt there, 3*s.* 4*d.* and a pair of shetes." At Faversham " my Lady ankeris " was succeeded by a male recluse ; Cromwell's *Remembrances* (1529-31) included petitions from the anker of Faversham and from his sister, Ann Sawsten, and as late as 1541, a legacy was made to Sir Thomas Crakynthorpe, anker. A will of 1538-9 shows that there were ankers both at the White Friars and Black Friars of Lynn.[2]

To such benefactions there was usually added a request for intercessory prayer ; e.g. at Faversham (1519) : " To the Ancres in the churchyard to the intent she shall pray for my soul and all Christian souls, 4*d.* " ; and at Sandwich (1535) : " To the Ancras being at Our Lady Church in Sandwich to pray for my soul, 6*s.* 8*d.*". Sums of money were bequeathed

---

[1] Nicolas, *Privy Purse Exp.*, 1, 67, 102 ; *L. and P. Hen. VIII*, IV., pt. iii., p. 2732 ; III., pt. ii., p. 1545.
[2] Consist. Court, Norwich, Reg. " Godsalve," f. 269.

to the priest enclosed in the Austin Friary at Northampton, known as "the ancre of our lady of Grace," or "the Armett of Saynt Austens". The parson of Creaton gave 20*d.* "to the good father Anker for to say v massys of ye v woundes of our Lord Jesu cryste'". At the time of the surrender of the house, Robert Barrett was anchorite.

The cell, as a recognized part of the chantry system, was doomed at the Dissolution of Monasteries. The inmates were quickly disposed of. In vain the nuns of Polesworth, with their abbess and an "ancress"—reported by the commissioners as women of a very religious sort—intimated their desire to continue there or to be transferred to other houses (1536). They were allowed, indeed, to buy a brief respite, but in 1539 they were forced to surrender. One of the nuns, possibly the recluse herself, was close upon 100 years old, and the commissioners themselves begged the Court of Augmentations to ratify pensions to all : " for most of them are aged, impotent, or friendless ".[1] The solitary Dominican sister at Worcester was dismissed under compulsion with a feint of acquiescence. The official visitor of the Blackfriars wrote to Thomas Cromwell that he had not a little business to get her out, " but owte she is ".

The Dominican anchoress of Norwich came under the influence of Thomas Bilney, the Protestant reformer, who presented her with a copy of the New Testament translated by Tyndale, and also with a book called the *Obedience of a Christian Man*, which was amongst those prohibited by Bishop Tunstall. When Bilney was convicted of heresy, there was a danger lest she should be incriminated. When therefore he was about to suffer for his faith at Norwich (1531), he made a solemn declaration at the stake, which was recorded by one who was present :—

" And where as that the lady Ankeres of the blak freres is put in grete trouble and surmysed that she shuld be an heretike and that I shuld teche and instructe her with heresyes as well by bookes as otherwise. Good cristen people here I take my deth upon it that I doo knowe her but for a good and vertuous woman. I beseeche god to preserue her in her goodnes. And I know non heresy in her nor I neuer taught her heresy. I wold god there were many more so good lyvyng in vertue as she is both men and women." [2]

---

[1] *L. and P. Hen. VIII*, x. No. 1191 (2).
[2] Foxe, *Acts and Mon.*, ed. Townsend, IV. 642, App. iii.

In all probability she was the " Kateryn Man late recluse in the house of the late Blak Freres " to whom in 1548 a pension of 20s. was granted by the Corporation for life, on condition that she relinquished such right as she had in the " ancressehouse ". Two years later the civic assembly passed another resolution : " It is agreed and graunted that Katheryn Manne syngle-woman shall have fre libertye to occupie within this cittie so long as she shall kepe her shoppe and be soole and unmarryed ". Some recluses, old and feeble, were dependent upon the alms of those who had known them in the old days ; thus in 1546-7 the parson of All Saints', Norwich, bequeathed 6s. 8d. to Mistress Kydman,[1] sometime anchoress of Carrow.

Buildings were disposed of in various ways. The " Ankeresse House" at Exeter was granted with St. John's hospital into private hands, whilst the " late ancres of Excettour," Alice Buttes, received an annuity from the Crown. The cell at Allhallows, London Wall, was suppressed in 1538, and was given to the City sword-bearer. In 1516, there had been an anchoress living at St. John's chapel, Wakefield, but a century later Dodsworth speaks of it as " now translated into a laythe (i.e. barn), on the south side wherof ther is a hollow place yett extant in the wall wher [an] anchoret lived ".[2] Such tenements were occasionally put to parochial uses, and became a vestry, or, as at Gateshead, a school. The four rooms at Chester-le-Street were occupied by widows, who paid a few shillings a year to the churchwardens. In 1619 these buildings were granted to the curate, but in 1626 the parish paid his house rent elsewhere " in lieu that formerly he solie have had the anchorage, which is imployed to support the poor ".[3]

There were hermits, too, scattered up and down the country during these years preceding the Dissolution of Religious Houses. Road and bridge hermits were still doing useful work, and were popular objects of charity. The private accounts of Sir Henry Willoughby in 1521 show "rewards" paid to the " armytts " called Egerton and Mytton, and to the " armytts " of Bindon and Polesworth ; and as late as 1542 he

---

[1] At the bishop's visitation in 1514, the sub-prioress had complained " that Dame Margaret Kidman is unkind ".

[2] *Church Notes* (Rec. Ser., 34), 51.

[3] W. O. Blunt, *Church in Chester-le-Street*, 13-5.

gave twopence to a poor hermit at the gates.[1] Persons travelling would give alms to hermits on the highway. Henry VIII
on a journey "paied in almes to an heremyte upon the waye"
4s. 8d. He also allowed £3 6s. 8d. to the hermit of Deptford
towards the repair of his chapel.[2]

The enterprising hermit of Lydd seems to have made
himself indispensable to the town, and to have remained on
at the hermitage from 1520 to 1558 in the capacity of agent in
connexion with church restoration.[3] John Bate supplied loads
of gravel, and even lead for the roofing of the chancel, e.g. :—

"1532. Itm receuyd of father armyte for Half a C and
20 lb. of Lede, 4s. 8d.

"1538-9. It pd. to the hermyte for certen Stonys of hym
Bought for to Amend the churche Wall, 2s. 8d."

But whilst some were honest, hard-working men, others
were idle and greedy of gain (pp. 61-2). William Thorpe, the
Lollard, had spoken in his *Testament* (1460) of " heremites and
pardoners, ankers and straunge beggers " who had leave to
defraud the poor.[4] There was some truth in his complaint,
for the system of indulgences was frequently applied to their
support, and some undoubtedly held positions which were
connected with superstitious uses. In 1443, for example, the
pope offered an indulgence to penitents who should visit and
give alms to a chapel[5] in the parish of Stalham, dedicated to
St. Andrew " at which John Kylburn, a hermit, has long
dwelt, and whither resorts a great multitude out of reverence
for the said saint, by whose merits divers of those who visit it
have been delivered from diseases ". Pilgrims to Bawburgh
were wont to resort to the oratory of the hermit near the
bridge, and after mass he " attended them to the town, sprinkling them with hyssop and holy water ". Another instance of
such service occurs at Hinxton, in the neighbouring county of
Cambridge. An Elizabethan inquisition on concealed lands
reported as follows :—

[1] *Hist. MSS. (Middleton)*, 1911 ; 331, 335-6, 346, 389.
[2] *Privy Purse Exp.* 42, 273 ; *L. and P. Hen. VIII*, v., p. 749.
[3] A. Finn, *Records of Lydd*, 346, 359, 376, 381-2, etc.
[4] Foxe, *Actes and Mon.*, ed. 1583, p. 543.
[5] Probably at the place now called Chapel field.

"We find lykwise that an Ermite . . . dwellinge there did cast hollywater on them that came to him fortye yeares sithence and tooke the proffitts thereof. . . . But whether the sayd howse and close were given or used to anye other superstitious use before or since that tyme we knowe not."

A similar commission held in the county of Northampton elicited the information that at Beston [1] in Brampton Ash there was a hermitage called the chapel of St. Augustine, where pilgrimage used to be made to an image of that saint, and where mass was many times celebrated in a superstitious manner. Pilgrimage was also made to the hermitage at Little Harrowden, whereof the hermit-chaplain, Sir Thomas, was the recipient of numerous bequests in the reign of Henry VIII.

The hermitage at Southampton, situated near the old ferry over the Itchen, was frequented by pilgrims ; the present Chapel Road was once the "causey of our Lady of Grace". Henry VII's charter presents a curious admixture of secular and spiritual interests. "Considering that by a confluence of our subjects and others the town may be greatly improved and advanced in wealth and prosperity," a yearly fair of several days' duration is granted to the mayor and burgesses, as also to William Gefferey, hermit of the chapel of the Holy Trinity and the Blessed Mary, "in which chapel the said glorious Virgin is very frequently honoured by the faithful". In 1510, Henry VIII visited this place and gave 6s. 8d. in alms.

The hermit of Colnbrook, near Windsor, was guardian of another shrine in honour of the Blessed Virgin. Elizabeth of York made an offering of 8d. at "Our Lady of Cabroke," and gave the same day to the hermit in alms 12d.

The chapel of Court at Street in Aldington sprang into fame about the year 1525 through its connexion with the "Holy Maid of Kent". Before becoming a nun at Canterbury, Elizabeth Barton had lived at Aldington. There she was visited with sickness which manifested itself in seizures and trances accompanied by wild speeches, and resulted (so says the statute-book) in "wekeness of her brayne". The parson of Aldington, Richard Master, encouraged the woman

---

[1] Or Bedstow. Sir John Holt of Brampton by Dingley by will dated 25 March, 1419-20, leaves " to the emendation of the hermitage of Bedstowe, xl s.' '. Linc. Reg. Repyndon, *Mem.* f. 190 *d.*

to believe herself inspired, and spread exaggerated reports, with intent to increase the number of pilgrims to the chapel " for hys own lucre and advauntage ".   Instigated to play the prophetess, she predicted that if the King's marriage with Anne Boleyn took place, she should be burnt and he would die a villain's death.   An immense crowd gathered at the chapel, in whose presence the nun became rapt :—

> " At her next voyage to our Lady of Court of Strete, she entred the Chappell with *Ave Regina Cælorum* in pricksong. . . . There fell she eftsoones into a marveilous passion before the Image of our Lady, much like a bodie diseased of the falling Evill, in the which she uttered sundry metricall and ryming speeches, tending to the worship of our Lady of Court of Strete, whose Chappell there shee wished to be better mainteined, and to be furnished with a daily singing Priest."

A hermit-chaplain, Sir William, was duly appointed, and "the Heremite was enriched by daily offering ".   When the fame of the place was at its height (1528) a typical bequest was made by Isabel, Lady Poynings :—

> "To the herymete of Curte of Strete vj*s*. viii*d*.   To our Lady Chapel . . . a yard and two nails and a half of cloth of gold, for a vestment." [1]

The chaplain himself was the subject of one of the nun's " revelations ".   Whilst she was at Canterbury, and he at Aldington, she announced " what meate the Heremite had to his supper, and many other things concerning him," whereat people marvelled greatly.   Lambarde's account, in his *Perambulation of Kent*, was written within thirty-six years of these events.

Elizabeth Barton herself may have been the victim of hallucinations, but her aiders and abetters who compiled the rolls of prophecies, were certainly guilty of fraud.   Bidden by an angel, she visited Henry VIII himself : possibly she told him the story repeated by Chapuys in a letter to Charles V, namely, that she had seen the seat prepared for him in hell (cf. p. 160).   She confessed many mad follies to the archbishop, but desired permission to go again to Court at Street,

---

[1] *Test. Vetusta*, 634.

and "there have a trance, and then know perfectly". At length she admitted her treason against God and the King, and publicly confessed her falsehoods at Paul's Cross. Cranmer declared, in 1533, that the feigned revelations of the false nun were had in abomination; and Sir Thomas More—who had once thought her pious, albeit strange and childish—now regarded her as "the wicked woman of Canterbury". Elizabeth Barton, the parson of Aldington, and their accomplices, were imprisoned, convicted of high treason, and executed (April,

Fig. 8.—Chapel of our Lady, Court-at-Street.

1534): "This day the nun of Kent, with two Friars Observant, two monks, and one secular priest, were drawn from the Tower to Tyburn, and there hanged and beheaded ".[1] The hermit escaped, but disappears from public notice. His ruined chapel, the scene of all this excitement, is still standing (Fig. 8).

One of the last of the Kentish hermits, an intelligent and hard-working man who dwelt by Richborough Castle, was visited by Leland and commended by him: "I had Antiquites of the Heremite the which is an industrius Man".

The last tenant of the hermitage near Southwick was Prior

[1] L. and P. Hen. VIII (1528-34); Act 25 Hen. VIII, c. 12.

William Noxton, who took refuge there from the sweating sickness (1534). Writing to Lady Lisle he says that the visitation of God is very sore, and that his letter is " scribbled with a comfortless heart in the eremitical habitation of St. Leonard ". In 1544, St. Leonard's Armytage, consisting of house, chapel, garden and closes, was disposed of by the Crown.

The last solitary of Sherborne died a few months before the expulsion of the monks from the abbey. One of the earliest entries in the parish register is the burial of William Howell, hermit of St. John the Baptist (1538). When visiting this town, Leland noted that "there was an heremitage of S. John by the mylle, now down ". Human bones have been found in the plot of ground near the saw-mill, still called " St. Jone's ".

There were a few survivors of the old days, in places not easily accessible to state officials. About the time of the suppression of Holme Cultram Abbey, in Cumberland, the following notice occurs : " There is a chapel called St. Cuthbert's Chapel with two garths containing one acre in the occupation of Richard Stanley hermit there, with a little moss thereunto belonging ". The Survey of Yorkshire chantries includes the pathetic memorandum concerning Tadcaster :—

"There ys a chappell in the sayd parishe, covered with stone, which in tyme past hath ben an hermitage, wherein a pore impotent man, sometyme heremyte thereof, doth dwel not able to pay the rent ; which chappell with th' appertenances ys worth to be letten by yere as appereth by the rentall, vj *s.* viij *d.*".

In the case of the last chaplain of Warkworth hermitage, the grant made by the Earl of Northumberland to Sir George Lancastre (p. 48) was ratified by the Court of Augmentations in 1537, save that in lieu of twenty marks, he was to receive ten marks yearly, with the profits of the Rood chapel, and of St. Leonard's hospital at Wigton. Before 1567, the place had ceased to be occupied. Clarkson's Survey observes that :—

"Ther is in the parke also one howse hewyn within one cragge, which is called the harmitage chapel : in the same ther haith bene one preast keaped, which such godlye services as that tyme was used and celebrated. The mancion howse ys nowe in decay : the closes

PLATE XXXVII

WARKWORK HERMITAGE

that apperteined to the said chantrie is occupied to his lordship's use." [1]

If, indeed, any solitary remained in his cell after the Dissolution of Monasteries (1536-9), he was almost inevitably homeless after the Suppression of the Chantries in 1546. It was reported in 1548 that the chapel of Horteley in Batheaston " wherein an Armyte sometyme dwelled " had for the last twelve years been inhabited by another tenant.

St. Brandan's chapel at Bristol—reported by Leland to be " now defacyd "—was secured by the town clerk, who built a windmill in its place. The site (which became a fort in the Civil Wars) is now occupied by the Cabot Tower. The chapel near Plymouth is referred to in 1591 as a barn and messuage called " the hermytage of our ladie at Quarrywell ". St. John's chapel, which had belonged to Tavistock Abbey—" a little cottage much ruyned, with two little garden plotts "—was used in the seventeenth century first as a pest-house and then as a poor-house. The premises of Malmesbury Abbey, sold in 1544, included " St. White's Armitage " upon Burton Hill. Leland mentions another " in the Dike of the Toune at the West Ende of the old Paroche Chirche," that is, in the Avon valley, south of Malmesbury. In the following century Aubrey noticed several ancient buildings, which looked like hermitages, about Malmesbury and Westport. In the parish of Stanton St. Quintin " stood a very fine hermitage, moted about in an oaken wood ". Alluding to a ruined chapel at Yatton Keynes, Aubrey says : " I think there was a Hermitage by it, but a pleasanter romancy place I know not easily where to find ".

The solitary now belonged to a bygone age—the true solitary, that is, for the " ornamental hermits " of the pseudo-gothic revival belong to a wholly different category. Recluses were swept away by the flood which carried off all that was in any way connected with monasticism. They had, however, fulfilled their purpose and justified their existence. They were not a class composed wholly of eccentric and fanatical, or selfish and morbid persons who shirked the duties of life. They were often men and women of strong and saintly character

[1] Percy's *Reliques*, ed. 1858, III. 333.

whose life commanded respect and won gratitude from their fellow-men, who recognized them as *workers*.   At its best, the contemplative life was a career and a noble one.   There were of course some whose conduct brought discredit on their profession, but there were others who lived up to the high ideal set forth by one of themselves :—

" Righteous hermits also have a single aim : in charity of God and of their neighbour they live ; worldly praise they despise ; as much as they may, man's sight they flee ; each man more worthy than themselves they hold ; to devotion continually their minds they give ; idleness they hate ; fleshly lusts they manfully withstand ; heavenly things they taste and eagerly seek ; and earthly they covet not but forsake ; in sweetness of prayer they are delighted." [1]

The passionate earnestness of purpose in such a life commands the admiration said to have been expressed in an outburst of enthusiasm by a Protestant moralist, Dr. Johnson : " I never read of a hermit but in imagination I kiss his feet ". Even the most cautious critic of the twentieth century, fearful of idealizing the " Dark Ages," may well echo the words of the hermit of Hampole :—

" Hermetis lyffe therfore is grett, if it gretely be done ".

[1] From Richard Rolle, *Fire of Love*, 29, 30.

APPENDIX A

THE OFFICE FOR THE ENCLOSING OF ANCHORITES
(according to the Use of Sarum)

[*Manuale ad Usum Sarum* (Surtees S. 63), 37*-43*. The office is "Servitium Includendorum," from the York Manual.]

THE SERVICE OF THOSE WHO ARE TO BE ENCLOSED

IN what manner those who approach the order of anchorites ought to approach and to order themselves, that which follows according to the Use of Sarum will make clear. No one ought to be enclosed without the advice of the Bishop ; but let him be taught and warned by the Bishop or some other presbyter that he must devoutly examine his own conscience, and in particular whether he desires holiness with a good or bad purpose, if he desires it to please God or to attain wealth or the praise of men ; lastly whether he have strength and endurance of mind enough to avail against the crafts of the evil enemy, and against manifold mischiefs of that sort. When he shall have promised to bear such things for the kingdom of God, and to set his hope on God alone, let the Bishop, or a presbyter by command of the Bishop, enclose him. But let the one who is enclosed learn not to think highly of himself, as though he deserved to be set apart from the mass of mankind ; but let him rather believe that it is provided and appointed for his own weakness that he should be set far from the companionship of his neighbours, lest by more frequent sin he should both himself perish and do harm to those who dwell with him, and should thus fall into greater damnation. Let him therefore think that he is convicted of his sins and committed to solitary confinement as to a prison, and that on account of his own weakness he is unworthy of the fellowship of mankind. This rule must be observed with both sexes.

HERE BEGINNETH THE ORDER OF ENCLOSING SERVANTS OR HANDMAIDENS OF GOD

Let him who is to be enclosed take care that he be confessed of all his sins which he can remember, and that on the day before the day of his enclosure he be refreshed only with bread and water. On the night following that day, he is bound to watch devoutly in prayer with his light burning in a monastery near his cell. On the morrow, after an exhortation to the people and to the one who is to be enclosed, the Bishop or priest must begin this Responsorium : Let us amend our ways. *The choir goes on—*For the amendment of our sins of ignorance, lest, taken suddenly by the day of death, we seek time for repentance, and find it not. Hear us, O Lord, and have mercy, for we have sinned against thee.

Verse. Help us, O Lord our Saviour, and for the glory of thy name deliver us, O Lord. Hear us, O Lord.

After this the Bishop or Priest prostrating himself on the carpet before the altar shall with the clerks, begin these Psalms: vi, lxxxviiii with Gloria Patri, *xx with* Gloria Patri, *xxxii, xxxv, xxxviii, xli, xliii, lvi, cii, ciii,* 1-5 (only), *cxxx, cxxxi, cxliii.* Lord have mercy upon us. Christ have mercy upon us. Lord have mercy upon us.

Our Father, etc. And lead us not, etc. But deliver, etc.

> O Lord, my God, save thy servant (*or* thy handmaid):
> Which putteth his trust in thee.
> Let not the enemy prevail against him:
> Nor the son of wickedness draw nigh to hurt him.
> Be unto him, O Lord, a strong tower:
> From the face of the enemy.
> Send him help, O Lord, from thy holy place:
> And strengthen him out of Sion.
> O Lord, hear my prayer:
> And let my cry come unto thee.

The Lord be with you. Let us pray.

Spare, O Lord, spare thy servant *N.* whom thou hast redeemed, O Christ, with thy blood, and be not angry with him for ever. Who livest, *etc.*

Another prayer with Let us pray.

O God of boundless mercy and great goodness, forgive his sins and heal all his weakness of soul, that having received forgiveness of all his sins he may rejoice in thy goodness. Through Christ, *etc.*

Let us pray.

Almighty and everlasting God, have mercy on thy servant *N.* and of thy great goodness guide him in the way of eternal life, that by thy grace he may love those things which are pleasing to thee, and may go on from strength to strength.

Prevent us, O Lord, in all our doings with thy gracious favour, and further us with thy continual help, that all our work may be begun, and ended in thee. Through our Lord, *etc.*

After this let the Bishop or Priest vest himself in a Chasuble and let any Mass he wills be at once begun; so that this prayer following be said for the one to be enclosed, with a single Per Dominum, *and a single* Oremus.

O God, who dost cleanse the wicked and willest not the death of a sinner; we humbly beseech thy majesty that in thy goodness thou wilt guard thy servant *N.* who trusteth in thy heavenly aid, that he may ever serve thee, and no trials may part him from thee. Through our Lord, *etc.*

After the Gospel the one who is to be enclosed must offer his taper which must always burn above the altar during the Mass. And the one who is to be enclosed must stand before the altar step and read his profession in a loud voice: if he is a layman some servant must read it for him. The profession must be of this sort:—

I, brother or sister *N.* offer and present myself to the goodness of God to serve in the order of an anchorite ; and according to the rule of that order I promise to remain henceforward in the service of God through the grace of God and the guidance of the church and to render canonical obedience to my spiritual fathers.

Then must the one who is to be enclosed make the sign of the cross on the deed of his profession with a pen, and placing it on his knees upon the altar, let him pray after the Bishop or Priest in this manner:—

Antiphon. Confirm, O Lord, that which thou hast wrought in us, from thy holy temple which is in Jerusalem. Alleluia, Alleluia. Let [God] arise.

Afterwards let the Bishop or Priest say :—

Let us pray.

O God, who dost quicken thy servant who has turned from the vanity of the life of this world to the love of thy heavenly calling ; cleanse the thoughts of his heart, and pour upon him thy heavenly grace, that trusting in thee, and guarded by thy mighty power, he may fulfil that which by thy grace he has promised, and the work of this life well done, he may attain at last to that which thou hast vouchsafed to promise to those who trust in thee. Through Christ, *etc.*

Then shall the Bishop or Priest bless the habit suitable to his profession with this prayer:—

We mark the sign of our Lord Jesus Christ on this garment that his profession may be kept, and that the Holy Spirit may rule in the heart and soul and in all the doings of him who receives it. Through the same Christ our Lord. Amen.

Then shall he sprinkle both the habit and him who receives it with holy water: and when he gives the habit let him say when it is being put on :—

May God put off from thee the old man with all his works, and may God clothe thee with the new man which after God is created in righteousness and true holiness.

And let all answer: Amen.

When he who is to be enclosed is clad in his habit, let him immediately prostrate himself before the altar step and let him remain thus prostrate in prayer until he be summoned by the Bishop or Priest to communion. After that let the Bishop or Priest chant over him still lying prostrate this hymn :—

Veni, Creator Spiritus, *etc.*

Verse. Send out thy Spirit and they shall be made : and thou shalt renew the face of the earth.

The Lord be with you. And with thy spirit.

Let us pray.

O God, who willest not the death of a sinner, but rather that he should, repent and be cleansed ; we humbly beseech thy mercy for this thy servant who has forsaken the life of the world, that thou wouldest pour upon him the help of thy great goodness that, enrolled among thy chaste ones, he may so run the course of this present life that he may receive at thy hand the reward of an eternal inheritance. Through Christ, *etc.*

Then shall the Bishop or Priest going to the altar finish the Mass for the one who is to be enclosed.

Secreta. We beseech thee, O Lord, that by the power of these holy mysteries thou wilt cleanse us from all our faults, and wilt grant to thy servant *N.* forgiveness of all his sins. Through our Lord, *etc.*

Postcommunio. May the sacraments which we have received, O Lord, make us pure, and grant that thy servant *N.* may be free from every fault, so that he whose conscience by sin is accused may rejoice in the fulness of pardon from on high. Through our Lord.

When the Bishop or Priest shall have communicated, let him also communicate the one to be enclosed. When Mass is finished, let the aforesaid taper be handed to the one who is to be enclosed; and when a procession has been formed, let the Bishop or Priest, vested in a chasuble, go before, then let him take by the hand the one to be enclosed carrying the taper, and let him lead him in goodly sort to his dwelling. Let the clerks meanwhile go before, singing a Litany. When they have reached the dwelling and the Litany is finished, the Bishop or Priest shall leave the one to be enclosed outside the dwelling and shall enter the dwelling alone, beginning, with holy water, the Antiphon Purge me, *or* I saw water, *as time permits.*

Then let him hallow and bless the dwelling with the following prayers.

This prayer shall be said over the altar with Let us pray.

O Lord, holy and merciful Father, who hast neither beginning of days nor end of years, whose greatness is bounded only by thy will ; O God whose majesty the heaven of heavens cannot contain ; we bless thee and humbly beseech thee that this altar may be such an one as that which Abel the forerunner in suffering, being slain by his brother, moistened and hallowed with fresh blood. May this altar be to thee, O Lord, like that which Abraham our father, who was permitted to see thee, made ; on which the High Priest Melchisedech set forth the pattern of a prevailing sacrifice. May this altar be to thee like that which Moses hallowed with seven days' purification and sanctified it with a threefold blessing ; as thou didst say unto him : Whosoever toucheth this altar shall be holy. On this altar then may all wantonness be destroyed, and every lust be smitten down ; and there be offered, instead of turtledoves, the sacrifice of purity, and for young doves the sacrifice of innocence. Through our Lord.

The Blessing on the house :—

Hearken, O Lord, to our prayers, and let the clear light of thy presence shine upon this house. Let a full measure of thy blessing fall upon those who dwell therein by thy grace, that, dwelling in all sobriety in these temples made with hands, they may ever be temples of thy Spirit. Through Christ our Lord. Amen.

Another prayer with Let us pray.

Hear us, O Lord, Holy Father, eternal God, that if there be any thing against us or opposed to us in this house of thy servant *N.* it may be cast out by the power of thy divine majesty.   Through our Lord Jesus Christ, thy Son, who with thee liveth and reigneth, In the unity.

Another with Let us pray.

Bless ✠ O Lord, this house and this place, that in it may dwell health, holiness, chastity, power, victory, devotion, humility, gentleness, meekness, fulfilment of the law and obedience to God, Father, Son, and Holy Ghost. And let a full measure of thy blessing ✠ rest upon this place and upon all who dwell therein in thee, that, dwelling in all sobriety in these temples made with hands, they may ever be temples of thy Spirit.   Through our Lord Jesus Christ thy Son, who with thee liveth and reigneth in the unity of the Holy Spirit One God.

After this, let the Bishop or Priest go forth and lead in the one who is to be enclosed bearing his light, beginning this Responsorium :—

The kingdom of the world.   *The choir goes on*—and all the glory of it have I despised for the love of my Lord Jesus Christ, whom I have seen, whom I have loved, on whom I have believed, whom I have chosen for myself.

Verse.   My heart has indited a good matter : I speak of my work for the King.   Whom I have seen.

When this has been sung with its verse, let the Bishop or Priest say :—

The Lord be with you *and* Let us pray.

We beseech thee, O Lord, Holy Father, almighty and everlasting God, that thou wilt vouchsafe to pour the spirit of blessing upon this thy servant that, endued with power from on high, he may be enabled both to gain thy glorious gifts and to set an example of good living to others.

Response.   Amen.

Also another blessing over him.

May the Lord Jesus Christ be by thy side, to defend thee.   Amen. May he be within thee, to refresh thee.   Amen.   May he be about thee, to keep thee safe.   Amen.   May he be before thee, to lead thee forth. Amen.   May he be above thee, to bless thee.   Amen.   Who with God the Father and the Holy Spirit liveth and reigneth, In the unity.

Another blessing.

May God the Father bless thee.   Amen.   May God the Son preserve thee.   Amen.   May he guard thy body.   Amen.   May he save thy soul. Amen.   May he enlighten thy body.   Amen.   May he direct thy mind. Amen.   And lead thee forth to everlasting life.   Amen.   Who in threefold perfection liveth and reigneth one God for ever and ever.   Amen.

After this, let the Bishop or Priest go forth from the house, the recluse alone remaining within and keeping strict silence, while he is being firmly enclosed from without, and in the meanwhile let the Bishop or Priest begin an Antiphon after this fashion in a loud voice :—

We have received thy mercy, O God, in the midst of thy temple.

Psalms xlviii, cxvi, cxlvii, cl, with Gloria Patri.

Let the Antiphon be repeated.   We have received, O God.

When the Antiphon is finished, let the Bishop or Priest cause them all to pray for him, that Almighty God, for whose love he has left the world, and caused himself to be shut up in a most strait prison, may so guard him and strengthen him in that service, that after death he may be found fit to live with him to all eternity.

Our Father, etc.   And lead us not, etc.   But deliver, etc.

Show forth, O Lord, thy mercy towards us.

That our peace may be in thee.

The Lord be with you.   Let us pray.

We beseech thee, O Lord, to defend this thy servant, and through the intercession of the Blessed Virgin Mary and all the company of heaven, increase in him thy manifold gifts of grace, that being set free from the temptations of this world, he may have help in this life, and in the world to come everlasting joy.   Through Christ.

Let us pray.

Almighty God, unto whom all hearts be open, all desires known, and from whom no secrets are hid, cleanse the thoughts of our hearts by the inspiration of thy Holy Spirit, that we may perfectly love thee and worthily magnify thy holy name.   Through Christ our Lord.   Amen.

Let us pray.

Almighty and everlasting God, guide us, we beseech thee, in all our doings with thy most gracious favour, that in the name of thy beloved Son we may worthily serve thee in all good works.   Who with thee liveth and reigneth in the unity of the Holy Spirit one God for ever and ever.

Then let them all depart to enter into the Church, the Choir singing some Responsorium with its versicle concerning the Saint in whose name and honour the Church is founded, ending at the choir step by the Priest saying a verse and prayer on the same subject.   And if it be a Church of Saint Mary this Responsorium must be said :—

Happy art thou, O holy Maiden Mary, and most worthy of all praise. Because from thee arose the sun of righteousness, Christ our God.   *In Eastertide :* Alleluia.

Verse.   Pray for the people ; mediate for the clergy ; intercede for womenkind who honour thee ; that all who join in thy service may feel thy comfort.   Because from thee arose, etc.

Verse.   Holy Mother of God, Mary ever Virgin.

Strengthen our weakness, we beseech thee, O merciful God, and grant that we who plead in the name of Mary the maiden Mother of God may by the aid of her prayers be freed from all our sins.   Through the same Christ our Lord.

APPENDIX B

THE OFFICE FOR THE BENEDICTION OF HERMITS

(According to the Rule of St. Paul the first Hermit)

[Transcribed by Mr. F. C. Eeles from a sixteenth century Pontifical in his possession. It was written for Thomas, titular Bishop of Lydence, who was suffragan to Richard Fitz James, Bishop of London, in 1521, and afterwards to Cuthbert Tunstall.]

[Folio 68.

*F*orma *et ordo qualiter heremita a seculi vanitate cordialiter conuersus faciet professionem que ab episcopo vel eius commissario fieri potest quocunque celebri festo ad hoc ordinato. Primo episcopus ex more sacris vestibus indutus peragat missam vsque ad euangelium et interim dum* Alleluia *Tractus vel sequenc[ia] dicitur conuersus deuote veniens | in vestibus consuetis portansque scapulare et alia vestimenta* [fo. 68v *professioni heremitice conueniencia super brachium sinistrum incedendo nudis pedibus vsque ad gradum altaris et ibidem nudato capite genuflectendo ea ponat ad pedes episcopi vel eius commissarij. Episcopo statim cum circumstantibus hunc. psalmum. alternatim premittentibus* Miserere mei. | deus secundum magnam misericordiam tuam *cum* gloria patri *et* [fo. 69 sicut erat. *Dicto psalmo episcopus sedendo alloquatur eum de proposito castitatis et examinando de obseruacione regulari eiusdem concensum publice requirendo Declaretque omnia alia que sibi videntur ad salutem anime illius esse oportuna Quibus secundum dei timorem completis legat conuersus professionem | suam vel episcopo ipsum docente dicat* [fo. 69v *hoc modo episcopo in cathedra sedente vultu ad populum conuerso*

Ego N non coniugatus promitto et voueo deo beate marie et omnibus sanctis in presencia reuerendi in christo patris et domini. N.N. episcopi propositum castitatis perpetue iuxta regulam beati pauli. In nomine patris et c[etera]

Deinde faciat signum crucis in fine professionis et tradat episcopo Tunc | dicat episcopus hanc oracionem super eum prostratum [fo. 70.

Oremus

P RAESTA quesumus omnipotens deus huic famulo tuo . N. renuntianti seculi pompis gracie tue ianuas aperi qui despecto diabolo confugit sub titulo christi iube uenientem ad te sereno vultu suscipi ne de eo valeat inimicus triumphare tribue huic infatigabile brauium auxilij tui mentem eius lorica fidei circumda vt/felici muro vallatus mundum se gaudeat euasisse. Per [fo. 70v. dominum.

Oremus

DEUS qui filios israel in heremi solitudine manna ad pascendum celeste quadraginta annis manare fecisti quique vitam heremiticam tam per filium tuum quadraginta diebus et quadraginta noctibus prophetas et sanctos in heremo degentes tibi in heremo placere monstrasti concede propicius vt/famulus tuus . N. similem pro modulo suo eligens vitam sic in [fo. 71 proposito heremitice discipline mores suos mutet aptet et componat quatinus perseueranter proficiens ad huius vite perfeccionem attingere et ad gaudia perfectorum valeat peruenire.   Per eundem

Sequitur benediccio vestium cum

[℣] Dominus vobiscum

℟   Et cum [spiritu tuo].

Oremus

DEUS eternorum bonorum fidelissime promissor certissime /per-   [fo. 71v. solutor qui vestimentum salutare et indumentum iocunditatis tuis fidelibus promisisti clemenciam tuam suppliciter exoramus vt hec indumenta humilitatem cordis et contemptum mundi significandus quibus famulus tuus sancto visibiliter est informandus proposito propicius bene-✠-dicere digneris vt et castitatis habitum quem te inspirante suscepturus est te protegente custodiat et quem vestimen/tis venerande professionis induis perpetualiter beata   [fo. 72 facias inmortalitate vestiri   Per dominum et c[etera]

DEUS bonarum virtutum dator et omnium benediccionum largus infusor exaudi preces nostras vt hanc vestem quam famulus tuus pro conseruande castitatis signo se ad cooperiendum expossit bene✠dicere et consecrare digneris ad laudem et gloriam nominis tui. per christum dominum nostrum   ℟   Amen. /   [fo. 72 v

Deinde aspergatur aqua benedicta et postea det ei habitum episcopus et dum induit dicat.

Exuat te dominus veterem hominem cum actibus suis et induat te nouum hominem qui quit secundum deum creatus est in iusticia et sanctitate veritatis
℟   Deo gracias

Deinde dicat ei episcopus si fuerit literatus vel in materna lingua

FRATER ecce dedimus tibi habitum heremiticum cum quo/monemus   [fo. 73 te viuere caste sobrie et sancte in vigilijs in ieiunijs in laboribus in precibus in misericordie operibus et habeas vitam eternam et viuas in secula seculorum Amen

Cui conuersus . r[espondit]. genuflectendo deuote sic.

Et ego reuerende pater in nomine domini nostri Ihesu christi illum recipio promittens me secundum posse michi a deo collatum uestrum preceptum fideliter seruaturum adiuuante dei gracia et sanctorum eius oracione benigna

Tunc/sequantur benecciones super eum prostratum cum   [fo. 73v

.Oremus.

FAMULUM tuum domine tue custodia muniat pietatis vt castitatis sancte propositum quod te inspirante suscepit te protegente semper illesum custodiat.   Per dominum

Oremus

A DESTO domine supplicacionibus nostris ut hunc famulum tuum bene-
dicere digneris cui in nomine sancto tuo habitum religionis/impo- [fo. 74
nimus vt te largiente et deuotus in ecclesia persistere et vitam per-
cipere meretur eternam. Per dominum

Deinde episcopus conuersus ad orientem dicat hunc ympnum.

U eni creator spiritus. *ut supra in benediccione vidue et dicatur vsque
ad finem. deinde dicatur*

K yrieleyson
C hristeleyson
K yrieleyson
Pater noster
[℣.] Et ne nos [inducas in temptacionem].
[℞.] Sed libera [nos a malo. Amen.]
[℣.] Saluum fac/seruum tuum. [fo. 74v
[℞. Deus meus sperantem in te.]
[℣.] Mitte domine ei auxilium de sancto.
[℞. Et de syon tuere eum.]
[℣.] Esto ei domine turris fortitudinis.
[℞. A facie inimici eius.]
[℣.] Domine exandi [oracionem meam].
[℞. Et clamor meus ad te veniat.]
[℣.] Dominus vobiscum.
[℞. Et cum spiritu tuo.]

Oremus

A DESTO quesumus omnipotens deus famulo tuo de tua misericordia con-
fidenti eumque tua proteccione custodi vt a cunctis aduersitatibus
liberatus benediccione eterna dignus inueniatur. Per christum dominum.

D EUS qui iustificas impium et non vis mortem pec/catoris [fo. 75
maiestatem tuam supplices deprecamur vt famulum tuum . N. de tua
misericordia confidentem celesti protegas benignus auxilio et assidua
proteccione conserues ut tibi iugiter famuletur et nullis temptacionibus a te
separatur. Per christum dominum

O MNIPOTENS sempiterne deus miserere famulo tuo et dirige eum secundum clemenciam tuam in viam salutis eterne vt te do/nante tibi [fo. 75v
placita cupiat et tota virtute perficiat et omnipotens dominus te benedicat
et graciam bene viuendi tibi tribuat et ad vitam eternam perducat   Per christum

Deinde benedicat eum episcopus genuflectentem sic dicendo

B enedicat te omnipotens deus pate ✠ *et filius* ✠ *et spiritus* ✠ *sanctus.*

*S ed antequam recedat quia sub aliqua regula certa viuere minime
de|bet coartari ideo ne ignorans ignoretur exponatur ei modus* [fo. 76
*viuendi cum eius obseruancia speciali.   Primo iniungitur ei episcopus vt
palam et publice dicat. oracionem. dominicam salutacionemque euangelicam
et fidei simbolum quibus ab omnibus perfecte auditis det sibi episcopus in*

mandatis quod pro qualibet hora diei statut[a] *ab ecclesia certum dicat |
numerum oracionum pro salute anime sue et omnium benefactorum* [fo. 76v
*suorum deuote impetranda videlict primo pro vesperis xx*ᵃ Pater noster *cum
totidem* Aue maria *pro completorio xiij* pater noster *cum totidem* Aue maria *pro
matutinis.* xxx pater noster *cum totidem* Aue maria *pro laudibus.* xv pater noster
cum totidem Aue maria *pro hora prima* xxiiij pater noster *cum totidem* Aue
ma/ria *pro qualibet hora videlicet iij*ᵃ *vj*ᵃ *et ix*ᵃ xv pater noster *cum* [fo. 77
totidem Aue maria *In ferialibus vero diebus dicet pro placebo.* l. pater noster
cum totidem Aue maria. *pro dirige* xxxiij pater noster *cum totidem* Aue maria
pro commendacione xxiiij pater noster *cum totidem.* Aue maria. *zymbolum
vere suum singulis diebus cum noctibus dicat xiij vicibus et cotidie audiat
missam Si vero fuerit literatus ita quod sciat | dicere horas beate* [fo. 77v
*marie virginis cum vij psalmis et letania ac placebo et dirige pro defunctis.
Extunc cum qualibet horarum illarum dicat ter* Pater noster *cum* Aue
maria *et cum dimidio Nocturni. psalterij semel in die omnibus alijs
pretermissis. Et quia ociositas inimica est anime et ne diabolus eum
inueniat ociosum suis labori manibus temporibus inter medijs circa
vic/tualia acquirenda aut vias et pontes firmiter construendas* [fo. 78
*In aduentu domini et in xl*ᵃ *ac decem diebus ante pentecosten abstineat a
carnibus vt in fine eorum communicetur confessione semper precedente In
omnibus ferijs quartis piscibus vtatur vel lacticineis Et in feria sexta
ieiunet pane et aqua nisi pro graui infirmitate aut nimio labore
secum | dispensetur In sabbato ieiunabit solis contentu piscibus* [fo. 78v.
*lineis vti non licebit exceptis femoralibus pedulis eciam cum sotularibus
solum vti debet caligis semper omissis Et post habitum ex ordinacione
episcopi sibi competentur datum in nomine domini recedat in pace.*

APPENDIX C

TABULATED LIST OF CELLS

EXPLANATION OF HEADINGS, REFERENCES

Description.   i.e. dedication or situation of cell.
H.   = hermit, hermitage.
A.   = anchorite (male or female), anchorage.
Date.   i.e. the earliest accredited reference; $c.$ = circa; c. = century; *bef.* = before; *tp.* = temp.
Patron.   = patron, benefactor, source of endowment.
Italics.   The use of italics implies uncertainty. When a name is italicized it signifies that the person is described not as hermit but keeper, chaplain, etc.
Name.   With name of inmate, D. = Dame; Br. = Brother; pr. = priest; $d.$ = died; n.d. = no date recorded.

N.B.—The numbering of cells is for purposes of reference. In some cases two or more numbers may refer to one cell, e.g. in Norfolk, Nos. 19, 27, 29, 30.

ABBREVIATIONS USED IN REFERENCES

B.	Blomefield, *History of Norfolk.*
B.M.	British Museum.
Bodl.	Bodleian Library.
Cart.	Cartulary.
Ch.	Charter.
Close.	Calendar of Close Rolls.
Dugd.	Dugdale, *Monasticon Anglicanum.*
Ex. Reg.	Exeter Episcopal Registers, ed. Hingeston-Randolph.
Fœd.	Rymer, *Fœdera.*
Itin.	Leland, *Itinerary,* ed. Hearne, 1770.
Linc. Wills.	A. W. Gibbons, *Early Lincoln Wills.*
Nov. Leg.	Nova Legenda Angliæ, ed. C. Horstman.
Pat.	Calendar of Patent Rolls.
P.R.O.	Public Record Office.
R.	Roll.
Rec.	Records.
Reg.	Register.
Rolls.	Rolls Series of Chronicles and Memorials.
S.	Society.
S.S.	Surtees Society.
Ser.	Series.
V.C.H.	*Victoria County History.*

I. BEDFORD

	Place.	·	Description.
1	Bedford	A.	—
2	”	A.	at St. Mark's
3	Bletsoe Wood	H.	St. Mary
4	Bushmead [in Eaton Socon]	H.	on site of priory
5	Dunstable	A.	at priory
6	”	H.	—
7	Farley, nr. Luton	H.	—
8	Houghton Regis	H.	chapel of St. Wilfrid
9	Kempston	A.	at church
10	Markyate Wood [in Caddington]	—	afterwards priory
11	Moddry Wood [in Clophill]	H.	St. Mary [site of Beaulieu]
12	Newnham Priory, in or nr.	H.	—
13	Oakley (" Ocle ")	H.	—
14	Turvey (bridge)	H.	chapel
15	Wilden	A.	—

1. B.M. Harl. 3656, f. 22 *b*.   2. C. H. Hartshorne, *Antiq. of N'humb.* II. 226.
3. P.R.O. Anc. Deeds, C. 1454, C. 1738, C. 2188.   4. Leland, *Collect.* I. 68.   5. *Ann.
Mon. Dunst.* III. 77, 109.   6. *Linc. Wills*, 172.   7. J. Amund. *Ann.* I. 59; cf. Pat.
1253, 1255.   8. Pat. 1330.   9. Reg. Hugh de Wells, ann. 8.   10. *Gest. Abb.* I. 97-105,

II. BERK

	Place.		Description.
1	Cookham	A.	—
2	Faringdon	A.	—
3	Hinksey	A.	—
4	Losfield [in Clewer]	H.	chapel of St. Leonard
5	Maidenhead (bridge)	H.	—
6	*Pewsey* (" Peuesia ")	A.	—
7	Poughley (Clenfordmere)	H.	site of priory
8	Reading	H.	chapel of St. Edmund M.
9	Sandleford, nr. Newbury	A.	—
10	Seacourt (" Seukewrthe ")	A.	—
—	Stratfield Saye, *v. sub.* Hants	—	—
11	Wargrave	H.	chapel of Corpus Christi

1. Pipe R.S. XVIII-XXXIII.   2, 3. Bodl. Oseney ch. XIV.   4. Close, 1225; Pat.
1275, 1320; Hundred R.   5. Hoare, *Wilts*, II. 162.   6. Pipe R.S. IV-XII.   7. *V.C.H.*

SHIRE

Date.	Patron.	Name.
xiii c.	—	Isabella
1184-5.	Crown	—
xiii c.	—	Robert Parage and brethren
—	—	
1222	—	Simon, *d.* 1228
1442	—	—
bef. 1431	—	cf. brethren of St. William in the Desert, 1253.
1330	—	Peter de Whitteleye
1242-3	Elstow Abbey	Br. Walter, pr.
bef. 1123	St. Alban's Abbey	Roger, monk ; " five hermits " ; Christina of the Wood
bef. 1146	Private, St. Alban's	Ralph de Nuers, monk of Lichfield
—	—	Simon
1339	—	*John*, pr.
1405	—	John Combes
1194-5	Crown	—

127.   11. *Ibid.* I. 78 ; Dugd. III. 276 ; Misc. Biog. (S.S. 8), 84-5.   12. *V.C.H.* I. 350 ; B.M. Harl. 3656, f. 11.   13. P.R.O., K.B. Anc. Indictments, I. Beds. Edw. III. m. 3. 14. Gibbons, *Ely Rec.* 403.   15. See (2).

SHIRE

Date.	Patron.	Name.
1171	Crown	—
bef. 1254	—	Childluve
1271	—	—
bef. 1225	Private	William, 1225 ; John, 1320 ; William, 1355
1423	—	Richard Ludlow
1155	Crown	—
c. 1160	—	—
1204	Abbey	Laurence Burgeys
1179	Crown	—
1271	—	—
—	—	—
1339	—	Alan de Elsefeld

11. 85.   8. Coates, *Reading*, 199, App. IX. ; Berks, *Arch. J.* XII. 28-9.   9. Pipe R.S. XXIX. etc.   10. See (2).   11. Pat. 1339.

III. BUCKING

	Place.		Description.
1	Brill	H.	chapel of St. Werburg
2	Chetwode	H.	„ „ SS. Stephen and Laurence
3	Colnbrook, nr. Windsor	H.	chapel of Our Lady
4	Finemere, nr. Quainton	H.	—
5	Stony Stratford (bridge)	H.	—

1. Chart., Close, and Pat. R.   2. Reg. Grosseteste, ann. XII.   3. Privy Expenses, Eliz. of Yk. 31-2.   4. B.M. Harl. Roll O. 26 (3) ; Close, 1213, 1218, 1228, 1237 ; Reg. Bek., Mem. f. 64.   5. Pat. 1400.

IV. CAMBRIDGE

	Place.		Description.
1	Arrington and Royston (between)	H.	—
2	Barnwell	—	chapel of St. Andrew
3	Cambridge (without)	A.	at St. Peter's church
4	„	A.	at Carmelite friary
5	„ (Trumpington St.)	H.	chapel of St. Anne
6	„ (Newnham bridge)	H.	chapel
7	„ (Barnwell road)	H.	—
8	Ely	A.	at St. Mary's
9	„ Russells Pits (" Roucehill ")	H.	—
10	„ diocese of	A.	—
11	„ „	H.	—
12	Gamlingay	H.	—
13	Haddenham	H.	—
14	Hinxton (Whytford bridge)	H.	chapel of St. Anne
15	Huneia, nr. Ely	H.	—
16	Leverington	H.	chapel of St. John B.
17	Royston in Bassingbourne	H.	—
18	Shelford (bridge)	H.	—
19	Stuntney	H.	—
20	Swavesey	H.	—
21	Thorney (Ancarig)	—	—
22	Throkennolt	H.	St. Mary and St. Andrew
23	Waterbeach and Denny (between)	H.	—
24	Whittlesford Bridge	H.	chapel of St. Mary B.V.

1. Gibbons, *Ely Rec.* 401.   2. J. W. Clark, *Eccles. de Bernewelle*, 42.   3. Camb. Antiq. S. XLIV (1908), p. 73.   4. Bale, *Script.* 565.   5. *Ely Rec.* 400; H. P. Stokes, *Trumpington Gates*, 66-7.   6. Pat. 1399 ; T. D. Atkinson, *Camb.* 62.   7. *Trumpington Gates*, 66.   8, 10. Pipe R.S. xv. 96.   9, 13. *Ely Rec.* 399, 404.   11. *Ely Dioc. Remembrancer*, 1909, p. 46.   12. Pat. 1271.   14. P.R.O. Sp. Exch. Com. 2926 ; *Dioc.*

HAMSHIRE

Date.	Patron.	Name.
1205 1246-7	Crown, Chetwode Priory Private	Robert, 1205 ; Richard, 1251 Robert de Walthone, pr.
1502 c. 1179 1400	— Crown, Nutley Abbey —	— William, monk, 1213-28 John Blawemuster

SHIRE

Date.	Patron.	Name.
1401	—	William Brown
c. 1112	—	Godesone
xiii c.	—	Matilda, dau. of Hervey
1421	Friary	Agnes, widow of Jn. Granseter
bef. 1361	—	John Bernewell, pr., 1399
1399	—	Jn. Jaye, 1399 ; Thos. Kendall, 1406
—	—	—
1169	Bishop	—
1394	—	Adam Holme of Wisbech
1169	Bishop	6 inclusæ
1494	—	Rob. Michyll ; Jn. Smith
1271	—	Br. William
1406	—	John Spenser
1524	—	William Popeley
c. 679	—	Huna, pr.
1488	—	—
c. 1506	—	hermit, d. 1506.
1398	—	John Lucas, cf. (23).
1458	Bishop	William Grene
1392	—	John Beel
vii c.	—	Thorncred ; Thortred ; Bosa ; Saxulph ; Toret.
xii c.	Bishop, Thorney Abbey	Trokonolus
1400	—	William Rogere
1401	—	John Lucas, cf. (17).

Rem. 1911.   15. *Nov. Leg.* II. 538.   16, 18. *Ely Rec.* 413, 400.   17. J. Beldam, *Royston Cave*, 48.   19. *Dioc. Rem.* 1904, p. 234.   20. *Ely Rec.* 398.   21. Ingulph, *Chr.* 43, 48 ; Leland, *Collect.* I. 10, 28.   22. Dugd. II. 594, 600, 601 ; *Pap. Lett.* I. 187. 23. *Ely Rec.* 401.   24. *Dioc. Rem.* 1900, p. 160.

	Place.			Description.
1	Chester		A.	St. James, by St. John's church
2	,,		A.	at St. Chad's chapel
3	,,	(on cliff)	H.	—
4	,,	(bridge)	H.	chapel
5	,,	(Hand bridge)	H.	chapel of St. James
6	Frodsham		A.	—
7	Hilbre Is.		H.	—
8	Plemstall		H.	—
9	Stockport	(bridge)	H.	chapel
10	,,		A.	—
11	Tarporley		H.	chapel of the Rood or [St. Mary B.V. &] St. Leonard
12	Tarvin	(Stanford bridge)	H.	St. Agatha V.
13	Wilderspool, nr. Warrington		H.	chapel

1. Ormerod, ed. Helsby, *Hist.* I. 353-4 ; *Staffs Coll.*, O.S. I. 283 ; N.S. VIII. 21, 32, 42, 47 ; X. ii. 162.   2. B.M. Harl. 2162, f. 61 *b*.   3. Ormerod, I. 353-4.   4. *Staffs Coll.*, N.S. VIII. 24, 38.   5. R. H. Morris, *Chester*, 189—possibly identical with (4). 6. Close, 1275.

	Place.			Description.
1	Bodmin		H.	—
2	,,	(near)	A.	—
3	Hamstoke (now St. Neot)		H.	—
4	Liskeard	(park)	H.	chapel of St. Mary B.V.
5	Marhamchurch		A.	in churchyard
6	Penlyne [in Lanlivery]		H.	—
7	Restormel [in Lostwithiel]		H.	—
8	*Roche*		*H.*	*chapel of S. Michael*
9	St. Teath (" Stathe ")		H.	—

1. Leland, *Collect.* I. 75 ; Dugd. II. 459.   2. Ex. Reg. Stafford, 25, 394. 3. Gorham, *St. Neots*, p. xcvii *seq*.   4. Pat. 1339.   5. Ex. Reg. Stafford, 251, 394.

SHIRE

Date.	Patron.	Name.
bef. 1341	Various	Br. Hugh le Vernoun, 1341 ; Br. Wm. de Heytildesham, 1357 ; Br. Jn. de Chorleton, 1363.
c. 1300	—	—
1358	—	John Spicer
1365	—	John, 1367
1450	Crown	Jn. Benet, 1450 ; Ieuan, 1455
1275	Earldom	Wimark
1328	Crown	—
c. 890	—	Plegmund
c. 1355	—	Thos., pr., *c.* 1355 ; Ric. Webster, pr., 1366 ; Thos., pr., 1372.
1361	—	Br. Jn. Boner, pr.
bef. 1287	Private	John, 1287 ; Adam, 1301
1395-6	—	Richard de Clayton
1367	—	Simon de Goddesmer

7. Dugd. vi. 1616.   8. Gervase (Rolls 73), ii. 350.   9. *Staffs Coll.*, N.S. viii. 57, 68, 96.   10. Lancs. and Cheshire Wills (Rec. S. 30), 7.   11, 12. Ormerod, ii. 236-7, 313. 13. *Staffs Coll.*, N.S. viii. 37, 116.

WALL

Date.	Patron.	Name.
—	—	· St. Guron ; St. Petroc
1416	—	Margaret
—	—	St. Gwerir, St. Neot
1339	—	Roger Godman
1403	—	Cecilia Moys, Lucy Moys
c. 1301	Earldom	Br. Robert
,,	,,	Br. Philip
	—	—
1408	—	—

6, 7. Cal. Inq. p.m. Edw. I. iii. 458.   8. Gilbert, *Par. Hist.* (1838), iii. 391-3. 9. Ex. Reg. Stafford, 391.

14

VII. CUMBER

	Place.		Description.
1	Dalston	H.	chapel of St. Wynennus B.
2	Denton	H.	—
3	Derwentwater	H.	on St. Herbert's Island
4	Holme Cultram	H.	at St. Cuthbert's chapel
5	Ilekirk [in Englewood Forest]	H.	St. Hilda
6	Kirkland " on east of Eden "	H.	St. Andrew
7	Linstock [in Stanwix]	H.	chapel of St. Peter
8	Sebergham	H.	—
9	Wragmire [in Hesket in the Forest]	H.	—

1. Reg. Kirkley, f. 451. 2. Lanercost Cart., Pt. 1, No. 4 ; Dugd. VI. 237 ; *Pap. Lett.* V. 513. 3. Cumb. and W. Arch. S., O.S. VI. 342-3. 4. *Ibid.*, N.S. II. 339-41. 5. Dugd. V. 595, 604 ; Chart. R. 1227. 6. C. and W. Arch. S. Tract 6 (Wetheral),

VIII. DERBY

	Place.		Description.
1	*Anchor Church*, nr. Repton	H.	cave
2	Breadsall	H.	" heremitorium," afterwards priory
3	Chesterfield	H.	at chapel of St. Thomas
4	,, (bridge)	H.	—
5	Cratcliff [in Birchover]	H.	cave
6	Dale [Abbey], " Depedale "	H.	,, ; chapel of Mary V.
7	,,	A.	—
8	Derby (bridge)	A.	by chapel of St. Mary
9	,, ,,	H.	" Oure Lady of the Bryge "
10	*High Tor, Matlock*	*H.*	—
10a	Kirkwood	H.	St. Godarn
11	Lees Moor (" Leyes "), nr. Bakewell	H.	—
12	Morewood [in Ashover]	H.	—

1. F. C. Hipkins, *Repton*, 123-4. 2. Pat. 1266. 3. L. and P. Hen. VIII, XIII. (1), No. 1345. 5. *Arch. Journ.* IV. 156. 6, 7. Derbs. Arch. S. V. 17-20, 23. 8. *Staffs Coll.*, N.S. VIII. 53. 9. Nottingham Rec. II. 270 ; J. Cox, *Derbs. Churches*, IV. 70.

LAND

Date.	Patron.	Name.
1342	—	Hugh de Lilford
xii c.	Private, Lanercost Priory	Br. Leysing
vii c.	—	St. Herebert, *d.* 687
xvi c.	—	Richard Stanley
xii c.	Crown, Holme Cultram Abbey	Roger Goky
bef. 1156	Private, Wetheral Priory	—
bef. 1362	—	William, *d.* 1362
xii c.	Crown, Carlisle Priory	William Wastehose
1354	—	John of Corbridge

25·6 ; Denton, *Account of Cumb.* 106.   7. R. S. Ferguson, *Test. Karl.* 130.   8. Close, 1228, 1234.   9. Reg. Welton, f. 112.

SHIRE

Date.	Patron.	Name.
—	—	*St. Hardulph*, cf. Breedon, XX
1266	*Crown*	" brethren of the hermitage "
1538	—	William Ludelam
—	—	—
—	—	—
xii c.	—	a baker of Derby
—	—	Peter Cocus of Batheley
1370	—	Agnes Waley
1468	—	John Shenton, 1488
—	—	—
1238-9	—	*heremita S. Godarn in haia*
1333	—	—
bef. 1235	Dale Abbey	—

10 *Ibid.* II. 527.   10*a*. Pipe R. 83, Yeatman, *Feudal Derbs.* I. 209.   11. Hist. MSS. (Middleton), 1911, p. 275.   12. B.M. Wolley, VII. 1, 2.

IX. DEVON

	Place.		Description.
1	Colyford [in Colyton]	A.	chapel of St. Kalixtus
2	Crediton	A.	St. Mary, by chapel of St. Laurence
3	Dodbrooke, Kingsbridge	A.	chapel of Our Lady of Langewyll
4	*Exeter*	A.	—
5	Exeter (Larkbere)	A.	in St. Leonard's churchyard
6	„ (*Sidwell ?*)	A.	" atte Wille "
7	„	A.	by St. John's hospital
8	Holbeton (Anchorist Rock)	A.	capella S. Anecorite
9	Ottery (bridge)	—	nr. St. Saviour's chapel
10	Pilton (churchyard)	A.	chapel of St. Agnes
11	Plymouth (on Hoe)	H.	„ „ St. Katherine
12	„ (Quarrywell)	H.	St. Mary, Our Lady of Grace
13	Tavistock by	H.	at chapel of St. John B.
14	„ by	H.	„ „ „ St. Margaret
15	„	H.	—
16	Torrington, Great	A.	—
17	Devon, county of	A.	—

1. Ex. Reg. Grandisson, Pt. II. 650.   2. Oliver, *Monast.* 88.   3. Ex. Reg. Stafford, 134.   4. Cath. MS. 3675, Liber Obit. f. 5, 9 [per Miss E. Lega-Weekes].   5. Ex. Reg. Stafford, 20, 99, 393, 394 ; Wills (Somerset Rec. S. 19), 330 ; Reg. Lacy, III. f. 499. 6. Reg. Lacy, III. f. 500 [per E. L.-W.].   7. L. and P. Hen. VIII, XV. 299 ; XVIII. (1), p. 258.   8. Ex. Reg. Stafford, 132.   9. Oliver, 262.   10. Ex. Reg. Grandisson, Pt. I.

X. DOR

	Place.		Description.
1	Blackmoor Forest, now Hermitage	H.	St. Laurence, or Priory Hermitage
2	Branksea Is., Poole Haven	H.	chapel of St. Andrew
3	Cerne, nr.	H.	by St. Augustine's Well
3a	Hawkchurch (Brimley)	H.	chapel of St. Andrew
4	Holt [in Wimborne]	H.	chapel of St. James
5	Luccombe, *alias* Chelborough	H.	—
6	Mannington	H.	—
7	Shaftesbury (Nenlitton, by)	H.	—
8	Sherborne	A.	in abbey church
9	„ (by mill)	H.	St. John Baptist
10	*Tarrant Kaines*	*A.*	—
11	Wareham	A.	—
12	West Stour or Westover	H.	chapel called " the Hermit "
13	Winterborne	A.	in churchyard
14	Woodbury Hill [in Bere Regis]	A.	chapel and Anchorite's well

1. Close, 1273 ; Pat. 1314.   2. *Itin.* III. 84.   3. Nov. Leg. I. 362.   3a. Wilts Arch. S. XXXVIII. 29.   4. Eng. Wills (E.E.T.S.), 10.   5. Cal. Chanc. R. (Var.), 42. 6. Chart. R. 1237, 1242.   7. Pat. 1352.   8. See (4).   9. Wills (Somerset Rec. S. 19),

SHIRE

Date.	Patron.	Name.
1332	—	Beatrice of Colyford, widow
1242	Bishop	Br. Nicholas
1412	—	Margaret Holt, widow
—	connected with cathedral	Wluric ; Editha
1397	—	Alice Bernard
1425	—	—
xvi c.	—	Alice Buttes
1400	—	—
xvi c.	—	John Selman
bef. 1329	—	Alice
c. 1370	—	—
bef. 1518	—	David Waryn
1383	Abbey	David Bukketorre
1383	—	Robert Crese
bef. 1470	—	John
c. 1395-1419	—	William Tredewy
c. 1175	Earldom of Cornwall	—

538; II. 653. II. *Pap. Lett.* VI. 306 ; R. N. Worth, *Hist.* 233 ; *Itin.* III. 43. 12. Oliver, 131 ; Worth, *Hist.* 234. 13, 14. Ex. Reg. Brantyngham, Pt. I. 499 ; *Gent. Mag.*, 1830, I. 232-3. 15. Worth, *Tavistock Rec.* 13, 14, 18 ; cf. (14), (15). 16. Ex. Reg. Stafford, 352. 17. Pipe R.S. XXV. 153 ; XXVI. 9.

SET

Date.	Patron.	Name.
bef. 1273	Earldom of Cornwall, Cerne Abbey	—
xvi c.	Cerne Abbey	—
ix c.	—	St. Eduold
1340	—	William Dughecut
1395	Private	Friar Thomas; recluse
1297	—	*Rob. de Lodres, keeper*
bef. 1237	Private, Tarrant Abbey	—
1352	—	William Godwot
xiii c.	Abbey	Edmund Arthur, recluse, 1395
1405	—	Wm. Whityng, 1405 ; W. Howel, *d.* 1538
c. 1297-1315	—	—
xii c.	—	Matilda, *c.* 1125-54 ; Gertrude ; Christiana
xvi c.	—	—
xii c.	—	John
—	—	—

304, 315 ; Hutchins, *Hist.*, ed. 1873, IV. 235. 10. *Ancren Riwle* (Camden S.), p. vii *n*. 11. B.M. Cott. Faust. B. IV. Vita S. Wulfrici, II. f. 96. 12. Hutchins, III. 636. 13. See (11), f. 97 *b*. 14. Hutchins, I. 135.

	Place.		Description
1	Chester-le-Street	A.	in church
2	„ „	H.	—
3	Durham	A.	in cathedral
4	„	H.	—
5	„	—	*by St. Oswald's Church*
6	„ diocese of	H.	—
7	„ in or near	H.	—
8	„ „ „	H.	—
9	Eighton or Skottewell	H.	chapel of Holy Trinity
10	Finchale	H.	chapels, St. Mary V., St. John B.
11	„	A.	near „ „ „
12	Gainford (Barmore)	H.	chapel of St. Mary M.
13	Gateshead	A.	by church of St. Mary
14	Heighley [in Winston]	H.	—
15	*Norton*	*H.*	—
16	Pounteys Bridge [in Middleton St. George]	H.	chapel of St. John
17	Satley	H.	—
18	Staindrop	A.	adjoining church
19	Tyneside (nr. Bishop's Park)	H.	St. Cuthbert
20	Wolsingham	H.	—
21	Yareshale on Derwent	H.	St. Mary

1, 2. Boyle, *Guide*, 420; Chantries (S.S, 22), App. VI. p. lxiv. 3. Rites of Durham (S.S. 15, 107), I. 15 ; II. 17. 4. Close, 1238. 5. Surtees, *Hist.* IV. 84. 6. *V.C.H.* II. 131. 7. Yk. Pontif. (S.S. 61), App. V. 288. 8. Tres Script. (S.S. 9), App. p. ccclxxix. 9. *V.C.H.* II. 131 ; *Ely Dioc. Rem.*, 1900, p. 54. 10, 11. Reginald, Vita S. Godrici (S.S.

	Place.		Description.
1	Barking	A.	—
2	Bradwell (bridge)	H.	—
3	Colchester	A.	at church of St. James
4	„ (Hythe, nr.)	A.	at [St. Leonard's] church
5	„ (Hallywell)	H.	St. Anne
6	Hainault Forest (" Henold ")	H.	—
7	Maldon	A.	—
8	Radwinter	A.	—
9	Stanstead-Mountfitchet	H.	chapel of St. Mary B.V.
10	Stratford le Bow (bridge)	H.	„ „ St. Katharine
11	West Tilbury	H.	at a free chapel
12	Woodham	H.	St. John B. (afterwards Bicknacre priory)
13	Writtle	—	" called Bedemannesberg "

1. Pat. 1417, 1423. 2. Pat. 1336 ; Morant, *Essex*, 1768, I. 154. 3. Pipe R.S. I.-XXXIII. ; Morant, I. 152 ; *V.C.H.* II. 158. 4. B.M. Harl. ch. 44, E. 17. 5. Pat. 1388, 1402. 6. Pat. 1461. 7. Pipe R.S. VII. 37 ; VIII. 16. 8. " Juxta mansione dni.

HAM

Date.	Patron.	Name.
1383	—	John de Wessington
1400	—	John Blenkinsopp
—	Priory	—
1238	Bishop	Thomas
—	—	—
1373	—	William Shepherd
c. 1365	—	G.— M.—
1493	—	John Man, of Yorkshire
1387	—	Robert Lambe
c. 1110	Bishop, Durham Priory	St. Godric
—	—	Burchwene
1435	—	Rob. Perules ; *Thos. Apulby*, 1486
1340	—	—
bef. 1315	—	—
—	—	—
1426	Durham Priory	*Jn. Teysedall*, 1402 ; Wm. Byndelawes, 1426
bef. 1195	„ „	John
1336	—	John de Camera
1312	—	John " called Godesman "
bef. c. 1110	—	Aelric and Godric
bef. 1188	Bishop, Durham Priory	John

20). 12, 13. *V.C.H.* II. 131; Pat. 1486, 1510; Reg. Pal. Dunelm (Rolls, 62), III. 300·1. 14. Surtees, *Hist.* IV. 38. 15. *Gent. Mag.*, 1864, I. 710-2. 16. Surtees, *Hist.* III. 228. 17. Feod. Prior. (S.S. 58), 240. 18. Boyle, 700-1. 19. Reg. Pal. Dunelm. I. 197. 20. Vita S. Godrici, 45-52. 21. *Ibid.* 192-3; Feod. Prior. 240, 279, 280.

SEX

Date.	Patron.	Name.
1417	—	Matilda Newton
1336	—	William
1155	Crown	Cecily, 1272
1290	—	Agnes
1388	Private, Priory	John Newton
1461	—	John Rychard
1163	—	—
1374	—	Anne de Lexeden
1492	—	John Parrot
1344	—	Br. John de Ware
xvi c.	—	—
bef. 1157	—	Br. Jordan, canon
tp. Hen. I	Crown, Colchester Abbey	Robert, monk ; *inclusus*, 1189

Johis de Lenne," Rye MSS., L'Estrange Wills, I. f. 52 *b*. 9. Gibbons, *Ely Rec.* 415. 10. Pat. 1334. 11. *Valor Ecc.* I. 448. 12. Dugd. VI. 446. 13. Cart. (Roxburghe Club), I. 38-9, 52-3; II. 529; Pipe R., ed. Hunter, 20.

	Place.		Description.
1	Ardland [Forest of Dean]	H.A.	at a chapel
2	Ashchurch (" Estchurche ")	A.	—
3	Bristol	A.	at St. Michael's church
4	„ (in castle)	A.	chapel of St. Edward
5	„	A.	in Dominican friary
6	„	H.A.	hermitage of St. Brandan
7	„ (Redcliffe in Somerset)	H.	cave, by St. John's hospital
8	*Bristol*	*H.*	*St. Milburga*
9	Campden, Chipping	A.	in churchyard
10	Clifton (Ghyston Cliff)	H.	cave, chapel of St. Mary and St. Vincent
11	*Cromhall*	*A.*	—
12	Dursley	H.	—
13	Gloucester	A.	—
14	„	A.	nr. St. Kyneburga's chapel
15	„	A.	—
16	„ (Sembridge, Sandbridge)	H.	—
17	*Gloucester*, in or near	H.	—
18	Kingsholm (" Kingesham ") [in Kg.'s Barton]	A.	at the king's chapel
19	Meysey-Hampton	A.	—
20	Newnham (" Niweham ")	A.	—
21	*Quinton*	*A.*	—
22	St. Briavels	H.	—
23	St. Tiriac's Rock (nr. Beachley)	—	" capella S. Tiriaci anachoritæ "
24	Stapleton	A.	—
25	Taynton Wood	H.	—
26	Wickwar	A.	—

1. A. W. Crawley-Boevey, *Flaxley Cart.* 46, 78 ; Close, 1225, 1241. 2. Ann. Theok (Rolls, 36, i), I. 68. 3. *Ibid.* 105-6. 4. P.R.O. Liberate R., 34 Hen. III. 5. Wills (Somerset Rec. S. 19), 161. 6. Barrett, *Bristol*, 60 ; Latimer, *Annals*, 59 ; W. Worcester, *Itin.* (ed. Nasmith), 241. 7. W. Worc. 274 ; Smyth, *Berkeleys*, I. 337. 8. Birch, *Margam Abbey*, 203. 9. Reg. Giffard, f. 18 *b*. 10. W. Worc. 185-6, 275 ; B. and Glos. Arch. S. XXX. 204-5. 11. Rudder, *Glos.* 397. 12. Smyth, *Berkeleys*, III. 175-6. 13. Pipe R. S. XVI.-XXXIII. 14. Pat. 1390. 15. *Linc. Wills*, 196. 16.

CESTERSHIRE

Date.	Patron.	Name.
bef. 1189	Flaxley Abbey	William ; Panye de Lench, 1225 ; Juetta de Wiz, 1241
1226	Tewkesbury Abbey	—
1237	„ „	—
1249	Crown	—
1512	—	—
bef. 1313	Tewkesbury Abbey	Lucy de Newchurch, 1351 ; Reginald Taillour, hermit, 1403
1347	Private	John Sparkes
—	*Margam Abbey*	—
1269	—	Matilda de Campden
bef. 1480	—	Thos. Dene, warden, 1492
—	—	—
bef. 1516	—	—
1170	Crown	Adam, 1170-84
1390	Lanthony Priory	—
1481	—	—··
xvi c.	St. Peter's Abbey	
1387	—	William Pereshore
1228	Crown	Celestria
c. 1300	—	—
1158	Crown	—
c. 1419	—	*Joan, Lady Clopton, widow*
bef. 1131	Crown, Grace Dieu	—
1290	Private, Crown	*John Sterre, monk*
1382	—	—
bef. 1163	St. Peter's Abbey	—
1278	—	Wm. de Pershore, pr.

Rudder, 196 ; L. and P. Hen. VIII, XXI., Pt. i, p. 578.   17. Corp. Rec. 1018.   18. Close 1228.   19. Godstow Reg. (E.E. Text S.), 151-2.   20. Pipe R.S. I.-XXXIII ; Chart R.   21. B. and G. Arch. S. XIII. 167-9.   22. *Ibid.* VI. 82 ; XXIX. 13 ; Dugd. v. 685 ; Close, Chart R.   23. Pat. 1385, 1391, 1402 ; *Pap. Reg.* IV. 354, 511 ; VI. 24, 141 ; *Val. Ecc.* II. 501.   24. Bristol Corp. MSS., Orphan Bk. I., f. 6.   25. Cart. Mon. Glouc. (Rolls 33), I. 116 ; II. 137.   26. Reg. Giffard, f. 79 *b*.

XIV. HAMP

	Place.		Description.
1	Farlington	A.	—
2	Itchel [in Crondall]	A.	—
3	Mottisfont	A.	—
4	Southampton	H.	Holy Trinity or St. Mary de Grace
5	Southwick	H.	St. Leonard
6	Stratfield Saye (on Loddon)	H.	,,
7	Winchester	A.	St. Aedred
8	,, in diocese of	H.	—

ISLE OF

9	St. Catherine's Down, nr. Chale	H.	St. Katherine V.

1. Close, 1235.   2. Winchester Pipe R., ed. H. Hall, 38.   3. Dugd. VI. 481.
4. Davies, *Southampton*, 230-2.   5. L. and P. Hen. VIII. VII. 1153 ; XIX. (1), p. 618.

XV. HERE

	Place.		Description.
1	Clodock [in Ewyas]	—	—
2	Hereford	A.	St. Sepulchre
3	,,	A.	church of St. Giles's hospital
4	,,	A.	—
5	Ledbury	A.	—
6	Leintwardine	A.	—
7	,,	H.	—
8	Winforton Is.	H.	chapel of St. Kenedr
9	Wormeley, at or nr.	H.	—

1. Liber Landav, 446.   2. Pipe R.S. XVIII.-XXXIII ; Pipe R., ed. Hunter, 141.
3. Reg. Orleton (Cant. and Yk. S.), 205 ; Capes, *Cath. Rec.* 187 ; *Pap. Lett.* III. 504.
4. Wills (Somerset Rec. S. 19), 300 ; possibly identical with (3).   5. Close, 1323 ;

SHIRE

Date.	Patron.	Name.
1235	Crown	Joan
1209	Bishop	—
tp. John	—	Peter de Rievaulx
1496	Town	William Gefferey
1534	Priory	—
c. 1170	Private, Alien Abbey	Godard " inclusus et heremita " and brethren
1189	Crown	Geldewin
1404	—	Robert Northrygge professed

WIGHT

Date.	Patron.	Name.
1312	—	John, *alias* Walter de Langeberewe

6. Hist. MSS. 9th Rep. 355-6 ; Pat. 1332, 1341.   7. Pipe R., ed. Hunter, 204.
8. Lambeth, Reg. Arundel, Pt. I. f. 435 *b*.   9. Reg. Woodlock, f. 172.

FORDSHIRE

Date.	Patron.	Name.
—	—	Lybiaw and Gwrwan
1171	Crown	Richard, 1171-84
1320	—	Alice, dau. of Roger de Atferton
1400	—	—
bef. 1322	—	Katherine, Làdy Audley
1290	—	
bef. 1410	—	Thos. Shelve, cf. Ludlow, XXIX
bef. 1234	Private, Wormeley Priory	Walter, pr. ; Stephen
—	Priory	Edwyn " primus heremita "

Camden, Brittannia, ed. 1789, II. 456.   6. Swinfield R., *Household Exp.* (Camden S. 59), p. cxcix.   7. Dugd. VI. 402 ; B.M. Harl. 6726, f. 88 *b*.   8. Harl. 3586, f. 145 *b*.

	Place.		Description.
1	Barkway	H.	—
2	Barkway and Ware, between	H.	—
3	Flamstead	A.	—
—	Markyate, *v. sub* Beds.	—	—
4	Northaw (wood)	H.	—
5	Radwell	A.	—
—	Royston, *v. sub* Cambs.	—	—
6	St. Albans, nr. (Eywood)	A.	St. Mary (site of Sopwell nunnery)
7	,,	A.	at St. Michael's church
8	,,	A.	at St. Peter's church
9	,,	—	at St. German's chapel
10	,,	A.	nr. ,, ,,
11	Standon, or Seltburn	H.	chapel of St. Michael
12	Wogobiliche [in Cheshunt]	H.	—

1. J. Beldam, *Royston Cave*, 48. 2. *Archælogia*, XXV. 432. 3. Nov. Leg. II. 535. 4. T. Walsingham, *Gest. Abb.* I. 105 ; J. Amund., *Ann.* II. 302-3. 5. Pipe R.S. VIII. 17. 6. *Gest. Abb.* I. 80-1 ; Dugd. III. 362, 365. 7. *Gest. Abb.* I. 305 ; J. Amund. I. 66 ; *Chr. S. Alb. VI*, II. 257-8 ; *Herts Genealogist*, I., II. 8. *Gest. Abb.* I. 388-9 ;

XVII. HUNTING

	Place.		Description.
· 1	Alconbury	H.	—
2	Bodsey	H.	—
3	Coppingford (" Copmanford ")	H.	—
4	Earith	H.	—
5	Higney, nr. Ramsey	H.	—
6	Suameshei [in Graffham]	H.	—
7	Sudbury [archdeaconry of Hunts]	H.	—

1. Smyth, *Berkeleys*, II. 214. 2. Ramsey Cart. (Rolls, 79), I. 87 ; II. 221 ; Dugd. II. 552, 588. 3. Bushmead Cart. *penes* W. H. Wade Gery, f. 65, 65 *b*. 4. Gibbons, *Ely Rec.* 400, 401 ; *Ely Dioc. Rem.*, 1908, p. 180. 5. Ramsey Cart. I. 159, 162, 852 ;

FORDSHIRE

Date.	Patron.	Name.
xvi c.	—	—
1520	—	—
xii c.	—	Alfwina
—	—	—
bef. 1146	—	Sigar, monk
1163	—	—
—	—	—
c. 1140	Abbey	2 women
c. 1235	„	Kath. Dytton, 1421, d. 1437 ; Agnes Vertesance, 1452, d. 1478 ; Marg. Smythe, 1483
c. 1258	„	Alice, 1412, 1426 ; Eliz. Kath. Holsted, 1480
ix c.	„	Wulfa ; Abbot Eadfrith ; Thos. Fyschebourn, d. 1428
bef. 1421	—	house for anchoress founded T. Fyschebourn
bef. 1163	Private ; Stoke-by-Clare Priory	built by William, inclusus ; *Robert*, 1384 ; *Simon*, 1393 ; Jn. Benwell, 1398.
c. 1160	—	—

B.M. Cott. Nero D. 7, f. 139 ; Nichols, *Royal Wills*, 250.   9, 10. *Gest. Abb.* I. 21-2 ; J. Amund. II. 27-8, 301-2 ; Bib. Carmel. 472.   11. Dugd. VI. 1658 ; Pat. 1384, 1393, 1398 ; B.M. Seal, XLIII. 13.   12. B.M. Add. ch. 28335.

DONSHIRE

Date.	Patron.	Name.
bef. 1524	Private	—
1220	Private ; Ramsey Abbey	—
bef. 1314	„ Bushmead Priory	*Joseph*, pr.
1397	—	Ric. Grymston ; Hy. Bourne, 1401 ; Jn. Thompson, 1491
bef. 1153	Ramsey (?)	Edwin
bef. 1216	—	—
1254	Private	*Reymund*, pr. ; *Adam de Mepersale*

Dugd. V. 522.   6. B.M. Add. ch. 33281.   7. Grosseteste, Roll, ann. 7 ; Reg. Dalderby. f. 234 b.

Place.		Description.
1	Bredhurst	H.	—
2	Canterbury	H.	—
3	„	A.	*at St. Mary's church*
4	„	H.	nr. the Dane John
5	„	A.	in Dominican friary
6	„ in province of	H.	—
7	„ „ „ „	H.	—
8	„ „ „ „	H.	—
9	Court-at-Street	H.	at chapel of Our Lady
10	Dartford (bridge)	H.	chapel of [St. Mary and] St. Katherine
11	„	A.	—
12	Davington, at or nr.	A.	—
13	Deptford [in Greenwich]	H.	St. Katherine
14	Dover	A.	at St. Mary-in-the-Castle
15	„ (Arcliffe)	H.	chapel of Our Lady [of Peace]
16	„ Occlive, nr.	H.	—
17	Faversham	A.	in churchyard
18	„	A.	„ „
19	Hackington	A.	—
20	Hartlip	A.	—
21	Kearsney [in Ewell], at or nr.	A.	—
22	Longsole [in Petham]	H.	chapel of St. Laurence
23	Loose	A.	—
24	Lydd (the Nesse)	H.	*St. Mary B.V.*
25	Malling, West	H.	—
26	Milton, nr. Sittingbourne	H.	—
—	Occlive *v.* Dover	—	—
27	Plumstead	H.	—
28	Puxton [in Stodmarsh]	H.	—
29	Reculver	H.	chapel of SS. Peter, James, and Anthony

1. B.M. Add. 4607.   2. *Ely Dioc. Rem.*, 1895, p. 55.   3. Hasted, *Kent*, IV. 478. 4. J. Brent, *Canterbury*, 129.   5. L. and P. Hen. VIII, VI. Nos. 1333, 1336, 1381.   6-8. Lambeth, Reg. Langham, f. 63 ; Islip, f. 110 *b* ; Arundell, Pt. I. f. 395.   9. L. and P. Hen. VIII, VI. No. 1468.   10. J. Dunkin, *Dartford*, 190-2.   11. *Fœd.* IX. 275. 12. *Arch. Cant.* XI. 25-6.   13. Pat. 1403 ; Hasted, ed. Drake, 64 *n*.   14. Close, 1232, 1234 ; Pat. 1259.   15. P.R.O. Duc. Lanc. Accounts (various), Bdle. 4, No. 1, f. 28. 16. Pat. 1308, cf. (15).   17, 18. Test. Cant. Pt. II. 128-9 ; L. and P. Hen. VIII, VI.

KENT

Date.	Patron.	Name.
bef. 1549	—	—
1374	—	William Cower
—	—	—
1446	—	—
1533	—	Christopher Warener
1367	—	Br. John de Dutton, " created " by Abbot of Westminster
1353	—	Thos. Stapelow " of parish of St. Leonard, Eastcheap "
1401	—	Jn. Langfeld of Northflete, professed
1525	—	Sir William, pr.
xiii c.	—	Jn. Sodeman, 1438 ; Jn. Colebrant, 1509
1415	—	
xiv c.	connected with priory	Celestria, nun ; Adilda, nun
1403	Crown	Rob. Darley, n.d. ; Walter Combe, 1518
1232	,,	Emma de Skepeye
1360	restored, Sieur de Vaux	David Welkes, 1399 ; *Jean*, chaplain, 1535
1308	—	John de Warwyk
1465	—	anchoress, 1465-1523
1472	—	Wm. Thornbury, pr., 1472 ; br. of Ann Sawston, *c.* 1531 ; Sir Thos. Crakynthorpe, 1541
1233	—	Loretta, Countess of Leicester, 1235
—	Rochester Priory	Robert
1285	Kearsney Manor	Mariun
1350	Private	*Stephen Fynamour, chaplain*
bef. 1228	Archbishop	Sarah
bef. 1510	—	John Bate
1496	—	—
1400	—	Wm. Fayreford, 1400 ; Wm. Hart, 1498
—	—	—
bef. 1207	Southwark Priory	—
1516		—
1415	Archbishop	Henry Gate, 1415 ; Thos. Hamond, 1486

135, VII. 347-8.   19. Close, 1233 ; Pat. 1235, 1256, 1259.   20. J. Thorpe, *Reg. Roff.* 124.   21. Cal. Inq. p.m. Edw. I, Vol. 2, No. 605.   22. *Reg. Roff.* p. 155 ; Hasted, II. 177 ; P.R.O. Anc. Deeds, C. 537.   23. Close, 1231-2.   24. Hist. MSS. 5th Rep. 496 ; Hasted, III. 517 ; Test. Cant. 202.   25. Test. Cant. Pt. I. 52.   26. *Ibid.* II. 215-7 ; Gibbons, *Ely Rec.* 401.   27. B.M. Harl. 55, E. 18.   28. Test. Cant. Pt. II. 365.   29. Lambeth, Reg. Chicheley, f. 64 *b* ; C. R. Smith, *Reculver*, 193, 202.

	Place.		Description.
30	Richborough	H.	nr. Castle
31	Rochester, diocese of	H.	chapel of St. Katharine
32	St. Margaret's-at-Cliffe	H.	" hermitagium S. Margarete atte Staire "
33	Sandwich	H.	at chapel of St. James (Jacob)
34	„ (Gascoign Lane)	H.	chapel or hermitage
35	„	A.	at St. Mary's church
36	Shamwell [in Sittingbourne]	H.	chapel of St. Thomas M.
37	Sutton [Valence]	A.	—
38	Whitstable	H.	St. Anne in the Wood
39	Wickham [Breaux]	A.	at St. Andrew's church
40	Wye	H.	—

30. *Itin.* VII. 138. 31. *Ely Dioc. Rem.*, 1894, p. 181. 32. Lambeth, Reg. Langham, f. 63. 33. Boys, *Sandwich*, 188, 328, 360; Test. Cant. 292. 34. Boys, 188. 35. Test. Cant. 286. 36. Pat. 1255, 1266; cf. Close, 1288, 1308. 37. Close, 1225. 38. Test.

XIX. LANCA

	Place.		Description.
1	Chatburn	H.	chapel of St. Martin
2	Cockersand	H.	—
3	Heaton	H.	nr. St. Cuthbert's chapel
4	Kersall	H.	St. Leonard
5	Lancaster (Lune bridge)	H.	chapel
6	„	A.	in Dominican friary
7	Pilling [in Garstang]	A.	nr. chapel of St. John B.
8	Ribble Bridge [in Walton le Dale]	H.	chapel
9	Ribchester, at or nr.	A.	—
—	Singleton, *v.* Lancaster; Ribble	—	—
10	Warrington (bridge)	H.	chapel
11	Whalley	A.	chapel in churchyard
12	„ at or under	H.	—
13	Wigan	A.	—
—	Wilderspool, *v. sub* Cheshire	—	—
14	Wirpelesmosse, nr. Burscough	H.	—

1. *V.C.H.* II. 103. 2. W. Farrer, Lancs. Pipe R., etc., 395; Cart. (Chetham S., N.S. 38), p. ix. 3. Roper, *Church of Lanc.* (Chetham S., N.S. 31), II. 279. 4. Dugd. v. 110, 112; *V.C.H.* II. 113. 5. Reg. J. of Gaunt (Camden S., 3rd Ser. XXI.), II. 179; Rot. Parl. v. 546. 6. *V.C.H.* II. 103. 7. Chetham S. LVII. (2), 29, 30. 8. *Staffs*

KENT—*continued*.

Date.	Patron	Name.
xvi c.	—	—
1346	—	John le Maure
1367	—	Br. Nicholas de Legh
1447	Wardens ; Town	Sir William, *d.* 1447 ; Sir Jn. Steward, 1533
—	—	—
1535	—	—
1255	Crown	Silvester ; *Br. Walter*
1225	„	—
1514	—	Robert Wodroff, 1519
c. 1220	—	—
1449	—	John Bernard

Cant. 362-3, xv. 39. B.M. Harl. 48, C. 25. 40. Hist. MSS. 4th Rep. 433 ; cf. Test. Cant. Pt. I. 61, 62.

SHIRE

Date.	Patron.	Name.
bef. 1372	Duchy	Br. Ric. de Goldbourne
bef. 1184	—	Hugh Garth
c. 1280	—	Br. William
bef. 1184	Lenton Priory	Hugh de Burun, monk
1373	Duchy	John, " h. of Singleton "
1390	—	Br. Ric. Pekard, pr.
1493	Cockersand Abbey	Agnes Booth or Shepard, nun
1366	—	John, 1366, 1371, cf. Lancaster
1292	—	Cecilia
—	—	—
1369	—	Br. John, 1369 ; Thurstan de Okenshaw, 1406
1354	Duchy and Abbey	Ellen, *c.* 1396 ; Isold Heton, widow, 1437
1353	Abbey	William de Wygan
c. 1322	Private	Alina
—	—	—
1361	—	Thos. de Huddeswell, pr.

Coll., N.S. VIII. 28, 57. 9. Whittaker, *Whalley*, II. 461. 10. *Staffs Coll.*, N.S. VIII. 48. 11. *V.C.H.* VI. 360 ; *Whalley*, I. 97, 102. 12. Lichfield Reg. Norbury (Act Bk. 5), f. 210, 211. 13. P.R.O. Anc. Petitions, 7470. 14. *Staffs Coll.*, N.S. VIII. 99 ; cf. Lanc. Pipe R. 349.

15

	Place.		Description.
1	*Breedon*	*H.*	*in cliff by R. Trent*
2	Charley [in Charnwood]	H.	St. Mary
3	Haliwell Haw „	H.	—
4	Leicester	A.	by St. Peter's church
5	„	H.	in church ; in wood ; at chapel of St. John B.
6	„	H.	chapel by St. James's Well
7	Mirabel Wood [in Stockerston]	H.	chapel
8	Ulverscroft	H.	—

1. Lord Kenyon's Library, see chapter III.   2. Reg. Hugh de Wells (Cant. and Yk. S.), I. 255 ; Dugd. VI. 565.   3. Nichols, *Leic. III*, Pt. I. 122 ; II. 822.   4. *Ibid. I*, Pt. II. 265 ;   Lambeth, Reg. Courteney, f. 139 *b*, 142 *b*, 143.   5. Walsingham, *Hist.*

XXI. LINCOLN

	Place.		Description.
1	Acke [in Sibsey] (?) Hakerley	H.	" heremitorium Ache or Hacchæ "
2	Ancaster (nr. castle)	H.	by St. Mary's chapel
3	Asfordby	H.	—
4	Belchford (" Beltesford ")	A.	—
5	Boston	A.	in Carmelite friary
5a	Brygdyke (? Briggend in Horbling)	H.	—
6	Broughton, nr. Brigg	A.	in St. Mary's church
7	Burreth (" Silverys " in)	H.	chapel
8	Caistor	A.	—
9	Carlton le Moorland	A.	by church
10	Crowland, Isle of	—	
11	Freiston	H.	chapel
12	Gainsborough	A.	—
13	Grantham	A.	by St. Peter's chapel
14	Grimsby	H.	St. Andrew by St. Leonard's Priory
15	Halton Marsh, nr. Miningsby	H.	—
16	Holland Marsh (" Hoyland ")	H.	chapel of St. Thomas M.
17	Lincoln (Greesen foot)	A.	in Holy Trinity - at - the - Stairs
17a	Ludborough	H.	—

1. Dugd. V. 455 ; Chart R. 1328.   2. *Itin.* I. 29.   3. Reg. Bokyngham, Mem. f. 30 *b*.   4. Pipe R.S. XXXIII. 23.   5. Bale, *Script.* 622-3.   5a. Will of Robert Pell of Newton.   6. Arch. Cant. XI. 37.   7. Reg. Bokyngham, Mem. f. 423 II. 79.   8. *Fœd.* IX. 275.   9. Reg. Beck, Mem. 91.   10. Birch, *Mem. of St. Guthlac ;* Gir. Camb. Op. III. 419 ; Nov. Leg. II. 698.   11. Reg. Bokyngham, Mem. f. 372.   12.

CESTERSHIRE

Date.	Patron.	Name.
— *bef.* 1174	— Luffield Priory, Private	*Hardulph* 3 brethren
— *bef.* 1388	Private, Garendon Abbey Duchy of Lanc.	— Matilda, 1388 ; Maude Wardesale, 1400 ; Isolda N., *c.* 1405
1382	—	Wm. de Swinderby, pr.
— *c.* 1231	Abbey Private	— *Elias, monk, warden ; Ric. de Keten, pr., etc.*
bef. 1220	,,	3 priests

II. 53-6 ; Fasc. Zizan. 334-40 ; Foxe, *Acts and Mon.* III. 195-6.   6. Nichols, I, Pt. II. 328.   7. Reg. Hugh de Wells, II. 321 ; Nichols, *II*, Pt. II. 815.   8. Reg. Hugh de Wells, I. 255.

SHIRE

Date.	Patron.	Name.
c. 1142	Revesby Abbey	—
xvi c.	—	—
1366	—	
1183	—	Matilda
c. 1488	—	George or Gregory Riplay
1524	—	" Armett," pr.
1409	—	John Kyngston, monk
1395	—	Thomas de Gretham
1415	—	
1347	—	Jn., son of Geoffrey of Knaresboro', pr.
c. 700	—	Guthlac, *d.* 714 ; Cissa ; Beccel ; Egbert ; Tatwin ; Lady Altrida, 794 ; Wulsi, *c.* 1035
1390	—	John Frere
1415	—	—
1338	—	Emma of Stapleford
1342	Crown	Simon de Scopwick ; cf. Peter, h. of Grimsby, 1348
—	Revesby Abbey	founded by Ralph, monk
1189	Sempringham Priory	—
1382	—	Isabella, 1383 ; D. Matilda, 1453
1530	—	Robert Fen

See (8).   13. Reg. Burghersh, Mem. 379 *b*.   14. Pat. 1342, 1348.   15. J. C. Walter, *Horncastle*, 139.   16. *Pap. Lett.* IV. 431.   17. J. E. Stocks, *Market Harborough Rec.* 58 ; *Linc. Wills*, 67 ; Insrtuctions for Priests (E.E. Text S.), 90.   17*a. Linc. Consist. Court*, 1520-31, f. 323.

XXI. LINCOLN

	Place.		Description.
18	Lincoln (Danesgate)	A.	at church of St. Andrew *super collem*
19	„ (Wigford)	A.	at St. Andrew's-in-Wigford
20	„	A.	by chapel of St. Mary M. in Holy Innocents' hospital
21	Lincoln, in diocese of	H.	—
22	„ „	H.	—
23	Nettleton by Caistor ("Twang-castre ")	H.	St. Mary
24	Newsham [in Brocklesby]	A.	—
25	Owston	A.	—
26	Revesby, nr. (Northdyke bridge)	H.	—
27	Saltfleet Haven [in Skidbrooke]	H.	chapel of St. Katherine
28	Skegness	H.	—
29	Stamford	A.	by St. Paul's church
30	„	A.	in parish church
30a	Strubby	H.	chapel
31	Tealby ("Tevelby Moor ")	H.	chapel of St. Thomas A. and St. Thomas M.
32	Thornton [Curtis]	A.	within abbey
33	Willingham, S. by	H.	on "Lymberghill"
34	Winterton	A.	by church

18, 19. *Linc. Wills*, 74. 20. Pat. 1339. 21. *Pap. Lett.* v. 59. 22. Reg. Cantilupe (Cant. and Yk. S.), II. 310. 23. Pat. 1348. 24. Somerset Ho., P.C.C. Luffenham, 20. 25. *Linc. Wills*, 153. 26. *V.C.H.* II. 141. 27. Pat. 1337 ; Reg. Bokyngham, f. 37. 28. W. O. Massingberd, *Ingoldmells R.* 117. 29. *Market Harborough Rec.*

XXII. MIDDLE

	Place.		Description.
1	Charing Cross	H.	St. Katharine
2	Hadley, Monken	H.	—
3	Harrow on the Hill	H.	St. Edmund and St. Catherine
4	Highgate [in Hornsey]	H.	chapel of St. Michael
5	*Highgate Rise, West Hill*	*H.*	—
6	Holborn	A.	at St. Giles-in-the-Fields
7	Islington	H.	—
8	Kensington	A.	—
9	Kilburn	H.	afterwards nunnery
10	London (Wall)	A.	at Allhallows' church
11	„	A.	„ „ Colman

1. Pat. 1263, 1267 ; R. R. Sharpe, *Cal. of Wills*, II. 107 ; Issue R., p. xxxi ; Macmichael, *Charing Cross*, 15. 2. Dugd. IV. 133, 149. 3. *Notes and Queries*, 10th Ser. III. 467. 4. Newcourt, *Repert.* I. 654 ; *Gent. Mag.*, 1834, I. 380-5. 5. W. Howitt,

SHIRE—*continued.*

Date.	Patron.	Name.
1394	—	—
1391	—	Isabella
1339	—	Elizabeth de Elm
1397	—	Thos. Bristow, pr.
1280	—	Br. Ric. de Chadelington
1348	—	Richard Dryng
1434	—	Sir Walter Bekeby
1419	—	—
bef. 1527	Revesby Abbey	—
1337	—	Rob. de Billesby ; John, 1366
1345	Private	William de Clederhowe
1382	—	Emmota Tonge of Bourn, 1435
1415	—	—
—	—	—
1331	—	Roger de Stamford and Ric. de Burle
1367	—	Petronilla de Wutton
1461	—	cf. Sir William *in monte*, 1434
1435	—	Beatrice Frank, nun

58 ; Reg. Gray, Mem. f. 187 *b*; Northampton Prob. Office, Bk. B. 12. 30. See (8). 30*a*. P.R.O. Rentals and Surveys (Duchy of Lanc.) Bdle. 6, No. 22. 31. Pat. 1331, 1336 ; Reg. Burghersh, Mem. 232 *b*. 32. Reg. Bokyngham, f. 53 *b*. 33. *Linc. Wills*, 180 ; Episc. Rec., Terriers, IV. f 138 ; cf. P.C.C. Luffenham, 20. 34. Reg. Gray, Mem. f. 186, 186 *b*.

SEX

Date.	Patron.	Name.
1263	Crown	*Simon de Brageham, pr.* 1267
bef. 1136	Walden Abbey	—
xv c.	—	—
bef. 1386	Bishop	Wm. Lichfield, 1386 ; Wm. Forte, 1531
—	—	—
1371	—	—
xvi c.	—	—
1290	—	—
bef. 1135	Westminster Abbey	Godwyn
1459	City	anchoress, xv c. ; Wm. Lucas, *d.* 1486 ; Symon, *c.* 1513
1228	—	—

N. Heights of London, 413. 6. Sharpe, II. 148, 158. 7. Pat. 1546. 8. Swinfield R. (Camden S. 59), p. cxxix. 9. Dugd. III. 422, 426. 10. C. Welch, Churchwardens' Accounts. 11. *Arch. Journ.* XXIV. 343.

	Place.				Description.
12	London			A.	at St. Benet Fink
12*a*	,,			A.	under St. Dunstan
13	,,	without Bishopsgate		A.	at St. Botulph's
14	,,	,,	Temple Bar	A.	,, St. Clement Danes
15	,,	,,	Cripplegate	A.	,, St. Giles
16	,,	Jewry		A.	chyd. of St. Laurence
17	,,			A.	at St. Margaret Pattens
18	,,			A.	,, *St. Mary de Manny*
19	,,	Cornhill		A.	,, St. Peter's
20	,,	Cripplegate		H.	St. James
21	,,	within Bishopsgate		H.	—
22	,,	,,	,,	A.	in wall beside Bishops-gate
23	,,	in Tower		A.	St. Eustace (by St. Peter's chapel)
24	,,	in wall nr. Aldgate by Tower		H.	St. Mary and St. Nicholas
25	,,	"Swannesnest" by T.		—	nr. St. Katharine's hosp.
26	,,	nr. Tower		A.	—
27	,,			A.	by St. Bartholomew's hosp.
28	,,			A.	(professed in Holy Trinity Priory)
29	,,			A.	professed in Dominican friary
	Stratford *v. sub* Essex				—
30	Tottenham			H.	chapel of St. Anne
31	Westminster			A.	by St. Margaret's in Abbey
32	,,			A.	—

12, 13. Sharpe, I. 483 ; II. 107, 146 ; Rye MSS. L'Estrange Wills, I. f. 609; Magd. Coll. Oxford, MSS. 77, 156. 12*a*. Pat. 1267. 14. Nicolas, *Royal Wills*, 250 ; *Hist. Collections* (Camden S.N.S. 17) p. xliii. 15. Sharpe, II. 107. 16. *Ibid*. II. 147, 197 ; *Arch. Cant.* XI. 36. 17. Close, 1236 ; *V.C.H.* London, I. 587. 18. Sharpe, II. 107. 19. *Ibid.* I. 483, 638 ; Reg. Baldock (Cant. and Yk. S.), 54 ; Parl. R. I. 418. 20. Pat. 1255-6, 1259, 1265, 1275, 1281, 1286, 1290, 1291, 1292, 1296, 1335, 1341 ; Reg. Baldock, 140-2. 21. Pat. 1342, 1346. 22. *Linc. Wills*, 117 ; *Royal*

SEX—*continued.*

Date.	Patron.	Name.
1345	—	—
1267	—	Maud Malet
1370	—	" wht. Bpsgate," D. Joan, 1449
1426	—	D. Joan
1361	—	—
1361	—	Ric. le Coupe, pr., and Geoffrey Richard, 1370
1236	—	—
1361	—	—
bef. 1307	Parish	Beatrice de Meaus, 1307 ; *Emma Cheyne, widow,* 1449
bef. 1199	Crown ; Garendon Abbey	Warin, pr., *d.* 1205 ; Rob. Bat ; Jordan de Eston ; Jn. le Megre ; Ric. de Ginges ; Laurence ; Rob. de S. Laurencio ; Wm de. Wyntreburn ; Jn. de Bello ; Thos. de Byreford ; Alan Chauns, Wm. de Lyons, 1332 ; Jn. de Flitwick, etc.
1342	Crown	Jn. de Warrewyk ; Robert, 1346
1415	—	—
1237	Crown	William, 1237 ; Idonea de Boclaund, 1252
1257	—	John ; Berengar ; Jn. le Megre
1360	—	John Ingram, 1371
1371	—	Sir Robert
1227	Crown	Katherine, wife of W. Hardel
1513	—	Simon Appulby, pr.
1521	—	Margerie Clyute
—	—	—
1408	Holy Trinity Priory	Thomas Hert
1241	Abbey	Br. Nicholas ; Br. Jn. Myrymouth ; Jn. London, *d.* 1429 ; Wm. Alnewyk, *c.* 1415.
1443	Crown	Cecily Norton, widow ; Alicia Rippas, 1486

Wills, 250 ; *Test. Vetust.* I. 356 ; Sharpe, II. 107.   23. Close, 1237 ; J. Bayley, *Tower,* 129.   24. Hund. R. I. 413, 420 ; P.R.O. Anc. Deeds, A. 1653 ; Pat. 1259 ; Cal. Lett. Bk. E. 49, 193.   25, 26. Sharpe, II. 147, 218, 228.   27. Close, 1227.   28. *V.C.H.,* London, I. 587.   29. Bodl. Tanner, CLXXVI. 132 *b.*   30. Gibbons, *Ely Rec.* 406 ; W. Bedwell, *Tottenham,* ed. 1818, 17-19.   31. Close, 1241 ; Pat. 1244, 1247 ; Sharpe, II. 260, 398 ; *Royal Wills,* 250 ; Stanley, *Mem.* 431, 447, 467, 641.   32. *Acts of P. Council,* V. 282 ; Pat. 1443, 1453, 1456, 1486 ; B.M. Harl. 433, f. 41.

	Place.			Description.
1	Acle	(bridge)	H.	site, " Hermitage Staithe "
2	Attlebridge		H.	—
3	Banham	(Stonebridge)	H.	—
4	Bawburgh	(bridge)	H.	chapel
5	Brandiston		A.	—
6	Cley-next-the-Sea		H.	chapel
7	Coxford		A.	—
8	Cressingham, Great		H.	chapel of St. George
9	Cromer		H.	—
10	Downham Hythe (Market) bridge		H.	—
11	*Erpingham*		*H.*	—
12	*Heacham, nr. Hunstanton*		—	—
13	Holm [in Horning]		A.	at St. Benet's
14	Houghton-in-the-Hole		H.	St. Catherine
15	Hunstanton		H.	—
16	Ickburgh	(Newbridge)	H.	St. Mary and St. Laurence (once hospital)
17	Langley		H.	—
18	Litcham		H.	—
19	Lynn, Bishop's		A.	—
20	,,	(Gaywood)	H.	chapel of St. Catherine
21	,,		H.	at " Lenne Crouch "
22	,,		H.	,, St. Margaret's
23	,,		H.	,, St. Nicholas
24	,,	(Eastgate)	H.	—
25	,,	(Southgate)	H.	—
26	,, South		A.	,, church of All Saints
27	,, ,,		A.	,, Carmelite friary
28	,,		A.	in Dominican friary
29	,,		A.	—
30	,,		A.	—
31	*Martham*, in or nr.		A.	—
32	Massingham		A.	—
33	,,		H.	—
34	Narford in Westacre		H.	chapel
—	Newbridge, *v.* Ickburgh		—	—
35	Norwich		—	church of All Saints

1. R. C. Taylor, *Index Mon.* 27.   2. Pat. 1405 ; B. X. 401.   3. B. I. 359.   4. B. II. 389.   5. B. VIII. 197 ; Taylor, 65.   6. Pat. 1343.   7. *Archæologia*, XXV. 524. 8. B. VI. 106.   9. *Pap. Lett.* VII. 421.   10. Ramsey Cart. II. 190, 215 ; B. VII. 344 ; Pat. 1398.   11. Hundred R. I. 514.   12. Taylor, 65.   13. *Mem. St. Edmunds* (Rolls 96), I. 38.   14. Pat. 1443 ; B. IX. 247.   15. *Archæologia*, XXV. 494 ; cf. B. X. 324. 16. B. II. 239 ; Pat. 1448.   17. Rye MSS. L'Estrange Wills, f. 795 *b*.   18. B. X. 14 ;

FOLK

Date.	Patron.	Name.
—	—	—
1405	—	Thomas Heremyte
—	—	—
1526	—	Margery de Boton, n.d.
1343	—	Rob. de Barton Bendish, pr.
1537	—	—
—	Parochial	
1425	—	John Hastyng
c. 1200	Private	Br. Aillet ; Jn. Skillynge, warden, 1398
1274-5	—	*Geoffrey*
—	Lewes Priory	—
xi c.	—	Aelfwen, nun
1443	Horsham Priory	*Walter White*
bef. 1530	Private	Thomas Cooke
1441	—	Ric. Ferneys, d. 1464 ; Jn. Bath ; Wm. Dane, 1481 ; *Jn. Canon ;* Sir Jn. Lyster, 1528
1455	—	William Sabyn
—	—	Thomas Cannon
—	—	Margery Kempe, n.d.
1381	Town, etc.	John Consolif
1349	—	John Puttock
1405-7	—	John ; Thomas
1373-4	—	John
1384-6	—	Ann Whyote, hermit
,,	—	Thomas
,,	—	—
1421	—	Joanna Catfelde, 1421 ; *Wm. Clays*, 1510
1440	—	Geoffrey, 1440 ; Jn. Lot, 1497
1392	—	—
1449	—	Isabella
xiii c.	—	Olive de Raveningham
1256	—	Ela and companions
1339	—	Br. John
—	—	—
1288	—	anchorite, 1288 ; Jn. Levot or Levolfe, hermit, d. 1509

Taylor, 65. 19. E. Underhill, *Mysticism*, 270, 554. 20-26. H. Harrod, *Deeds and Rec.* 30 ; B. VIII. 513-4 ; H. J. Hillen, *Lynn*, 250-1. 27. Bale, *Script*. 565. 28. *Arch. Journ.* XLI. 83-4. 29. Wylie, *Henry IV*, IV. 145 *n.* 30. L'Estrange Wills, f. 609. 31. Hist. MSS. (Holkam), 1907, Various, IV. 319. 32. B. III. 489. 33. Pat. 1339. 34. B. VI. 236 ; Taylor, 65. 35. Hudson and Tingey, *Rec.* I. 358 ; L'Estrange Wills, f. 1612 ; B. IV. 134.

	Place.			Description.
36	Norwich		A.	church of St. Christopher
37	,,	Conisford	A.	,, St. Edward
38	,,		A.	,, St. Etheldred
39	,,	Tombland	A.	,, St. George
40	,,	on the Hill	H.	,, St. Giles
41	,,	Timberhill	A.	,, St. John B.
42	,,		H.	,, ,,
43	,,	Conisford	A.	,, St. John E.
44	,,	,,	A.	,, St. Julian
45	,,	Carrow	A.	in priory
46	,,	Newbridge	—	church of St. Margaret
47	,,		A.	,, St. Mary Combust
48	,,	in Coselany	A.	,, St. Mary
49	,,		A.	,, St. Michael at Plea
50	,,		A.	,, St. Olave
51	,,	Hungate	A.	,, St. Peter
52	,,		A.	,, St. Saviour
53	,,		A.	under Holy Cross chapel
54	,,		A.	by St. Martin's bridge
55	,,		A.	at Dominican Friary
56	,,		H.	nr. chapel in fields
57	,,		A.	at St. Giles or Newport Gate
58	,,		H.	by Bishop's bridge
59	,,		H.	at Magdalen gate
60	,,		H.	by Berstreet ,,
61	,,		H.	at St. Stephen's gate
62	,,	Conisford	H.	,, South ,,
63	,,		H.	,, Heigham ,,
64	,,		H.	,, St. Austin's ,,
65	,,	Westwick	H.	,, St. Benet's ,,
66	,,		H.	,, St. Martin's ,,

36. *Rec.* II. 359. 37. B. IV. 70 ; Norf. and Norw. Arch. S. I. 124. 38. B. IV. 75. 39. See (36). 40-3. B. IV. 239, 128, 336, 102. 44-5. W. Rye, *Carrow Abbey ; Paston Lett.* II. 267. 46-7. Rye, *Norwich Deeds*, 100, 103 ; B. IV. 474. 48. Taylor, 65. 49. See (36). 50. B. IV. 475. 51. See (36). 52. B. IV. 444. 53. Bale, *Script.* 565 ;

FOLK—*continued*

Date.	Patron.	Name.
1247 xiii c.	— —	— Margaret ; D. Joan, 1428 ; D. Agnes Kyte, 1458
bef. 1305 1247 1428	— — —	— — Sir Richard, 1428
— xiv c. *c.* 1300 xiv c.	— Dominican Friary Franciscan „ Carrow Priory	— — — D. Julian, *c.* 1373-1413; D. Julian Lampit, *c.* 1428-1478; D. Ag- nes, 1472 ; D. Eliz. Scott, 1481 ; D. Agnes Edrygge, 1524
1429 1305	— Norwich Priory	D. Margaret Kydman, *bef.* 1546 Katherine, anchoress, 1305 ; Jn. Martin, hermit, 1429
1304 — 1247	— — —	Cecily " St. Anne's anchoress " —
1289 1247 *bef.* 1288 1421 1441	— — — Carmelite Friary „ „	Margaret and Alice — Sabine Lady Emma Stapilton, 1421-42 Thos. Bradley, 1441 ; Jn. Castle- acre, 1465 ; Thos. Barton, 1479
1471 1410	— —	Kath. Foster, 1471 ; Kath. Man, " late recluse," 1548 Sir Thomas, 1410 ; Richard, 1455
1244 — —	— Norwich Priory —	— — —
xiii c. 1435	— —	Thomas, 1455 Thos. Basset, *d.* 1435 ; Rob. Godard, 1483
1455 — — —	— — — —	John [*Felton*] — — —

Zimmerman, *Hist. Carm.* I. 408. 54. Bale, 629 ; L'Estrange Wills, f. 64 ; N. and N.
Arch. S. IV. 332, 337. 55. *Ibid.* III. 166 ; IV. 335 ; Kirkpatrick, *Relig. Orders*, 51-2.
56. Taylor, 65 ; L'Estrange, f. 794. 56-66. Kirkpatrick, 211 ; B. IV. 140, 165, 167,
250, 438. 60-2. L'Estrange Wills, f. 444 *b*, 795 *b*, 849 *b*.

	Place.		Description.
67	*Norwich*	H.	—
68	Norwich, diocese of	H.	—
69	Outwell	H.	chapel of St. Christopher
70	Pickenham, N.	H.	„ St. Paul
71	Pulham, St. Mary V.	H.	„ St. James
72	Shipdam	H.	St. Thomas of Canterbury
73	Stalham	H.	chapel of St. Andrew
74	Stow Bardolph (bridge)	H.	*St. Botulph*
75	Stratton, Long	A.	chapel
76	Suffield	A.	—
77	Thetford (Castle Hill)	H.	—
78	„	H.	in church of St. Giles
79	„	H.	St. John's chapel
80	Thornham	A.	—
81	Walpole	H.	chapel of All Saints
82	*Walsham*	*H.*	—
83	Walsingham, Little	A.	in Franciscan friary
84	Walsoken (" Sculedale ")	H.	—
85	„	H.	Holy Trinity
86	Weasenham	H.	St. Paul
87	Welney	H.	—
88	Wiggenhall St. Mary M.	H.	—
89	Winch, West	A.	—
90	*Worstead*	*H.*	—

67. *Ibid.* f. 1754 *b.* 68. *East Anglian,* IX. 107. 69. Pat. 1348. 70. B. VI. 69. 71-2. Gibbons, *Ely Rec.* 401, 413. 73. *Pap. Lett.* IX. 302, 333-4. 74. B. VII. 448 ; *Ely Dioc. Rem.,* 1901, p. 39. 75. B. V. 193. 76. B. III. 489. 77-9. T. Martin, *Thetford,* 10, 81 ; B. II. 75, 87-8 ; Pat. 1413. 80. B. III. 489. 81. *Ely Rec.* 403 ;

XXIV. NORTH

	Place.		Description.
1	Brampton Ash, Beston in	H.	chapel of St. Augustine
2	Fotheringhay (in wood)	H.	—
3	Grafton Regis	H.	St. Mary and St. Michael
4	Grimsbury (Banbury Bridge)	H.	—
5	Harrowden, Little	H.	at chapel of St. Andrew
6	Islip or Thrapston (bridge)	H.	chapel
7	Marholm	H.	St. Guthlac
7a	Newark by Northampton	H.	at chapel of St. Mary M.

1. P.R.O. Sp. Exch. Com. No. 1672 ; Bridges, *Northants,* II. 284. 2. *Ibid.* 451 ; B.M. Cott. Aug. II. 125. 3. Baker, *Northants,* II. 170-1. *Ibid.* I. 750 ; A. Beesley, *Banbury,* 161. 5. Northampton Probate Office, Bk. A. f. 415, B. f. 139 ; D.

FOLK—*continued*

Date.	Patron.	Name.
1516	—	" Maister Clyff "
1504	—	John Ferys
1348	—	—
xvi c.	—	—
1401	—	Walter Colman
1487	—	—
1443	—	John Kylburn
1406	Gild	Thomas Coteler
1256	—	—
1256	—	—
—	—	—
xv. c.	—	—
1413	Austin Friary	—
1256	Bishop	—
1404	—	Robert Downham
1274-5	—	*William*
1507	—	—
tp. John	—	—
c. 1390	—	Wm. Danyell ; *W. Crouch*, etc.
bef. 1465	—	Jn. Keating, "late hermit" ; Thos. Leek
xii c.	Private, Pentney Priory	—
—	—	John
—	—	Mabilia de Leverington, n.d.
1274-5	—	*Roger*

Dioc. Rem., 1901, p. 58.   82. Hundred R. I. 505.   83. L'Estrange Wills, III. f. 1600 ; B. IX. 281.   84. Ramsey Cart. III. 295.   85. Pat. 1390, 1408, 1414.   86. See (30).   87-8. Dugd. VI. 69 ; V. 69, 70.   89. B. IX. 157.   90. Hundred R. I. 508.

AMPTONSHIRE

Date.	Patron.	Name.
bef. 1420	—	— Chambers, xvi c.
bef. 1176	Saltrey Abbey	—
bef. 1205	Private ; St. James's Abbey, Northampton	Elias
xvi c.	—	—
1517	—	Sir Thomas, pr., 1519-33
1400	Crown	William Mareschal, pr.
1395	—	—
1446	Peterborough Abbey	John Grenefeld

f. 86 ; Sp. Exch. Com. 1672.   6. Pat. 1400 ; *Itin.* I. 8 ; Bridges, II. 239.   7. Pat. 1395. 7a. B. M. Lansd. 1028, f. 188.

	Place.			Description.
8	Northampton		A.	at church of St. Giles
9	,,		A.	—
10	,,		A.	at Carmelite Friary
11	,,		A.	at Our Lady of Grace in Austin Friary
12	,,	nr. S. bridge	H.	at chapel of St. Thomas
13	,,		H.	at St. James' End
14	,,	W. bridge	H.	—
15	,,	in or nr.	H.	at a chapel
16	,,	(Kingsthorpe)	H.	St. David (afterwards hosp.)
17	Oundle		A.	—
18	Peakirk		—	cell of St. Pega, or hermitage of St. Bartholomew
19	Peterborough		A.	—
20	Pipwell		H.	*St. Mary de Divisis*
21	Radstone		H.	—
22	Rockingham		H.	—
23	Rushden		H.	at chapel of St. James
24	Singlesole, nr. Peterborough		H.	—
25	Stowe Wood, nr. Bugbrooke		H.	—
—	Thrapston *v.* Islip		—	—
26	Towcester		H.	—
27	Weldon		H.	chapel

8. B.M. Add. ch. 7028.   9. Eng. Wills (E.E. Text S.), 48.   10. B.M. Harl. 3838, f. 37.   11. Nhp. Prob. Off., Bk. B. f. 33, 119 ;   D. 288 ; E. 21 ; P.R.O. Surrender Deeds, No. 169.   12. *Ibid.* D. f. 209.   13. Will of W. Henne.   14. J. C. Cox, *Borough Rec.* II. 523, 432.   15. Somerset Ho., P.C.C. 4 Blamyr.   16. P.R.O. Anc. Deeds, C. 2026.   17. Pipe R.S. XXVI. 105.   18. *V.C.H.* II. 519 ; Bridges, II. 577.

	Place.			Description.
1	Alnwick, nr. (?)		H.	—
2	Bedlington		H.	at lepers' hospital
3	Berwick-on-Tweed (Segden)		H.	chapel
4	Byker		H.	chapel of St. Mary V. and St. Anne
5	Caistron	(Maydenly, nr.)	H.	St. John
6	Coquet Is.		H.	—

1. Northumb. Assize R. (S.S. 88), 70 ; P.R.O. Assize R. 642 m. 10.   2. Pat. 1388.   3. Cal. Doc. Scotland, III. 45 ; J. Scott, *Berwick*, 348.   4. Pat. 1344.   5. New-

AMPTONSHIRE—*continued*.

Date.	Patron.	Name.
tp. Edw. I.	—	Eva
1420	—	—
1421	—	Alice Wakleyne, nun, *d.* 1426 ; Margaret Hawten
1510	—	Father Anker, 1522 ; Rob. Barrett, 1538
1528	—	Stonton
1519	—	—
—	—	—
1501	—	John Mason, pr.
xii c.	St. Andrew's Priory	—
1176	Peterborough Abbey	—
viii c.	Crowland Abbey	St. Pega
1176	Abbey	—
xii c.	—	—
1215	Private	Elyseus
xvi c.	—	—
xvi c.	—	—
bef. 1190	Peterborough Abbey	—
—	—	Alnoth
—	—	—
1534	—	John Littley
1516	—	Sir Gregory, pr. 1528

19. See (17). 20. Dugd. v. 431, 434 ; Bridges, II. 331. 21. Close, 1215-6, 1225 ; Pat. 1227 ; cf. Pat. 1260, "House of Radestan". 22. Sp. Exch. Com. 1672. 23. *Arch. Journ.*, 1901, p. 130. 24. Chart. R. 1332. 25. Nov. Leg. II. 423. 26. Nhp. Prob. Off., Bk. E. f. 154. 27. *Ibid.* A. f. 415, D. f. 288, 328 ; E. f. 21.

UMBERLAND

Date.	Patron.	Name.
1255-6	—	Seman de Botelesham
1388	Bishop	Ric. Holewey of Shypwassh
1311	Hosp. of St. Mary M.	Br. Roger of Wateby
1344	—	John Segerstane
1247	Newminster Abbey	Br. Hugh of Hepes
bef. 1127	Tynemouth Priory	St. Henry, *d.* 1127 ; Martin, *c.* 1300.

minster Cart. (S.S. 66), p. xvi, 138-40. 6. J. C. Hodgson, *Northumb.* V. 316-21.

XXV. NORTH

	Place.		Description.
7	Corbridge	H.	—
8	Farne Is.	H.	—
9	*Lilburn*	H.	—
10	Merkelldene [in Earsdon]	H.	St. Ninian, *alias* St. Ryn-yane
11	Newcastle-upon-Tyne	A.	at church of St. John B.
12	,,	A.	,, ,, ,, St. Nicholas
13	,,	A.	in Dominican Friary
14	Norham on Tweed	H.	—
15	*St. John Lee* (" Hernshow ")	H.	—
16	Warenford by Bamboro'	H.	at leper's hospital
17	Warkworth	H.	chapel of Holy Trinity

7. Pat. 1354.   8. Bede, *Vita S. Cuthberti ;* Symeon Dunelm, I. 295-325 ; Nov. Leg. I. 101-6.   9. Reg. Pal. Dunelm, III. 137, 190, 199.   10. Hodgson, IX. 120, 121. 11. Pat. 1260 ; J. R. Boyle, *Vestiges of Newcastle*, 160.   12. *Ibid*. 93.   13. *Fœd*. IX.

XXVI. NOTTING

	Place.		Description.
1	Blyth	A.	—
2	,,	H.	chapel of St. James
3	,,	H.	,, St. Michael
4	Clipston [Birkland in Sherwood]	H.	,, St. Edwin
5	Felley	H.	St. Helen
6	Halloughton (" Halton by South-well ")	A.	—
7	Kneesall	A.	—
8	Mansfield, East Thwaite	H.	—
9	Mansfield-Woodhouse	A.	—
10	Nottingham	A.	in church of St. Nicholas
11	,,	H.	" called Owswell "
12	,, (Sneinton)	H.	rock hermitage
13	,, in archdeaconry of	A.	—
14	Welbeck	A.	—

1. Close, 1241 ; Reg. Giffard (S.S. 109), 116 ; Reg. Wichwane (S.S. 114), 74. 2, 3. Pat. 1335.   4. Close, 1205, 1217 ; Pat. 1318 ; *V.C.H*. II. 62.   5. *V.C.H*. II. 109. 6. *Linc. Wills*, 97.   7. *Ibid*. 118 ; *Fœd*. IX. 275.   8. Walkerdine, *Mansfield Deanery*, 6.

UMBERLAND—*continued.*

Date.	Patron.	Name.
1354	—	Thomas de Anderstowe
676	Lindisfarne Abbey ; Durham Priory	Cuthbert, *d.* 687 ; Aethelwald, 687-99 ; Aelwin, *bef.* 1150 ; Bartholomew, 1150-93 ; Thos., *c.* 1163 ; Aelric
1337	Private	Robert
bef. 1497	—	Robert Coward, 1500
1260	—	Christiana Umfred
1408	—	
1415	—	
bef. 1329	Durham Priory	Roger de Ellesden, pr. ; *Rob. de Dunelmo,* 1337
c. 687	—	St. John of Beverley
1399	Duchy of Lancaster	Richard Hayzaund
1487	Earldom	Edward Slegg, 1515 ; *George Lancastre,* 1531

275. 14. Raine, *N. Durham,* 262. 15. Hodgson, IV. 143-4. 16. *Ibid.* I. 251. 17. *Ibid.* V. 134 ; C. H. Hartshorne, *Antiq. of Northumb.* II. 212-28.

HAMSHIRE

Date.	Patron.	Name.
1241	Archbishop	2 recluses, 1271 ; D. Joan, 1281
1335	—	Br. Peter de Lound
"	—	Br. Jn. le Mareschal
bef. 1205	Crown	Benedict, 1217 ; Roger de Trusseley, 1318
1156	Private ; Priory	Br. Robert
1401	—	
1411	—	
c. 1280	—	
1403	—	
bef. 1394	Crown	Joan de Aylston
1357-8	—	
xvi c.	—	
1267	—	
1411	—	John, recluse

9. *Linc. Wills,* 103, 118. 10. Pat. 1394, 1400 ; Test. Ebor. II. (S.S. 30), 131. 11, 12. Stevenson and Stapleton, *Religious Inst. of Notts,* 163, 208-9. 13. Reg. Giffard, p. 185. 14. *Linc. Wills,* 118.

	Place.		Description.
1	Bicester	H.	chapel of St. John B.
2	Cassington	A.	—
3	Crowmarsh	A.	—
4	Dornford [in Wootton]	A.	—
5	Ewelme	H.	at chapel
—	Finmere, *v. sub* Bucks	—	—
6	Henley (bridge)	H.	—
7	Horsepath	A.	—
8	Iffley	A.	—
9	Lockesley [in Wychwood]	H.	—
10	Loughboro', Low Barrow, nr. Leafield	H.	—
11	Muswell [in Piddington]	H.	chapel of Holy Cross
—	Newbridge *v.* Standlake	—	—
12	Oxford near	A.	at Holywell church
13	,,	A.	,, St. Budock's church
14	,,	A.	,, St. Ebbe's ,,
15	,,	A.	,, St. Giles's ,,
16	,,	A.	,, St. John's ,,
17	,,	A.	,, St. Peter's-in-the-E.
18	,,	A.	in a certain church
19	,, Grandpont, S. bridge	H.	chapel of St. Nicholas
20	,, Pettypont, E. ,,	H.	—
21	Pheleley	H.	chapel of St. John B.
22	Standlake (New Bridge)	H.	—
23	Tetsworth [in Thame]	H.	St. John Baptist

1. J. Dunkin, *Bicester*, 117.   2. Close, 1237.   3. Bodl. Oseney, ch. XIV.   4. Pat. 1236.   5. Pat. 1403 ; *Linc. Wills*, 193 ; *Valor Ecc.* II. 201, 265.   6. J. S. Burn, *Henley*, 196.   7. See (3).   8. Pat. 1234 ; Close, 1235, 1238, 1241.   9. Pat. 1337.   10. Close, 1232 ; Dugd. VI. 684 ; Reg. Giffard (Worc. Hist. S.), II. 537 ; V. J. Walney, *Cornbury*, 19.   11. Dugd. VI. 549 ; B.M. Harl. 3688, f. 128-9, 133.   12. Surius, *Vitæ S.S.* VI. 688 ; Close, 1236.   13. Pat. 1242 ; Oseney, Ch. XIV.   14. Magd. Mun.

	Place.		Description.
1	Langham	H.	—
2	Norewood [in Clipsham]	H.	—
3	Ryhall	—	—

1. Pat. 1314, 1326.   2. Reg. Hugh de Wells (Cant. and Yk. S.), II. 137.

SHIRE

Date.	Patron.	Name.
1355	—	Nicholas Jurdan
1237	—	Matilda de la More
1271	—	—
1236	Crown	Br. Robert
1403	Bruern Abbey	Simon Kirton, 1403 ; Thos. Wylkys, *d.* 1458
—	—	—
1505	—	—
1271	—	—
1234	Crown	Annora, 1238 ; Alienora, 1241
1337	Deerhurst Priory ; Crown	*Roger*, pr.
1232	Crown ; Lechlade Priory	Robert ; Ernald and Lucian, 1232
bef. 1154	Private ; Missenden Abbey	Ralph
—	—	—
c. 1180	—	Matthew
1242	—	Alice
bef. 1225	—	Basilia
1271	—	—
1271	—	—
c. 1227	—	—
c. 1194	—	—
1359	Town	Jn. Braye of Shiplake, 1365 ; Wm. Cardon, 1399
bef. 1358	,,	*Hugo Rose, custos,* 1321 ; Nic. Wadekyns, 1358
bef. 1135	Private ; Eynsham Abbey	—
c. 1434	—	Wm. de Cornubia, *c.* 1434 ; Thos. Brigges, *c.* 1462
1447	Gild	—

St. Ebbe's, No. 7. 15. Wood, Oxford (Hist. S.), II. 503. 16. *Ibid. ;* Oseney R. LIII.
17. Magd. Mun. St. Peter's, 21 B, 29 C ; New Coll. Mun. St. Peter's, No. 62, 68.
18. H. Salter, Eynsham Cart. II. 273, 334 ; cf. Vita S. Hugonis (Rolls S. 37), 239.
19, 20. Wood, II. 498 ; Bodl. Twyne, XXIII. 340, 390. 21. Dugd. III. 20 ; Eynsham Cart. I. p. XIV. 22. Twyne, IV. 243. 23. Pat. 1447.

LAND

Date.	Patron.	Name.
1314	—	Jn. de Norton, 1314 ; Jn. de Warrewyk, 1326
c. 1226	—	*Ric. de Beddestowe, pr.*
vii c.	—	St. Tibbe

3. Wright, *Rutland*, III. ; Women S.S. (E.E.T.S.), 73.

	Place.		Description.
1	Albrighton	H.	—
2	Astley Abbots (" Estlege ")	A.	—
—	Athelardston *v.* Bridgnorth		—
3	Bridgnorth (" Athelardston," by)	H.	Cave and oratory
4	Haughmond	H.	afterwards Abbey
5	Langley [in Acton-Burnell]	H.	—
6	Le Botwood	H.	—
7	Ludlow (Temebridge)	H.	St. Katharine
8	Mount Gilbert, the Wrekin	H.	—
9	Newport	H.	chapel of St. Katherine
10	Priors Lee	A.	—
11	Shrewsbury (Mount)	H.	by Cadogan's Cross
12	,,	A.	at St. Chad's church
13	,,	A.	,, St. Mary's ,,
14	,, Frankwell	A.	,, St. George's chapel
15	,,	A.	,, St. Romald's ,,
16	,, without	H.	,, St. Mary M.'s ,,
17	,,	A.	,, Dominican friary
18	,, six miles from	A.	in church

1. Cal. Inq. p.m. Edw. I, Vol. 2, No. 569. 2. Chart R. 1265. 3. Pat. 1328, 1333, 1335, 1346 ; *Staffs Coll.*, N.S. VIII. 40. 4. *Itin.* VIII. 106. 5, 6. Eyton, *Salop*, VI. 145, 245-6. 7. Pat. 1410. 8. Pat. 1265 ; Eyton, I. 310, IX. 149 ; *Staffs Coll.*, N.S. VIII. 154. 9. *Staffs Coll.*, N.S. VIII. 60, 154. 10. E. L. Cutts, *Scenes and Characters*,

XXX. SOMER

	Place.		Description.
1	Andersey [in Curry Rivel]	H.	—
2	Badgworthy [Exmoor]	H.	—
3	Bath and Wells, in diocese of	H.	—
4	Batheaston (" Horteley ")	H.	chapel
—	Bristol, *v. sub.* Glos.		—
5	Buckland [in Durston]	A.	nr. Hospitaller's church
6	*Congresbury*, nr.	—	chapel of Holy Trinity
7	Crewkerne	A.	by church
8	,,	H.	—
9	Glastonbury	—	—

1. Athelney Cart. (Somerset Rec. S. 14), 166. 2. Buckland Cart. (S.R.S. 25), 121, 196. 3. Reg. Radulf (S.R.S. 9), 245. 4. Chantries (S.R.S. 2), 151-2. Cf. Hartley Farm. 5. *Pap. Lett.* VII. 180. 6. Nov. Leg. I. 249-50. 7. Trokelowe, *Ann.*

SHIRE

Date.	Patron.	Name.
1284	—	
1265	—	
—	—	
1328	Crown	Jn. de Oxendon, 1328 ; Andrew de Corbrigge, 1333 ; *Edmund de la Mare*, 1335 ; Roger de Burghton, 1346 ; Ric. de Callyley, 1367
bef. 1101	—	
1180	—	
c. 1170	—	Bletherus, monk
1410	—	Thos. Shelve ; cf. Leintwardine
1265	Crown	Nicholas de Denton
1355	—	Br. William, pr., 1371
1409	—	Br. Richard Goldeston
1355	—	
1355	—	Alice Breton
1272	—	Petronilla
1310	—	Emma Sprenghose
1314	—	Isolda de Hungerford
1356	—	Br. Roger
1415	—	
1296	—	Emma, nun

100. 11, 12. *Staffs Coll.*, N.S. VIII. 29, 154 ; Salop Arch. S., 3rd Ser. V. 394, 400. 13. Eyton, VI. 89. 14, 15. Owen and Blakeway, *Shrewsbury*, I. 315 *n* ; II. 475. 16. Pat. 1356. 17. *Fœd.* IX. 276. 18. Chr. Lanercost (Bannatyne Club), 183-5.

SET

Date.	Patron.	Name.
bef. 1166	Private	Herduin
bef. 1184	—	" hermits "
1335	—	Jn. Worm of Glastonbury
xvi c.	—	
—	—	Jn. Toker, friar
1420	—	St. Cungar
—	—	Robert Cherde, monk
1402	—	
1523	—	St. Gildas ; St. Dunstan
—	—	

Edw. II, ed. Hearne, 263 ; Reg. Bowett (S.R.S. 13), 36-7. 8. Gerard, Description (S.R.S. 15), 67 ; Wills (S.R.S. 19), 224. 9. See (11).

	Place.		Description.
10	Haselbury [Plucknett]	A.	by church
11	Holme, Flat, Is. (Ronech)	H.	—
12	„ Steep, Is. (Echni)	H.	—
13	Neroche (or Rechych) Forest	H.	—
14	Oath (" Oth ") in Aller	H.	—
15	Polden Hill	—	at chapel of St. Thomas
16	Publow	H.	" called Clarelewe "
17	Rownham [in Long Ashton]	H.	—
18	*St. Decumans*, nr. Watchet	—	—
19	Spraulesmede or Burtle [in Moorlinch]	H.	chapel of St. Stephen
20	Twerton	A.	'at church
21	Winscombe	H.	" in loco qui S. Romani nuncupatur "

10. B.M. Cott. Faust. B. IV. f. 67 *b* to 123 *b ;* Nov. Leg. II. 511-20 ; Gervase, I. 130-1 ; Roger Wend. I. 4-9 ; M. Paris, *Chr. Maj.* II. 205-9.   11, 12. *Vitæ*, ed. Giles (Caxton S. 1854), 312.   13. Reg. Drokensford (S.R.S. 1), 167.   14. *Ibid.* 284 ; W. Hunt, *Dioc. Hist.* 92, B.M. Harl. ch. 57 D. 4, 5.   15. Close, 1241 ; Wills (S.R.S.

	Place.		Description.
1	Bethney (now Stafford)	H.	—
2	Burton ("Scaleclif," "Andreseia ")	A.	chapel of St. Andrew
3	Calwich [in Ellastone]	H.	—
4	Dunstall	H.	—
5	Fairwell	H.	(afterwards nunnery)
6	Handsacre (Armitage)	H.	—
7	Newcastle-under-Lyne	A.	in the church
8	„	H.	—
9	Radmore [in Cannock Chase]	H.	(afterwards monastery)
10	Stafford	A.	—
11	Sutton Wood [in Forton]	H.	" locus S. Johannis B."
12	Tamworth (" Muryhull," by)	A.	at chapel
13	*Walton, nr. Stone*	*H.*	—
14	West Bromwich (by Sandwell)	H.	(afterwards priory)

1. Nov. Leg. I. 165.   2. *Ibid.* II. 210 ; Shaw, *Staffs*, I. p. I.   3. Dugd. VI. 224 ; *Staffs Coll.* (W. Salt S.), N.S. XII. 102, 278.   4. *Ibid.* p. 76 *n*.   5. Dugd. IV. III.   6. B.M. Add. Ch. 24239 : Shaw, 207.   7. Close, 1237.   8. *Staffs. Coll.*, N.S. VIII. 154 ;

SET—*continued*

Date.	Patron.		Name.
c. 1125	—		St. Wulfric, *d.* 1154
—	—		St. Cadoc
—	—		St. Gildas
1317	—		*Richard Bozon, pr.*
bef. 1328	—		Br. Thomas, friar, 1328
1241	—		Elneva built *reclusorium*, 1241 ; John, hermit, 1505
c. 1228	Private		—
1406	—		William Popylton
—	—		St. Decuman
bef. 1199	Private ;	Glastonbury Abbey	Br. Walter
1337	—		Sibilla of Bathford
1331	—		Phillip Schipham

19), 88.   16. Collinson, *Somerset*, II. 428.   17. *Ibid.* 296 ; Bristol Corp. MSS. Orphan Bk. f. 103 *b ; W. Worc.*, ed. Nasmith, 275.   18. Nov. Leg. I. 264.   19. Dugd. I. 34·5 ; Reg. Drokensford, 54.   20. Reg. Radulf (S.R.S. 9), 303.   21. *Ibid.* 70.

SHIRE

Date.	Patron.		Name.
—	—		St. Beccellin
—	—		St. Modwen
bef. 1148	Various		—
bef. 1162	Trentham	Priory	Walter
c. 1140	—		Roger, Geoffrey, and Robert
bef. 1307	—		*John, pr.*
1237	—		Avice
1355	—		*David Hawardedyn,* 1465
xii c.	—		Clement and Hervey
1415	—		—
bef. 1227	Private ;	Shrewsbury Abbey	—
1360	—		Br. Roger de Henerebarwe
—	—		*St. Wulfade*
xii c.	—		—

Pat. 1465.   9. Dugd. v. 446.   10. *Fœd.* IX. 275.   11. Dugd. III. 523.   12. *Staffs Coll.*, N.S. VIII. 93.   13. *Ibid.* XII. 111 ; O.S. I. 178.   14. Dugd. IV. 189, 190.

XXXII. SUF

	Place.		Description.
1	Blythborough	H.	—
2	Brandon Ferry (on bridge)	H.	*chapel of SS. Mary and Etheldreda*
3	Bury St. Edmunds	A.	in cemetery
4	,,	A.	—
5	,, W. gate	H.	chapel
6	Catiwade (bridge)	H.	chapel of St. Mary B.V.
7	Cowlinge	A.	—
8	Exning	H.	chapel of St. Mildred
9	Gorleston, Southtown	H.	near ferry
10	Ipswich	A.	at Carmelite friary
11	Sudbury	H.	in St. Gregory's chyd.
12	Thrandeston (" Randeston ")	A.	—

1. T. Gairdner, *Dunwich*, etc., 125.   2. *Ely Dioc. Rem.* 1903, p. 179 ; 1904, p. 150, 189 ; cf. 1905, p. 21.   3. Madox, *Form. Angl.* 423.   4. Pat. 1449.   5. R. Yates, *St. Edmundsbury*, 49.   6. Pat. 1360.   7. Close, 1234.   8. *Dioc. Rem.* 1897, p. 97.

XXXIII. SUR

	Place.		Description.
1	Bletchingley	H.	—
2	Brookwood [in Windsor Forest]	H.	—
3	Dorking	A.	—
4	Ewell	H.	—
5	Ottershaw (" Hoteressaham ")	H.	—
6	Sheen	A.	in house of Bethlehem
7	Southwark (Horsleydown)	H.	—
8	Thames Ditton, in or nr.	H.	—

1. Close, 1233.   2. Gervase, *Chr.* II. 295 ; Pat. 1367.   3. Close, 1240.   4. MS. Memoriale [per Canon Deedes].   5. Surrey Arch. Coll. *Feet of Fines*, 10.   6. Pat.

XXXIV. SUS

	Place.		Description.
1	Arundel	H.	at chapel of St. James
2	,,	A.	in Dominican Friary
3	Camber, the (Is. by Winchelsea)	H.	chapel of St. Anthony
4	Chichester	—	chapel of St. Ciriac

1. Tierney, *Arundel*, 679.   2. *Pap. Lett.* IV. 352 ; v. 470.   3. *W. Worcester*, 110 ;

FOLK

Date.	Patron.	Name.
1516	—	Robert Leake, *d.* 1517
bef. 1406	Bishop of Ely	Wm. Bussheby, 1406 ; Jn. Newton ; Ric. Passhlew ; Thos. Passhelawe, *d.* 1459, etc.
tp. John	—	Lucy
bef. 1449	—	— Cheyne
1360	—	Br. John atte Welle
1234	—	Nicholaa
1389	—	Philip de Cliston
xvi c.	—	Agnes, n.d.
1433	Parish	J. Levynton (& Ric. Appelby ?)
1157	—	*inclusus* 1157-81

9. C. J. Palmer, *Yarmouth*, III. 257 ; Suckling, *Suff.* I. 378.   10. B.M. Harl. 3838, f. 37.   11. B. II. 241 ; Suff. Inst. Arch. VIII. p. xxvii.   12. Pipe R.S. I-XXXI.

REY

Date.	Patron.	Name.
1233	Crown	Roger.
1289	—	Prior Thomas, 1289 ; *Jn. Tylman*, 1367
1240	—	—
bef. 1408	Merton Priory	—
1218	—	Geoffrey
1417	Crown, Priory	Jn. Kyngeslowe, pr. 1417 ; Jn. Dygoun, pr. *reclusus quintus*, n. d.
xvi c.	—	—
1294	—	Richard le Eremite

1417 ; Magd. Coll. Oxford, MSS. 77, 154, 156.   7. Surrey Arch. Coll. I. 176.   8. *Feet of Fines*, p. 64.

SEX

Date.	Patron.	Name.
1459	—	—
1402	—	John Bourne, friar
bef. 1536	—	
1247	Alien Abbey	anchoress, 1247 ; Ric. Petevyne, hermit, 1405

L. and P. Hen. VIII, XII. (1), 1095.   4. D. and Ch. Mun. Y. f. 135 *b ;* Reg. Rede, f. 14.

	Place.			Description.
5	Chichester		A.	in cathedral
6	„ in diocese of		H.	—
7	Hardham (" Heringham ")		A.	in church
8	Harting		A.	—
9	Houghton		A.	—
10	Lewes		A.	*at St. John-sub-Castro*
11	„	(Westout)	A.	at St. Mary's church
12	Pagham		A.	—
13	Seaford	(on cliff)	H.	—
14	Stedham		A.	—
15	Stopham		A.	—
16	Westbourne		H.	chapel of St. Anthony
17	Winchelsea		A.	at church of St. Thomas

5, 6. Reg. Rede, f. 105, 116 ; *V.C.H.* II. 16. 7. Sussex Arch. Coll. I. 174 ; XLIV.
78-80. 8. Pipe R.S. XXX. 145, etc. 9-12. S.A.C. I. 174-6 ; XII. 132, 134. 13. Pat. 1272.

	Place.			Description.
1	Berwood, nr. Birmingham		H.	*chapel of Our Lady*
2	Binton (" Bindon ")		H.	—
—	Bridgtown *v.* Stratford bridge		—	—
3	Coventry	(Bablake)	A.	by chapel of St. John B.
4	„		H.	St. Anne
5	Fletchamstead Wood [in Stone-leigh]		H.	St. Mary
6	Guy's Cliffe (" Gibbecliff ")		H.	cave ; chapel of St. Mary Magd.
7	Packington, Little, or Maxstoke		H.	" Hemeric's church "
8	Polesworth		A.	by abbey church
9	„	(Tamworth road)	H.	by St. Edith's well
10	Stratford-on-Avon	(bridge)	H.	chapel of St. Mary Magd.
11	Warwick		H.	—
—	„ *v.* Guy's Cliffe		—	—
12	Wolvey Heath		H.	—

1. Dugd., *Mon.* VI. 466. 2. Hist. MSS. (Middleton, 1911), 336. 3. Dugd.,
Warw., ed. 1730, p. 193. 4. Dugd., *Mon.* VI. 16. 5. *Ibid.* IV. 345, 348 ; VI. 835.
6. Pat. 1334 ; *Staffs Coll.* N.S. VIII. 280, 285, 289. 7. Dugd., *Warw.* II. 978 ; Ann.

SEX—*continued*

Date.	Patron.	Name.
1402	—	William Bolle, pr.
,,	—	Robert Rydley, professed
1253	—	—
1180	—	—
1253	—	—
—	—	Magnus, n.d.
1253	—	—
,,	—	Br. Hunfred
1272	—	Peter
1180	Crown	—
1253	—	—
bef. 1527	Earl of Arundel	Simon Cotes, *d.* 1527
1242	—	—

14. Pipe R.S. xxx. 146, etc. 15, 16. S.A.C. I. 175; XII. 79, 80; XXII. 98. 17. Chart R. 1242.

WICKSHIRE

Date.	Patron.	Name.
xii c.	Leicester Abbey	—
1521	—	—
—	—	—
1357	—	Robert de *Worthin*, pr.
bef. 1381	—	—
xii c.	Crown ; Templars ; Luffield Priory	Gerald, monk
c. 927	—	Guy of Warwick ; Br. Wiger, *c.* 1205-21 ; Thos. de Lewes, 1334 ; Rob. Maudith, 1373 ; Jn. Burry
bef. 1135	Private ; Worcester Pr.	—
bef. 1457	Abbey	Margaret Salle, 1457
1521	—	—
1367	Private	Br. Jn. Richeman, 1367 ; Jn. Rawlyn, 1443 ; Jn. Whythede, 1472 ; Thos. Smyth, 1495 ; Jn. Butteler, 1497, 1503
1283	—	Gilbert, sub-deacon
—	—	—
1395	Private ; Combe Abbey	Wm. de Scregham, 1395 ; *Jn. Iddezeard,* 1501

Mon. Wigorn. IV. 487. 8, 9. Dugd., *Warw.* II. 1117; Hist. MSS. (1911), 331, 349, 381, 384. 10. J. Halliwell, *Rec.;* Bloom, *Rec.;* Lambeth, Reg. Langham, f. 63. 11. Reg. Giffard (Worc. Hist. S.), II. 204. 12. Dugd., *Warw.* I. 67.

XXXVI. WEST

	Place.		Description.
1	Kendal (Kirkland)	A.	by " Anchorite's well "
2	Shap (" Heppa ")	H.	chapel of St. Mary
3	Windermere, Ladyholm in	H.	„ „

1. C. Nicholson, *Annals*, 78.   2. B.M. Harl. 48 C. 25.   3 Inq. p.m. 1272, 1354 ;

XXXVII. WILT

	Place.		Description.
1	Bentley Wood, by Clarendon	H.	—
2	Bradford-on-Avon	H.	chapel of St. Andrew
3	„	H.	St. Mary (now Tory chapel)
4	Britford	A.	—
5	Castle Combe	H.	—
6	Chippenham (Monkton)	H.	—
7	Codford, East	H.	chapel of Holy Cross
8	Edington	H.	chapel
9	Fisherton Anger	H.	chapel of St. Anne
10	„	A.	at Dominican Friary
11	*Hazelbury* [in Box]	H.	(now Chapel Playster)
12	*Lydiard Tregoz*	—	" *by Antedoch's well*
13	Malmesbury (Burnvale)	H.	chapel of St. Michael
14	„ (South)	H.	" in the dike of the toune "
15	„ (Burton Hill)	H.	St. White
16	Marlborough	A.	—
17	„ (Sun Lune)	H.	—
18	„	H.	St. White, St. Clement, and St. Novalis
19	Preshute	A.	—
20	Salisbury	A.	—
21	„ in diocese of	H.	—
22	„ „	H.	—
23	„ „	H.	—
24	„ „	H.	—
25	*Stanton St. Quintin*	*H.*	*in wood*
26	Sunning	A.	at the church
27	*Yatton Keynes*	*H.*	—

1. Pat. 1330-6.   2. Reg. Metford, f. 123 *b;* Wilts Arch. S. XIV. 103.   3. *Ibid.* 1. 148 ; v. 35 ; XX. 319-20.   4. Close, 1226, 1241 ; Reg. Osmundi (Rolls 78), I. 259 *n.* 5. Scrope, *Castle Combe*, 161.   6. J. J. Daniell, *Chippenham*, 95-7.   7. Hoare, *Wilts,* I. 231, 319.   8. *Itin.* III. 98.   9. Hoare, II. 161-2.   10. Somerset Ho., P.C.C. Logge, f. 101 ; P.R.O. Minister's Accounts, 30-1 Hen, VIII, *n.* 136.   11. *Itin.* II. 55. 12. Aubrey and Jackson, *Wilts Coll.* 183.   13. Dr. G. F. Browne, *St. Aldhelm*, 43-4.

MORLAND

Date.	Patron.	Name.
—	—	—
c. 1220	—	—
1272	—	—

'at. R. 1334, 1381, etc. ; Close, 1344.

SHIRE

Date.	Patron.	Name.
1330	—	Br. John de Warrewyk
1397	—	—
xvi c.	—	—
bef. 1226	Crown	D. Joan Malewyn
1358	Private	John
xvi c.	—	—
1317	—	Br. Henry de Mareys, pr.
xvi c.	—	—
1348	—	Thomas, 1396 ; John, anchorite, 1418
1483	—	—
xvi c.	—	—
—	—	—
c. 637	—	Maildubh
xvi c.	—	—
„	Abbey	—
1517	—	John Benton
bef. 1548	—	—
1523	Town	Nicholas Heage
1215	Crown	Eve
xvi c.	—	D. Alice Curson
1326	—	7 hermits professed
c. 1410	—	J. Spenser „
1487	—	Geoffrey Middleton professed.
1495	—	Richard Pury „
—	—	—
bef. 1220	—	Alice
—	—	—

14. *Itin.* II. 54. 15. L. and P. Hen. VIII, XIX (2), p. 414. 16. *Ibid.* III. (1), p. 500 ; IV. (3), p. 2732. 17. Wilts Arch. S. 561, 567. 18. Corp. MSS. 19. Pat. 1215. 20. Birch, *Hyde Abbey*, Liber Vitæ, 185. 21. Reg. Mortival, II. f. 187. 22. Reg. Halam, f. 47. 23. Reg. Langton, f. 24. 24. Reg. Blythe, f. 40. 25. *Wilts Coll.* 288. 26. Reg. Osmundi, I. 275. 27. *Wilts Coll.* 123.

	Place.		Description.
1	*Blackstone, nr. Bewdley*	*H.*	*cave*
2	Droitwich	A.	in church of Austin Friary
3	Evesham	A.	—
4	„ in or nr.	A.	chapel of St. Kenelm
5	Malvern, Great	H.	„ St. John B.
6	„ „	H.	on site of priory
7	Redstone, nr. Astley	H.	cave, chapel
8	Severn Stoke	A.	—
9	*Southstone [in Stanford on Teme]*	*H.*	*chapel of St. John B.*
10	Worcester	A.	by church of St. Nicholas
11	„	A.	by cathedral
12	„	A.	in Dominican Friary
13	Worcester, in diocese of	H.	—

1. Nash, *Worc.* II. 47. 2. *Ibid.* I. 332. 3, 4. Evesham Chr. (Rolls 29), 219 *n*, 266, 267 *n*, 322. 5. Leland, *Collect.* ed. Hearne, I. 65. 6. W. Malm., *Gest. Pontif.* 285-6. 7. Habingdon, Survey (Hist. S.), II. 17. 8. Pipe R.S. XVI.-XXX.; Pat. 1264.

	Place.		Description.
1	Ainderby [Richmondshire]	A.	adjoining church
2	Beeston, nr. Leeds	A.	—
3	*Beverley*	*H.*	—
4	Beverley	A.	—
5	„	A.	by church of St. Giles
6	„	A.	in house of St. Juliana
7	„	A.	at St. Nicholas le Frary
8	Bolton	A.	—
9	Bridlington or Flamborough	H	—
10	Burneston	A.	—
11	Byland	A.	—
12	Cadeby [in Sprotburgh]	H.	St. Margaret
13	Campsall	A.	—
—	Conisboro, *v.* Sprotburgh; Cadeby	—	—
13*a*	Cave, North	A.	—
14	Coverham [in Coverdale]	H.	chapel of St. Simon and St. Jude

1. Reg. Thoresby, f. 287; Perry, *R. Rolle*, p. xxvi. 2. Reg. Romeyn, f. 45 *b*; Reg. Melton, f. 156 *b*; Test. Ebor. (S.S. 30), II. 26, 178. 3. (?) *Fœd.* VIII. 296. 4. B.M. Stowe, Ch. 432; Test. Ebor. III. (S.S. 45), 32. 5. Test. Ebor. II. 98. 6. *Linc.* Reg. Buckingham, f. 107. 7. *V.C.H.* III. 15; Test. Ebor. II. 98. 8. Will of

CESTERSHIRE

Date.	Patron.	Name.
—	—	—
bef. 1388	Private	Br. Henry de Stokebrugge
xi c.	Abbey	Aelfwin ; Basing
c. 1042	,,	St. Wulsi, *d. c.* 1097
xi c.	—	St. Werstan
c. 1085	—	Aldwyn (*d.* 1140) and Guy
—	Private	—
1170	Crown	—
bef. 1353	*Evesham Abbey*	—
bef. 1256	Private ; Bishop	Juliana, 1256-69
—	Priory	2 recluses
bef. 1538	—	
1431	—	Ric. Spetchley professed

9. Habingdon, I. 382.   10. Pat. 1256, 1266 ; Reg. Giffard, f. 25 *b*.   11. Reg. Worc. Pr. (Camden S.), 120 *b*, 124 *b*, p. cii ; J. Noake, *Worc. Cath.* 119.   12. Ellis, *Orig. Lett.* CCCXXVIII, 3rd Ser. III. 190.   13. Reg. Pulton, f. 137.

SHIRE

Date.	Patron.	Name.
1367	—	D. Margaret Kirkby, cf. Layton
1294	—	Denise of Barneby, 1294 ; Joan Sperry, nun of St. Clement's, York, 1322.
1403	—	—
1397	Duchy of Lancaster	Robert Riell, 1397-1415
1444	—	—
1392	—	—
c. 1321	—	Agnes Migregose and Marg. de Punchardon, nun
1385	—	—
xii c.	—	Simon, n.d. ; hermit, 1403
1400	—	—
1392	—	—
1226	Private	—
1240	,,	Muriel
—	—	—
1286	—	Agnes Muscregros
—	Coverham Abbey	—

Jn. de Gisburne.   9. W. T. Lancaster, *Bridlington Cart.* 179 (? *Fœd.* VIII. 296). 10. Test. Ebor. I. (S.S. 4), 274.   11. See (6).   12. P.R.O. Anc. Deeds, A. 5074 ; cf. (79, 80).   13. Close, 1240 ; Pat. 1244.   13*a*. Reg. Romeyn (S.S. 123), 196. 14. *Yks. Arch. Journ.* XX. 484.

XXXIX. YORK

	Place.		Description.
15	Crayke	A.	—
16	Cudworth, nr. Barnsley	H.	—
17	Dalby [in Pickering Forest]	H.	—
18	Darton	A.	—
19	Doncaster	H.	—
—	,, *v.* Sprotburgh	—	—
20	*Easington, or Newton,* in or nr.	H.	—
21	Ecclesfield (Kimberworth)	H.	St. John
22	Egton [in Lythe]	H.	St. Leonard
23	Elland	A.	—
24	Eskdaleside	H.	—
25	Farndale-head	H.	—
26	Goathland	H.	*St. Mary*
27	Guisborough (" Gysburne ")	A.	—
28	Hampole	H.	—
29	,,	A.	—
30	Harum [in Helmsley]	H.	—
31	Haverah (" Haywra ") [Knaresboro' Forest]	H.	—
32	Healaugh Park	H.	—
33	Hedon	A.	in churchyard of St. Nicholas
34	Helmsley	A.	—
35	Hessey [in Moor Monkton]	H.	—
36	Holme on Spalding Moor	H.	—
37	Hood [in Kilburn]	H.	—
—	Howden, *v.* Ringestainhirst	—	—
38	Huntington, nr. York	H.	chapel of St. Augustine
39	Kexby Ferry	A.	in chantry chapel
40	Kirkburton	A.	in churchyard
41	Kirkby Wiske	A.	—
42	Kirkstall	H.	afterwards abbey
43	Knaresborough, nr.	H.	chapel of St. Giles ; chapel of Holy Cross
44	,,	H.	chapel of St. Robert
45	,, Grimbald bridge	H.·	—
—	,, *v.* Haverah ; Rudfarlington	—	—
46	Layton, East	A.	in a house in the chapel

15. *Ibid.* IV. 435. 16. Yks. Deeds (Rec. Ser. 39), 156. 17. J. C. Cox, *Royal Forests*, 108. 18. Reg. Gray (S.S. 56), 65. 19. Pat. 1328. 20. Wills (S.S. 116), 17. 21. Dugd. v. 416, 419. 22. *Ibid.* v. 392 ; Chr. Melsa (Rolls 43), I. 84. 23. Reg. Giffard, p. 123. 24. Whitby Cart. (S.S. 69), 3. 25. Rievaulx Cart. (S.S. 83), 36. 26. Whitby Cart. 161. 27. *Proc. Arch. Inst. Lincoln*, 313. 28. Horstman, *R. Rolle ;* Perry, *R. Rolle* (E.E. Text S.). 29. *Mkt. Harboro' Rec.* 58 ; *Linc. Wills*, 97 ; *Fœd.* IX. 275. 30. *Linc. Wills*, 71. 31. *V.C.H.* III. 91. 32. Dugd. v. 437-8. 33. J. R.

SHIRE—*continued.*

Date.	Patron.	Name.
c. 767	—	Etha or Eata, *d.* 767
—	—	Richard
1323	—	William
1234	—	Cecily
1328	—	Geoffrey de Bolton
	—	
1417	—	—
—	Private ; Kirksted Abbey	—
bef. 1150	„ ; Meaux Abbey	Sedeman ; Ivo
1270	—	—
c. 1158	Whitby Abbey	
xii c.	Private	Edmund
bef. 1114	Crown ; Whitby Abbey	Osmund, etc.
1386	—	John
bef. 1349	Priory	Richard Rolle, *d.* 1349
1382	—	
1392	—	John
1267	—	Lambert le Fleming, etc., 1315
bef. 1184	Private	Gilbert, monk
1267	—	Alice de Falketon
1392	—	Agnes
1348	—	Stephen Hamondes
xii c.	Selby Abbey	—
bef. 1138	—	Robert de Alneto, monk
—	—	Rob. de Skitheby, cf. Skeeby
1333	—	Thomas Coke, pr.
1398	—	Agnes, dau. of Wm. de Burton
1293	—	—
1382	—	Seleth, etc.
c. 1147	—	Knight ; St. Robert, *d.* 1218 ;
bef. 1199	Crown ; Priory	Ive
		Br. Robert de Eboraco
1339	—	Roger, 1336 ; William, 1398
1336	—	—
1348	—	Marg. la Boteler, nun of Hampole, 1348 ; Marg. de Kirkby, *bef.* 1357, cf. Ainderby

Boyle, *Hedon*, 155 and App.   34. See (30).   35. Pat. 1348.   36. Selby Cart. (Rec. Ser. 13), 27 ; Reg. Zouche, f. 210.   37. Dugd. v. 343, 349 ; VI. 322.   38. Pat. 1333.   39. Test. Ebor. I. 244 ; *Fœd.* IX. 275.   40. Reg. Romeyn, I. 126.   41. *Mkt. Harboro' Rec.* 58 ; Test. Ebor. I. 274, III. 32 ; *Fœd.* IX. 275.   42. Kirkstall Cart. (Thoresby S.).   43. Close, 1216, 1219 ; Chart. R. 1227 ; *Mem. of Fountains* (S.S. 42), I. 167-71 *n*.   44. Pat. 1339, 1340.   45. Pat. 1336 ; Wheater, *Knaresboro'*, 158.   46. Reg. Zouche, f. 72 ; Reg. Thoresby, f. 287.

	Place.			Description.
47	Leak by Upsall		A.	—
48	*Lindholme [in Hatfield Chase]*		*H.*	—
49	Mulgrave [in Dunsley]		H.	St. James
50	*Newton [in Cleveland]*		*H.*	—
51	Newton-upon-Ouse		H.	—
52	Nostell [in Wragby]		H.	St. James
53	Nun Appleton		A.	—
54	Pontefract	(by castle)	A.	in St. Helen's chapel
55	,,		A.	—
56	,,		H.	on hill of " St. Thomas "
57	,,	(nr. Blackfriars)	H.	rock hermitage and chapel
58	,,		H.	—
—	,,		H.	—
59	Rameshagh [in Sproxton]		H.	—
60	Ravenser (" Ravenserespourne ")		H.	chapel of St. Mary and St. Anne
61	Ribblehead and Gearstones (between)		H.	" domus heremitæ "
62	Richmond		A.	—
63	,,		A.	by chapel of St. Edmund K.
64	,,		A.	—
65	Richmondshire, in		A.	—
66	Ringestainhirst, by Howden		H.	chapel of St. Mary M.
67	Ripon Bishopton bridge		H.	*chapel of St. Mary*
68	Rudfarlington [Knaresborough Forest]		H.	at chapel of St. Hilda
69	Saltburn-by-sea		H.	—
70	Selby	in wood	H.	chapel of St. German
71	,, nr. (" Scablu ")		H.	—
72	Sherburn in Elmet		H.	St. Mary M. " hospital or hermitage "
73	Shipton [in Overton]		H.	chapel of St. Helen

47. Test. Ebor. I. 376 ; *Fœd.* IX. 275.   48. *Gent. Mag.*, 1747, XVII. 23.   49. Whitby Cart. (S.S. 72), II. 525-7.   50. Ord, *Cleveland*, 423.   51. Chart. R. 1294.   52. Dugd. VI. 89.   53. Test. Ebor. I. 376.   54. Close, 1240 ; Reg. Zouche, f. 58 *b ;* Pat. 1359, 1486 ; Parl. R. v. 546.   55. Pap. Reg. v. 471.   56. *Reg. J. of Gaunt,* II. 40 ; *Fœd.* IX. 275 ; Test. Ebor. II. 26.   57-58. B.M. Stowe, Ch. 468-470 ; G. Fox, *Pontefract*, 291-2.   59. Chart. R. 1336.   60. Pat. 1399, 1427 ; *Fœd.* VIII. 89-90.   61.

SHIRE—*continued*

Date.	Patron.	Name.
1414	—	*William of Lindholme*
bef. 1244	Private ; Whitby Abbey	—
1294	—	—
c. 1121	—	Gilbert and brethren
1414	—	Sybille, 1240 ; Joan Haliday,
1240	Private ; Duchy of Lancaster	1351 ; Alice Ripas, 1464 ; Margaret Multon, 1486
bef. 1401	—	Emma Scherman
1372	—	Wm. de Byngham ; John, 1415
1368	Private	Br. Adam, 1368 ; Laurence Grene, pr., 1404
1404	Private ; Nostell Priory	John de Crayk (?), *alias* Queyks
1405-6	—	William Portyngton
xii c.	Private ; Kirkham Priory	Godwyn ; Edwin
1399	—	Matthew Danthorpe, 1399 ; Ric. Reedbarowe, 1427
c. 1190	Furness Abbey	
1393	—	D. Joan Sampson
1274	Private ; Crown	Margaret Askham, 1439 ; Alice Howorth, 1446
1490	Town	Margaret Richmond ; Alison Comeston, 1490
c. 1361-79	—	Thos. de Osgoteby, 1284 ; *Ric. de Cavill*, 1366 ; Rob. de Sakerston, 1391
1284	Bishop of Durham	
bef. 1521	—	St. Robert, cf. Knaresborough
c. 1200	—	
bef. 1211	Private ; Whitby Abbey	Br. Archillus
c. 1069	—	Benedict, first abbot
c. 1123	—	Abbot Hugh de Lacy
1352	—	John de Kildesby
1327	—	Adam de Whenby

Furness Cart. B.M. Add. 33244, f. 123.   62-4. Test. Ebor. I. 189, 274 ; II. 115 ; III. 202, 297 ; *Itin.* v. 116 ; Whittaker, *Richmond*, I. 100-1 ; Pat. 1439, 1446.   65. Nov. Leg. II. 71-2.   66. Pat. 1284 ; Reg. Pal. Dunelm. I. 429 ; *V.C.H., Durham*, II. 131 *n.;* Test. Ebor. I. 156.   67. *Memorials* (S.S. 74), I. 114, 183, 274.   68. B.M. Harl. 3775, f. 76.   69. Whitby Cart. I. 177.   70-1. Coucher Bk. (Rec. Ser. 13), Cap. xiii, xiv, xxx.   72. Pat. 1352.   73. Pat. 1327, 1330, 1332.

	Place.		Description.
74	Skeeby, nr. Richmond	H.	chapel of St. Augustine
75	Skip Bridge ; cf. Hessey	H.	—
76	Snaith	A.	—
77	Sowerby, nr. Thirsk	H.	—
78	Spaldingholm	H.	—
79	Sprotburgh, Doncaster bridge	A.	by St. Edmund's chapel
80	,, or Conisborough	H.	St. Margaret
81	Staddle Bridge ("Stalebrig")	H.	—
82	Stainforth Bridge, nr. Barnby on Don	H.	at chapel
83	Tadcaster	H.	,, ,,
84	Thorganby by Cottingwith	A.	at the church
85	Wakefield (Northgate Head)	A.	by chapel of St. John B.
86	Wath	A.	—
87	Weighton	A.	—
88	Westcroft in Hutton Bushell	H.	—
89	York North Street	A.	at All Saints' church
90	,,	A.	,, St. Cuthbert's church
91	,,	A.	,, St. Giles's ,,
92	,, Fishergate	A.	,, St. Helen's ,,
93	,, Walmgate	A.	,, St. Margaret's ,,
94	,, Clementhorpe	A.	,, St. Clement's ,,
95	,, Bishophill	A.	—
96	,, Hungate	A.	—
97	,, Layerthorpe bridge	A.	—
98	,, Peaseholm	A.	—
99	,, in diocese of	H.	—
100	,, ,,	H.	—

74. Pat. 1328. 75. Pat. 1335-6. 76. Reg. Gaunt, II. 243. 77. Test. Ebor. I. 206 ; cf. Wakefield R. (Rec. Ser. 36), 156, 185. 78. B.M. Cott. Claud. D. XI. f. 34. 79. Hunter, S. Yorks, I. 348 ; Reg. Giffard (S.S. 109), 116. 80. L. and P. Hen. VIII, V. p. 700; Chantries (S.S. 92), II. 426. 81. Yks. Arch. Journ. XVIII. 266. 82. Pat. 1348. 83. Chantries, II. 375. 84. Test. Ebor. I. 186 ; II. 26 ; Fœd. IX. 275. 85. Reg. Zouche, f. 59 ; Test. Ebor. I. 286, V. 74 ; Halifax Wills, 217 ; Itin. VII. 43-4.

SHIRE—*continued*

Date.	Patron.	Name.
1328	—	Rob. de Skytheby, cf. Huntington
1335	—	Br. Thomas
1374	—	—
1395	—	[cf. Hugh, 1308]
bef. 1179	N. Ormsby Priory	
1271	Private ; Archbishop	Amabil and Ellen, 1279 ; Sibil Lisle, 1294 ; Beatrice, nun, *bef.* 1304 ; Joan of Easingwold, 1328
xvi c.	—	—
1484	—	—
1348	—	William de Epworth
xvi c.	—	—
1393	—	D. Agnes, 1433
1352	—	Elizabeth de Coppelay
1393	—	—
1415	—	—
bef. 1187	Private ; Whitby Abbey	—
1430	—	D. Emma Rawghtone, *c.* 1422
1393	—	—
1386	—	John
1433	—	—
1435	—	—
1465	Priory	D. Alice Darby, 1475
1385	—	—
”	—	—
1381	—	—
1415	—	—
1343	—	Walter de Thorp ordained subdeacon, deacon, priest
1404	—	Nicholas Humanby professed

86-7. *Ibid.* I. 186, 274 ; *Fœd.* IX. 275.   88. Whitby Cart. I. 49.   89. Test. Ebor. II. 26, 56 ; *Old York Church : All Hallows*, p. 94.   90. *Ibid.* I. 186.   91. See (27). 92-3. Test. Ebor. II. 26, 56, 271.   94. *Ibid.* II. 271, 145 *n.* ; Madox, *Form. Anglic.* 437.   95. See (8) ; Test. Ebor. V. 214.   96-7. *Ibid.* I. 186, 118.   98. *Fœd.* IX. 275. 99. York, Ordination List, Zouche.   100. Lambeth, Reg. Arundel, Pt. I. f. 435 *b.*

	Place.		Date.
I	Basing, Basinch, or Acres chapel: St. John B.	H.	1138
2	Cen	A.	x c.
3	Childris : St. Bridget	H.	1207
4	Colemanshegg : chapel	H.	1256-7
5	Cruke	A.	1176
6	Dodford	H.	*bef.* 1199
7	Fordham	A.	1260
8	Hauescumba	H.	*bef.* 1166
9	Hungate	H.	1433
10	Leye or Reye : chapel	A.	1315
11	Magdalen, La	H.	—
12	Mosehuda	H.	*bef.* 1260
12a	Tanfield (in wood)	H.	1409
13	Vestheton	A.	1393
14	Warham	A.	1183-4

1. Gloucester Abbey Cart. (Rolls 33), I. 224, 228, 352 ; II. 169.   2. St. Dunstan (Rolls 63), 381-2.   3. Pat. 7 John m. 3.   4. F. Devon, *Excheq. R.*, p. xxx, 34.   5. Pipe R.S. XXVI. 10, etc.   6. Dugd. VI. 836, 839.   7. Pat. 1260.   8. B.M. Campbell,

FIED

Patron.	Name.	
St. Peter's, Gloucester	—	Oxon or Bucks
—	pilgrim	—
—	brethren of hermitage	—
Crown	Richard, hermit	—
	—	? Creech, co. Dorset
„ ; Templars	—	? co. N'hants or Worc.
	Isabel and Olive, recluses	? co. Cambs
—		
Private ; Farley Priory	—	? Hawcomb, co. Glos.
—	—	—
—	Isabella	dioc. Hereford
—	Prior Humfrid	? co. Derbs.
Templars	Geoffrey	Berks or Oxon
—	—	probably W. Tanfield, Yorks
—	—	? West Heaton
Crown	—	probably co. Norfolk

Ch. XIII. 12.   9. *Linc. Wills*, 158.   10. Reg. Swinfield, Camden S. 213, and Cant. and Yk. S. 501.   11. Derbs. Arch. S. v. 23.   12. Bodl. Wood Empt. No. 10, f. 83. 12*a*. See p. 176 ; cf. Pat. 1314.   13. Test. Ebor. I. 186.   14. Pipe R.S. XXXIII. 110.

INDEX

(a. = anchorite, anchorage; h. = hermit, hermitage).